—*Kirkus Reviews*

"Ben Fong-Torres ran and wrote the music section of *Rolling Stone* and at the same time kept his other foot in the dark, secret world of San Francisco's Chinatown. It's an amazing story." —Jann Wenner

"Moving . . . peppered with colorful anecdotes . . . demonstrates a broad knowledge of and sympathy for both Chinese and American traditions." —*Publishers Weekly*

"Ben Fong-Torres's voice rocked over the radio waves, and a whole generation listened to one of the pioneer voices to break out of Chinatown. Now Fong-Torres fills his memoir, *The Rice Room*, with worlds of feeling, both tender and tragic, to reveal the fire behind that voice." —Fae Myenne Ng, author of *Bone*

"One man's journey into the heart of contemporary America with a Chinese-American soul . . . a witty, moving, heartfelt read." —Philip Kan Gotanda, writer and director of *The Kiss*

"I am a fifty-three-year-old Caucasian woman, and I feel as if a forty-seven-year-old Chinese man has just told my story—that of a generation of Americans. Thank you, Ben." —Grace Slick of The Jefferson Airplane

"A poignant examination of Ben's life. I couldn't put it down." —Steve Martin

BEN FONG-TORRES has been a writer at *Rolling Stone* and the *San Francisco Chronicle*, a deejay for KSAN, the pioneer FM rock station in San Francisco, and has been published in such magazines as *GQ*, *Playboy*, *Esquire*, and *Sports Illustrated*. He currently lives in San Francisco.

ALSO BY
BEN FONG-TORRES

Hickory Wind:

The Life and Times

of Gram Parsons

THE RICE

ROOM

GROWING UP

CHINESE-AMERICAN

—FROM NUMBER TWO SON

TO ROCK'N'ROLL

BEN FONG-TORRES

A PLUME BOOK

PLUME
Published by the Penguin Group
Penguin Books USA Inc., 375 Hudson Street,
New York, New York 10014, U.S.A.
Penguin Books Ltd, 27 Wrights Lane,
London W8 5TZ, England
Penguin Books Australia Ltd, Ringwood,
Victoria, Australia
Penguin Books Canada Ltd, 10 Alcorn Avenue,
Toronto, Ontario, Canada M4V 3B2
Penguin Books (N.Z.) Ltd, 182-190 Wairau Road,
Auckland 10, New Zealand

Penguin Books Ltd, Registered Offices:
Harmondsworth, Middlesex, England

Published by Plume, an imprint of Dutton Signet,
a division of Penguin Books USA Inc.
This is an authorized reprint of a hardcover edition published by Hyperion.
For information address Hyperion, 114 Fifth Avenue, New York, New York 10011.

First Plume Printing, May, 1995
10 9 8 7

The author gratefully acknowledges permission to use excerpts
from the following books and song lyrics:
"That's Amore," copyright © Paramount Music Corporation and Four Jays Music Company,
1953. Copyright renewed © Paramount Music Corporation and Four Jays Music Company, 1981.
"Daniel," written by Elton John and Bernie Taupin. Copyright © Songs of PolyGram International, Inc., 1972. Used by permission. All rights reserved.
"It's All Right, Ma (I'm Only Bleeding)" by Bob Dylan, copyright © Warner Bros. Inc., 1965.
Copyright renewed © Special Rider Music, 1993.
"In old age, life's affairs" by Yuan Mei, from *The Columbia Book of Later Chinese Poetry*, translated by Jonathan Chaves, copyright © Columbia University Press, 1986. Reprinted with permission of the publisher.

REGISTERED TRADEMARK—MARCA REGISTRADA

LIBRARY OF CONGRESS CATALOGING-IN-PUBLICATION DATA:
Fong-Torres, Ben.
The rice room: growing up Chinese-American: from number two son
to rock 'n' roll / Ben Fong-Torres.
p. cm.
ISBN 0-452-27412-5
1. Fong-Torres, Ben. 2. Chinese American—Biography.
3. Journalists—United States—Biography I. Title.
E184.C5F65 1995
973'.04951'0092—dc20
[B]   94-43472
CIP

Printed in the United States of America

Original hardcover design by Barbara M. Bachman

BOOKS ARE AVAILABLE AT QUANTITY DISCOUNTS WHEN USED TO PROMOTE PRODUCTS
OR SERVICES. FOR INFORMATION PLEASE WRITE TO PREMIUM MARKETING DIVISION,
PENGUIN BOOKS USA INC., 375 HUDSON STREET, NEW YORK, NEW YORK 10014.

For my family

IN HONOR OF OUR PARENTS,

IN MEMORY OF BA-BA (1903–1994) AND BARRY (1943–1972),

IN LOYALTY TO SARAH, SHIRLEY, AND BURTON,

AND

IN LOVE OF DIANNE

•• ACKNOWLEDGMENTS ••

I'd like to thank everyone who's been in my life. But since I can't, I'll single out a few who were particularly helpful to me in the writing of this book, from jogging memories to reading the manuscript.

In the early stages of research and recollection, I received invaluable assistance and support from Serena Chen, Betty Ko, Darlene Joe, Maeley Locke, William Fung, Dexter Waugh, Milly Hurlimann, and the Asian American Studies Library at the University of California, Berkeley.

Numerous friends from grammar school through college, and beyond, surfaced over the course of my writing of this book, and although some chose to accept my offer of anonymity or an assumed name, all the people represented in the text have my deep gratitude. I extend special thanks to Ann Wai Wong, Karen

Lim Lum, Dale Evans Drew, Paul Forrest, Helen Pulver Rosenberg, Marsha Warren Addiego, Judith Smith Cushner, Lindi Bortney, Carolyn Giffin Conrad, Mary Keith, Dave Swanston, Geoffrey and Fran Link, Pat Sullivan, Leslie Yee-Murata, Amie Hill, Karen Thorsen, and my all-time favorite roommate, Tom Gericke. Thanks to Jann Wenner for all those years and stories at *Rolling Stone*; to all my radio friends—especially Gary Owens, Russ Syracuse, Tom Saunders, and Wes "Scoop" Nisker. Wherever she may be, hello to Candace Barnes. And for helping keep the memory of my brother alive, love to Norma Yee Don, Jacklyn Jordan, Patricia Higa, Skip Skeen, Ruby Webbe, Laurie Wu, and, especially, Gail Katagiri.

Gordon Lew deserves a separate thank you, not only for being my friend through these years, but for being a friend to the family as well. In the most pivotal and critical moments of my life, he's always been there.

I had many uncertain moments throughout this strangest of endeavors, this telling of one's own story, but I was fortunate to have my friend and agent Sarah Lazin keeping me on track, and I was blessed to have as my editor Leslie Wells, who encouraged me to tell it all, and then helped me to tell it as well as I could.

Finally, thanks to my loving and amazingly patient wife, Dianne; to all our friends whom we couldn't see while I was mired in self-examination, and to my family. This book is, ultimately, for all of us.

·· CONTENTS ··

Prologue 3

1 ·· THE MAI FONG 7

2 ·· CONNIVERS 11

3 ·· THE ALL-AMERICAN CITY 23

4 ·· BROTHERS AND SISTERS 32

5 ·· THE GAMBLER 51

6 ·· LIFE WITHOUT FATHER 57

7 ·· ROUTE 66 70

8 ·· WORKING FOR A LIVING 82

9 ·· A NEW HOUSE 92

10 ·· THE PINK PRISON 96

11 ·· SUMMERTIME BLUES 106

12 ·· A SUMMER SONG 116

13 ·· COLLEGE DAYS AND NIGHTS 120

14 ·· GROOVY KIND OF LOVE 130

15 •• ON OUR OWN 1 3 8

16 •• ENDINGS AND BEGINNINGS 1 4 5

17 •• 1968 .... 1 6 0

18 •• ALMOST CUT MY HAIR 1 6 3

19 •• DAZED AND CONFUSED 1 8 2

20 •• INTO A MINE FIELD 1 9 6

21 •• AN UNCOMMON DEATH 2 0 7

22 •• DO YOU STILL FEEL THE PAIN 2 1 5

23 •• LOVE THE ONE YOU'RE WITH 2 2 2

24 •• GOING HOME 2 3 8

25 •• FULL CIRCLES 2 5 2

THE RICE ROOM

PROLOGUE

I was walking with my father on Eighth Street in Chinatown, Oakland, toward the dim sum restaurant where *Ma-Ma* was waiting. Every few steps, I had to remind myself to slow down in order to stay with him.

Behind us, by just a few blocks, was the flat where we'd lived forty years, a lifetime ago. Around the corner, on Webster Street near Seventh, is where our family restaurant, the New Eastern Cafe, used to be.

It was spring, and my father had been extremely sick last summer; he had a whole doctor's checklist of ailments. Now, I was asking about his gout. "How's your foot?" I said.

"The same," he said. Then he added: "I sure can't lift a hundred pounds any more. Old days, I'd carry sacks of potatoes . . ."

"And onions," I said, remembering the red net sacks.

"And rice," he said. Always there was rice.

That's all we said to each other on our two-block walk to the Jade Villa, but I felt excited by the simple exchange. It seemed to be as much as we'd ever said to each other.

I thought about a remark my brother-in-law, Dave, had made once when we were talking about language barriers. Dave is a Caucasian who had it none too easy being accepted by my parents, who wanted their five children to marry five Chinese. And here was the first child running off with a *bok-guey*—a white devil.

Dave told me he felt okay. "I don't really know how your mom feels about me," he said. "And your dad . . . your dad would be a great guy to know. He seems like a regular, fun-loving guy. I would love to be able to talk with him."

"Yeah," I said to Dave. "Me, too."

Over the years, I've talked with my parents many times, but we've never really communicated.

When we talk, it sounds like baby talk—at least my side of it. The parents say what they will in their native dialect of Cantonese. I pick up the gist of it, formulate a response, and am dumbstruck. I don't know half the words I need; I either never learned them, or I heard but forgot them. The Chinese language is stuck in its own place and time. When we were growing up, we learned to say police in Chinese: *look yee.* That means "green clothes," which referred, we'd learn years later, to the uniforms worn by the police in Canton. There are no Chinese words for "computer," "laser," "Watergate," "annuity," "AIDS," or "recession." When the telephone was invented, the Chinese, who concocted so many things that the rest of the world had to find words for, simply called it "electric line."

What I speak, then, is patchwork Cantonese, with lots of holes, some of them covered up, to no avail, by occasional English words that they may or may not understand.

What we have here is a language barrier as formidable, to my mind, as the Great Wall of China.

The barrier has stood tall, rugged, and insurmountable between my parents and all five of their children, and it has stood through countless moments when we needed to talk with each other, about the things parents and children usually discuss: jobs and careers; marriage and divorce; health and finances; history, the present, and the future.

This is one of the great sadnesses of my life. How ironic, I would think. We're all well educated, thanks in part to our parents' hard work and determination; I'm a journalist and a broadcaster—my *job* is to communicate—and I can't with the two people with whom I want to most.

Our language barrier stood, heartless and unyielding, when we suffered the first death among us. When we most desperately needed to talk with each other, to console and comfort one another, words failed us.

And yet, that death led to the first chipping away of the language barrier. Through a trusted family friend who acted as interpreter, I was able to talk with my parents about their lives in China; about their early years in San Francisco and Oakland; about their goals for themselves and their family.

I talked to my parents for our entire family, to allow all of us to have a good, long look over that wall. I also did this for my parents; to let them sit atop the wall for a moment, to give them a chance to learn a few things about us, things we'd never been able to express fully, fluidly, with all intended nuances.

For so long, I had wanted to tell them the most basic things— why I chose the work that I did; what that work involved; why I didn't marry the Chinese woman they'd wanted me to; why I married the woman I did. I'd wanted to let my father know that, whatever hardships he endured, his children admired him, and that I, in particular, traced my own successes to him. The long stretches of silences; the clumsy give-and-takes notwithstanding, I had learned from him.

And I wanted to explain the conflicts we all felt, growing up both Chinese and American, and the choices I made, of wading not only into the American mainstream, but then into the counterculture of the sixties. I wanted to explain the frustrations my sisters, brothers, and I felt over our obligations to our family businesses throughout our young lives.

They never understood why most of us ultimately rebelled, in one way or another. But we had our reasons. We had to deal with numerous contradictions in the instructions they gave us in life. We would succeed in school and in white-collar careers, but we would also spend after-school hours studying Chinese and working at the restaurant, leaving us little time for homework and next to none for socializing. We were made to feel guilty if we wanted to do what others did; to have what others had. We were torn between obligations to the family and the freedom we naturally wanted.

I didn't explain all of this during the conversation with the interpreter between us. That's a lifetime of talking. But we concluded the talk with a sense of many missions accomplished.

They learned enough about me, and I learned enough to tell my story. It is an equally Chinese and American story. It is told by the son of a mother who always wanted the best for me and whose influence I sense every day, and of a father who worked endlessly throughout his life. As it turns out, my brother-in-law Dave is right. He *is* a great guy to know.

·· 1 ··

THE MAI

FONG

The rice room—the *mai fong*—was the generic name for an area in the back of our father's restaurant.

From the time of my birth in 1945 until they sold the restaurant ten years later, the cafe at 710 Webster Street was my home away from home.

Sometimes, it was just plain home.

It is a bank now, but when I see the numbers over the doorway, it's my place. Outside is where I stood and played with firecrackers and came close to blowing off a thumb. Inside, straight past the row of tellers, I can still make my way through to the kitchen and beyond, past the door on the left that led out to the backyard. Straight ahead was the bank of iceboxes where we stored the soda pops and beer, and to their right were the cantankerous generators, the boxes on boxes of canned water chestnuts and bamboo shoots—and Old Dutch cleanser, whose label featured a scary, witchlike Dutch girl who always gave me the creeps. I'd get past the stacks of Dutch girls, the shiny, squared tin cans of soy sauce and peanut oil, and the crinkly paper packages of dried bean curd, turn left, and there I'd be again: the *mai fong*.

To the right was a tiny room with a bed, a chair, and a table, where we spent our infancies. To the far left was the rice room, a cold, concrete-floored, chicken-wired area. And setting them apart, but not very far, was our study room, where, under the light of a bare light bulb strung from the low ceiling, we read and drew pictures and listened to a Mitchell table radio that shared a shelf with jars of fermented bean cakes and tins of salted fish.

Our babysitters were *The Lone Ranger* and *The Great Gildersleeve*; the machine-gunning *Gangbusters*, who were known as "G-men" as they went after criminals, and the *T-Man*, a rugged Federal Treasury agent who had his own bad guys to chase every week.

"Ah-*Ha-Nui!*—Sarah!"—we'd near in the distance, and my sister would dash out of the room, headed to the kitchen.

"Ah-*Haw-Doy!*" and I'd be off, to the *chui fong*—the kitchen—to wash rice, or to a table at the rear of the dining room, where I'd sit and help shell prawns or strip the spines off sugar peas. Whatever we were old enough to learn to do, we did.

To us, the kitchen was a mysterious place. Our kitchen at home was so simple: an old Sparks stove, a refrigerator, sink, and table. At the New Eastern, it was a bustling *factory*. Almost an entire wall was taken up by a line of gigantic black woks. This was my father's stage. He strode the length of the four woks, each one fired up by gas flames underneath. Beneath him, planks of wood, raised off the ground an inch or two, served to give his legs and feet some spring, and to allow food particles to drip through, to be swept off the floor later.

The sink was the size of a bathtub; the refrigerator had glass doors and stretched three times as wide as the one at home. Every appliance was bigger, and there were things we never saw anywhere else, like the big cylindrical metal oven in which my father draped rods holding large marinated pieces of pork loin. We could hear the fire roaring from the bottom of this *loo-how*. My dad would go about his business, and then, always at exactly the right time, he'd wander over, lift off the top, and pluck out several rods of barbecued pork—glowing bright red, with black at the tips.

If I happened by at that magical moment, I'd stop. *"Yeet-gow!"* I'd say. One piece. And, taking a big Chinese cleaver, he'd deftly chop off a piece of the succulent, sweet meat. "One dollah!" he'd shout, then hand it over.

My father made the best food in town. Every now and then, he'd make a batch of *Jah-Don*—which meant "bombs," but which tasted infinitely better. They were Chinese cream puffs without the cream, but liberally dipped in sugar.

There was nothing he wouldn't try. If he tasted a candy he liked, he'd try to duplicate it himself. He was proud of a rock candy he whipped up once and determined to sell at the front counter of the New Eastern. We, of course, served as his guinea pigs, and we couldn't bring ourselves to tell him the sad truth: The candy was so hard that it was inedible. I rolled a piece around my mouth. "Tastes good, *Ba-Ba*," I said. Then, when he looked away, I spat it out.

Life in a Chinese restaurant gave us access to some strange snacks, most of which we grew to like. There were the *moy*, the salted or sugared preserved plums given so freely as gifts. The salted ones set off ticklish explosions inside our mouths, but once we adjusted, nothing rivaled the satisfaction of working the plum around, getting down to the plum seed.

There were the pickled scallions we'd pluck out of the jar, bulbous onion heads that we thought of as candy. Sometimes, Dad would get a sugar cane or two at the produce market and chop off inch-long pieces for us to suck on.

When we ventured beyond the rice room and kitchen, into the dining room, we'd run into the waiter, Gim Bok. He was a tall, spindly man with rimless glasses and thinning hair who liked to spin stories to us. Watching my little sister Shirley nibbling on an apple, he'd lean over.

"Don't eat the seed," he said, "or an apple tree will grow inside you."

"What?"

"Yes. Right inside your stomach, an apple tree!"

As kids we didn't stray from the restaurant, except to go across the street to the store where they sold comic books. As we grew, we did chores that took us up Webster Street, to the store where they cultivated bean sprouts and bean cake, or down Eighth Street, in the direction of home, where we'd pop into Hoy Chang and Company to pick up cigarettes and gum to sell at the front counter.

Beyond the immediate environs, there lay the unknown.

Everyone in Chinatown knew about Freddy, a shaggy-haired kid who lived just about a block below us, on Seventh Street on the lower skirt of Chinatown, Oakland. He was seven years old when he died. Our parents gave us some of the gruesome details a few days later. Freddy had been run over by a car and dragged for blocks. It was the first time I'd heard about death, and I couldn't get him out of my mind. It was the same for my older sister and brother. We couldn't blot out the visions of Freddy losing his life ... right in our neighborhood, just around the corner from the New Eastern. I wondered what it had been like to be Freddy at that moment. I wondered about death.

·· 2 ··

CONNIVERS

For all these years, it has been so hard for them to talk. It's not the language, and it's not that they don't remember. They remember too well. The silences—about who and what they were in China, and about what they wanted to be when they arrived in America—were born of the guilt and fear shared by all who left their homeland in the southern part of China for what they universally knew as *Gum Sahn*, the "Golden Mountains" of the United States.

They came from the districts surrounding Canton—Nam Hoi, Pun Yu, Shuntak, Toishan, Sun Ning, and Hoi Ping—and, in leaving their villages, they were leaving a country being torn apart by both inner and outside forces. They were encouraged by their families to go, to seek a greater fortune and then to return to fetch them, too.

They left with uncertainty. So many who'd gone to America before them had never returned. So many had failed to amass a fortune; so many had died.

And almost all of them had entered America as outlaws.

My parents connived their way into the United States, using false identities. For most of their existence here, they feared being found out, and the shame of being sent back home.

And so they were silent about their pasts, even to their own children; sometimes, especially to us.

My father was born Fong Kwok Shang in 1903 in a village called Gow Bay Hong, in the Hoi Ping district in southeast China. Fong Shang was a mythical figure in early Chinese history, when Fongs were, in fact, few. The Fong surname came into prominence during the Ming dynasty (1368–1644), primarily in the fields of art and academics, but it was not until the last Chinese dynasty, the Qing (1644–1911), that the surname blossomed, through highly regarded artists, scholars, and Confucianists named Fong.

China, in 1903, was a country in turmoil, ruled by a reactionary, isolationist dowager empress whose short-sightedness and stubbornness left the country open to foreign incursions and to revolutions among its own people. The empress died in 1908 and her son—China's last emperor—was a child who ruled less than four years before he was forced to abdicate. Enter Sun Yat-sen, who began to rally China's middle class. The country was ready to give up the remnants of the Manchu Dynasty, to take its first few steps into the modern era.

But for my father's family, it was too late. The Fongs were poor. My dad's grandfather, Fong Zhe Hou, farmed rice and grew vegetables, and his father, Fong Fu-man, sold sundry goods—food, clothing, and stationery—traveling on foot to villages both near and far. By the time he was twelve, the Fongs—with four boys and a girl in the family—had determined that their best future was not in Gow Bay Hong. Their home consisted of a single dirt-floored room. They slept on straw mats, their heads resting on brick pillows. As the children grew older, they would take wooden boards and chairs to a nearby ancestral hall and sleep there, along with children from other families.

My father wanted to get away from the village, to find a place where he could make substantial money and then return. He heard about Manila, the port and capital city of the Philippine Islands.

In the early 1900s, the United States had taken control of the Philippines in the aftermath of the Spanish-American war. In Manila's main business district, Binondro, much of the most menial manual labor was being done by Chinese coolies. Some of the young men from my father's village had gone to Manila and reported that a hard-working person could save some money there. It was 1921, and my father was eighteen.

He went to Manila, where he worked ten hours a day delivering bread by horsewagon, earning a paltry fifteen dollars a month. He then became a cashier at an export company, tripling his salary. After work, he often went to the Far East, a Chinese restaurant next door. There, helping out, he learned to cook, and he was soon preparing banquets.

But he was growing restless. He made enough money to send some back to his village and to bring a younger brother over to Manila, to be a companion and business partner. Instead, the brother soon married and moved to a town outside Manila.

And my father's prospects for starting up a store of his own grew dim. Early on, he had insisted to his family that he'd never go to America. "I don't want to lose my Chinese ways," he had said. But after six years in the Philippines, he'd had enough. He'd heard stories about fellow villagers in Gow Bay Hong who had made the trip and done well.

He wrote to some village relatives in the United States. "Life is very hard in the village and in the Philippines," he said. "If I could come to America, could you be of assistance?" The relatives, who had settled in Oakland, California, promised to help.

Now, he needed to circumvent the Exclusion Act that Congress had enacted in 1882 to bar all Chinese—except for sons of United States citizens or Chinese merchants—from entering the country.

He learned that because the Philippines were a colony of the United States, any citizen of the islands could enter. All he needed was a birth certificate bearing a Filipino name.

He obtained a copy of a birth certificate with which he could claim to be "Ricardo Torres." The name belonged to a deceased Filipino. For $1,200, it now belonged to my father.

He traveled by boat to the United States, stopping first in Seattle, where he got his first inkling that his ruse had succeeded. A Chinese cook glanced at him, taking note of his smooth, dark complexion. Then, speaking a Cantonese dialect he figured my father had no way of understanding, he turned to a friend and shouted, "He's a Filipino; you can mix some dog shit into his food."

My father knew a few Filipino phrases, but didn't speak up; an accent could expose him as Chinese. He went without that first meal and continued his journey to San Francisco, where he arrived with a dollar in his pocket and no job prospects. It was 1927.

In his first days in the city, my father stayed at the Fong family association. Early Chinese immigrants had formed various associations—usually by clan names—as a way of unifying, governing, and defending themselves. Some built majestic halls, where meetings and clan rituals were conducted, and where a room was set aside to house those who had no work or home.

Through family friends, my father got a job washing dishes. But he wanted to be a cook—especially after he heard that another family association was willing to pay fifty dollars for a cook to go to San Mateo, on the Peninsula south of San Francisco, to prepare a banquet for fourteen tables of ten diners each. My father, who was making sixty dollars a month, got the assignment. When he received a fifty-dollar tip, he thought he was on his way; he'd had his first glimpse of the gold of the Golden Mountains.

Looking for a chance to cook, my father moved across the bay, to Oakland, where he took a dishwashing job at the New Shanghai restaurant. Within a few months, the boss could see, by the advice my father gave the cooks, that he belonged in chef's whites, and he was promoted.

To earn more money, he stayed at the restaurant after work and, using a pair of long bamboo sticks, whipped and stretched wheat flour into noodles, which he sold to other restaurants.

By 1930, he'd saved enough to become a partner in a restaurant, the New China on Eighth Street in Oakland's Chinatown. He was owner, chef, and, occasionally, delivery man. Chinatown restaurants often delivered food without benefit of boxes or cars. Food would be served on dishes, as in the restaurants, and be placed on a large, round, metal tray. A waiter would then hoist the tray above his head and deliver the meal by foot. At the New Shanghai and other restaurants where he worked, when waiters were busy or sick, my father would take the trays through Chinatown himself. If it was raining, he'd cover the dinner with an oilcloth, the tray itself serving as his umbrella.

For all his work, my father's timing was off. He and his partners opened shop in the midst of the Depression, and, although charging only twenty-five cents for a full lunch, they barely broke even.

My father finally found some good fortune in 1936 when, on a Chinese Keno lottery ticket that cost him $1.50, he marked enough lucky numbers to win $1,800. He put most of the money into another restaurant with a friend named Ah Wing. My father named the restaurant the New Canton, but any optimism he had was dashed when Mr. Ah was killed by his younger brother over a family "misunderstanding."

Shattered by the loss of his friend, my father stepped away from restaurants. He took a job marking Keno tickets in the South Bay, and worked at a nearby racetrack.

Between his earnings and his rare winnings, my father had enough money to send some back home, to help siblings get married, purchase gifts for Spring and Moon Festivals, and for living expenses. He kept just enough to live on and to bank for future business opportunities.

Soon, his relatives were telling him that it was time that he, too, considered marriage.

"Ai-ya!" they'd cry. "You're not young any more. You'd better start your family." From China, his sister-in-law wrote encouraging him to get married and offering to help find someone for him.

In 1940, my father was thirty-seven. Only five feet six, he was thin and wiry. His face was calm, unmarked, and unlined, but his hands were rough and spoke of hard work. Under a high forehead, his small brown eyes gazed out steadily, and when his full lips were closed and downturned, he could appear stern. Yet, he loved to joke and laugh. He had a strong, commanding voice and a keen ear for comedy and mimicry, and he'd mime local drunks or pompous politicians, American customers and Chinese opera singers. At that point, he hadn't given much thought to marriage, but others had.

A young woman who worked at a Chinatown coffee shop tried to befriend my father, and there were several girls who showed up at whichever restaurant he was cooking at. They'd call him "Cooky," chat with him, and wind up with heftier portions than the average customer. But he'd tell them he had no time for any kind of social engagements.

To his friends, he would say that, when the time came, he didn't want any brash, American-born Chinese. He wanted to find a girl from China. He wrote back to his sister-in-law and said he hadn't met any girls he liked in the United States. Could she help him to find a village girl?

My mother, too, came to America with false papers bearing a false name.

Although somehow I accepted my dad having the name "Ricardo," I never understood how my mother came to be known as "Joe": Joe Tung Low Torres.

Her real name was Tui-Wing, her surname, Soo Hoo. Born in 1921 in Chek Hom, a small village of a hundred households near my father's, she was the youngest of five children. Their father was a schoolteacher, and their mother was an educated housewife who practiced some medicine—writing prescriptions and treating minor ailments—in spare hours.

When she was eight, my mother saw an aunt who had managed to emigrate to the United States. Back in the village for a visit, she stunned my mother with the way she was dressed. Others talked about hard times in America, in the throes of the Depression, but the aunt talked about how much better life was in the United States than in the village. My mother liked what she heard. The Chinese not only thought of the United States as the land of golden mountains, but called America *Mai Gok*— which meant "beautiful country."

In the late twenties, China was once again under siege by the Japanese, but my mother was not concerned with war—or with thoughts about work or a career.

For a girl in a tiny village in China, there wasn't much to occupy one's mind. She went to school for a few years. In idle moments, she did embroidery and needlepoint with the girls in the village. Every young woman's goal, it seemed, was a marriage proposal from someone in the United States.

By 1937, the Japanese encroachment into China was palpable, as major cities fell. Interest in leaving for America increased.

In 1939, when my mother was eighteen, a photograph of my father arrived in her village. My father's brother and sister-in-law had begun scouting local girls; they sought a good girl, one who was willing to go to America, one who was not afraid of work. When they heard of such a specimen, they would arrange a time and place for a quick look.

My mother's look-see took place at a clock shop. She didn't know it, but she was being watched. She suspected something was up; the word had gotten around and a small crowd had gathered at the store to view this early stage of matchmaking. "Why so many people?" she thought to herself. She wondered if she was the target of a potential suitor. The only young man she noticed was one in a blue *cheong-sam*, a long gown, walking back and forth, avoiding her eye. My mother was right. She was under scrutiny, but the young man was my father's brother.

By now, he had already seen more than twenty young women. In my mother, he saw an attractive girl in a flowered *cheong-sam*, with a modified pageboy brushed back to leave only a petite row of bangs over the forehead. She looked healthy and well fed, but not big. If my father's brother could have put them side to side, my father would have been taller by no more than an inch. She seemed purposeful, and with her big, wide eyes, she looked like she was ready to take in the world.

In Oakland, my father went to a photography studio downtown and posed for a portrait. Dressed in a suit and tie, he stood, slightly bow-legged, in front of a panel of curtains, then put on a stylish overcoat and a hat for another shot. He sent the photos to his family, and they forwarded them to the family of Soo Hoo Tui-Wing.

On paper, my father looked acceptable to my mother's family. Her sister then went to my father's village to do some research on him. There, she was told that Fong Kwok Shang was a good, kind man, a hard worker who sent money not only to his family but one year, when he was in Manila, to every household in the village during Spring Festival—Chinese New Year. My mother's family quickly approved the marriage. Tui-Wing was going to the beautiful-sounding *Mai Gok*.

As much as she'd fantasized about America, she worried about leaving her mother behind. Her family kept telling her that her marriage was the best thing for all of them. Too many village girls wound up marrying in farm towns far away from home, forced into a life of hard labor. If she could make money in the United States, she would have a good life. And, of course, she would send money back to them.

My mother knew these things to be true, and she felt lucky to have been chosen.

By bus and sedan chair, she traveled from her village to Canton and on to Hong Kong. The road to Hong Kong was very difficult to walk, and highways had been destroyed to keep Japanese invaders away. Problems with paperwork stalled her for five months. My father had spent the two thousand dollars he had saved up over the thirteen years he'd been in America to purchase a false paper transforming Tui-Wing into Joe Tung Low, headed for a reunion with her "father" in San Francisco. But by the time my mother set sail for the Golden Mountains, he would have to borrow and scrape up another four thousand dollars.

She left just in time. In 1940, there was a war going on, and shortly after she left, no ships from Asia were allowed into the United States.

Even as she rode the liner to America, my lucky mother knew what was in store for her—one last but imposing barrier to entry. She'd been told that all the Chinese who tried to get to the Golden Mountains first had to be locked up in "the wooden house."

My mother's first sight of America was a cruel illusion. From her boat, Angel Island looked like paradise, a richly forested mountain isle. As the boat docked at the wharf on the northern tip of the island, her first close-up view of American land encompassed a stand of four sturdy palm trees fronting several grand-looking structures like none she had seen in China or even during her stay in Hong Kong.

This was the immigration station on Angel Island, which, with an area of a square mile, was the largest island in San Francisco Bay. From here, it was a fifteen-minute boat ride to the city. In 1910, the federal government had built several buildings to serve as a detention center for thousands of would-be immigrants. Here, they were examined and interrogated to ensure that they weren't getting in with either communicable diseases or false identities.

She was sent to the women's dormitory in the Administration Building. It looked like an army barracks. There were several dozen bunk beds stacked up three to a space, and above the highest bed, clotheslines were draped with just-washed garments. Below each lower bunk sat a bedpan. "Several tens of beds," she thought. "And what a stink."

This was the room my mother would have to live in for six weeks, the forty-one days between the time her ship reached American shores and the time she was allowed to meet my father.

My mother made a few friends among the women there. When she had extra food, she'd share it with dormitory mates. But, aside from meals in the dining room and walks within a yard, the detainees were not allowed out of their barracks building. Women were segregated from men, children from adults, all in the interest of deterring cheating on the interrogation process.

Bathrooms had a couple of sinks and a long row of toilets with no stalls. With guards always nearby, women had no privacy, and some resorted to placing paper sacks over their heads so that they couldn't see themselves being observed.

At Angel Island, you were guilty until proven innocent.

In her time there, the officials sent three women back to China. The fact that one of them had even managed to learn English didn't help her. They'd been on Angel Island for two to three years. One woman, having failed the examination and despairing over losing face back home in China, hanged herself in the bathroom. Another killed herself by sticking a chopstick through an ear.

Stories about suicides and ghosts made their way from barrack to barrack, and my mother, fearful of ghosts, refused to go to the toilet without a friend.

By the time she reached this island, she felt she loved my father, even though she hadn't yet met him. He had written her faithfully while she was held up in Hong Kong. Once he knew that she was on Angel Island, he shipped food to her, which some of the Chinese cooks on the island would help prepare for her.

Once, as she handed over fresh vegetables and fish, one of them looked at her and raised an eyebrow. "You have a father who's so nice?" he asked. She nodded shyly. She knew better than to say that she had a husband waiting. The cooks and kitchen staff, who lived in San Francisco, were known to help smuggle messages between the island and Chinatown, including notes for detainees to use in their interrogations, but she'd been warned not to trust anyone.

My mother had a packet of information about her false family—her father, her story went, was in San Francisco, and that's who she was joining—and she studied the family's history from Hong Kong to Angel Island. Twelve people in the family, and she had to know them intimately—their names, their own histories, their home and neighborhood in China—so that she could convince the officials that she was indeed part of that family.

She took her turn before the officers from the Immigration and Naturalization Service, with a Chinese man sitting at their table to interpret.

The officers struck her as hostile, and she was frightened. At one point, her face reddened.

"Why are you turning red?" an officer asked. "Is it because you're not who you say you are?"

My mother flushed deeper, then snapped: "Of course not. It's just hot in here."

They asked her the questions she expected—"There is this man in your village. Which house did he live in? Where was it located?" She answered such questions for several hours, then repaired to the women's dormitory, uncertain.

A week later, on August 6, 1940, forty-one days after she'd arrived, an official entered the dormitory and shouted out her false name. She was stunned. While an official called to alert her "father," other women rushed to her bunk. Several helped her pack, while one quickly ironed her dress. Suddenly faced with the life she'd been waiting for, she nervously made her way down to the dock, accompanied by several of the women with whom she'd been living. A worker handed her the suitcases that had been taken from her six weeks before. She clutched her belongings and looked at the women, all of them working to hold back their envy, to only wish her well. She looked beyond them and back to the wooden house. Several more women waved to her. She wondered which among them would be as lucky as she was.

Her ferry circled the east coast of the island and, from the southern tip, made its way to the Ferry Building in San Francisco. My father was on the dock. He greeted her with an outstretched hand and a happy shout: "Oh, Tui-Wing! You've landed!"

They were immediately attracted to each other. "I am *hoi-them*"—my heart is open and happy, my mother thought. She had already been won over by his letters, by his kindnesses while she was on Angel Island. She was already convinced that he was a good man. Now, as she visited with him, she found him handsome as well. She was just about to turn nineteen, and he was a month short of thirty-seven, but she didn't think of him as old.

It didn't matter what she thought, of course. If he had turned out to be a brute, or so grotesquely deformed that she couldn't bear life with him, her only recourse would have been to escape to a boarding house, where she'd have to work out her future in America or a way to return to China.

They met some of my father's family friends from his village; by the time they had dinner, it was getting late. Still, my father, anxious to show her more of the kind of life to be lived in America, took her to the Great China Theater on Jackson Street, one of two movie houses that showed Chinese films. They saw a musical, *Night Thief of Red Scarf*, featuring two acclaimed Cantonese opera stars, Mac Bingwing and Xu Renxing. In addition to this musical reminder of the land she had just left, my mother saw an American newsreel and a few comedy film clips. They were the first movies she had seen since she was a child in the village.

"I'm so lucky to be here," she said to my father as they emerged from the theater. She thought about her village; how her family and his had made all arrangements for her to come to America. She'd felt sure that once they had met, they'd marry.

My father felt the same commitment; before my mother arrived at Angel Island, he had rented a two-bedroom flat just blocks from Oakland's Chinatown, at 206 Eighth Street. Within a few weeks, they went to City Hall, took out the necessary papers, and exchanged vows in a civil ceremony. Back in Chinatown, villagers and friends hosted a twelve-table wedding banquet for them.

THE ALL-

AMERICAN

CITY

My father and mother began their lives together in an Oakland that was mostly white, mostly middle-class, Republican, and solid, churchgoing Protestant. Oakland was, it liked to say about itself, an all-American city. The Chinese had their little enclave, and there were pockets of Irish and Portuguese, but the post–World War II influx of blacks was yet to come.

The Chinese seemed content to stay in Chinatown, where, in their view, it was the non-Chinese who were the unknowing foreigners, the *bok guey*—the white demons.

Sometimes, they made my father laugh. He told my mother about the morning he was at the New Shanghai and two white women entered the empty restaurant. They wanted to know when it'd be open. My father picked up the word "open," but didn't speak any English. He grabbed a broom to indicate eleven o'clock on the overhead clock, but as he raised the broom, the women turned and fled, fearing for their lives.

History books show that it took Oakland a long time to think of the Chinese as anything other than laborers, either wanted or unwanted. The Chinese helped build some of the town's most vital pipelines, introduced intensive farming to the Bay Area, and provided restaurants and homes with fresh produce.

But, like Chinese throughout California and the rest of the country, the Oakland Chinese became targets of "anti-coolie" clubs, movements, and demonstrations as unemployment rose in the 1870s. The protests, which closed down Chinese settlements, also led to Congress passing the Chinese Exclusion Act in 1882. And when the Immigration Act of 1924 barred any Chinese woman from entering the United States as a permanent resident, a bachelor society was created in various Chinatowns, driving some men to prostitution and opium.

But most of the Chinese in Oakland persisted, and when the 1906 earthquake and fire destroyed San Francisco's Chinatown, Oakland's Chinese welcomed wealthy refugees who helped them to build a strong Chinatown centered at Eighth and Webster Streets.

Still, they were trapped. Realtors in various parts of town kept Chinese from buying, owning, or leasing property. The only way they could live in houses outside of Chinatown was as servants.

But in their own part of town, the Chinese could operate businesses, and just before my mother's arrival, my father opened the New Eastern Cafe at 710 Webster Street.

This was good timing. In 1940, Chinatown's population, steadily declining since it became a bachelor society, had a reversal in fortunes as San Francisco's Chinatown, jammed with nearly 18,000 residents, found many of them crossing the four-year-old Bay Bridge to Oakland.

It had been three years since my father had owned his own

place, and he was sparing none of his energy to make it work. But his devotion to the New Eastern Cafe left my mother to make a fitful adjustment to *Mai Gok*.

At first, she resisted leaving the house—she was just too shy—and suffered from loneliness. She allowed herself to think, "I had more fun at Angel Island."

Soon, she met Grace Fung, a waitress from the New Eastern, who lived with her husband Jack just across Eighth Street. When my mother knew she was pregnant, another neighbor woman offered to help prepare for the birth of Sarah in June of 1941, and Grace became her godmother.

Just before my mother entered the Oakland Maternity Hospital on Pill Hill, a cluster of medical buildings north of downtown, my father was talking to Benson Fong, a Chinese community leader who was known as the honorary mayor of San Francisco's Chinatown. My father mentioned his quandary: His legal name was Torres, but his real name was Fong. He was planning to give his children only his legal name; otherwise, the immigration authorities might come after him.

Being a Fong himself, Benson was not about to let my father proceed. "Your real name is Fong," he said. "You must include it." They resolved the matter by concocting a double last name: Fong Torres. (The hyphenation would come later, when the children learned punctuation and tired of having their names filed under "Torres.")

Five Fong Torreses would appear between 1941 and 1949. The three boys were named *Jeen-Hoong*, *Jeen-Haw*, and *Jeen-Geet*—for Chinese heroes. The girls were *Wai-Ha* and *Wai-Sehng*, the *wai* meaning wit and wisdom. *Ha* meant dew and *Sehng*, goddess.

Mother and Father had no clue about American names. At the hospital, they looked over a book of baby names. My father liked the look of the letter *S* and picked one of the first names on the list: Sarah. Two years later, for the first boy, he tapped the *B* list and chose Barry, then, another year and a half later, Benjamin. For the second daughter, he and Mother went back to the *S*'s and chose Shirley, then went back once more to the *B*'s and selected Burton.

At Lincoln School, teachers assumed that our middle name was Fong and our last name was Torres. And they got to wondering how Chinese kids could have a Spanish name.

We'd shrug. All we knew was that Fong wasn't our middle name, because our parents didn't give any of us middle names. Through those early years, a story materialized and, like Sarah's and Barry's clothes, got handed down. In just the way we'd put on the clothes with no questions, we began to tell what we thought to be the truth about our name.

Our father, we would say, was born in the Philippines. He's Chinese, we'd add, but because of his birthplace, he was given a Filipino name on top of his Chinese name. Simple as that.

Our friends would nod and accept it. Older people would look puzzled, but if we just kept shrugging to any further questions, they, too, would come to accept our explanation.

It would be many years before we learned that we were passing on a lie.

Sarah, Barry, and I were born into an America at war. Sarah was born in June 1941, six months before Pearl Harbor; Barry came along in May 1943, exactly a year after the United States ordered all Japanese—Americans or not—to be evacuated to internment camps.

Throughout the war, Oakland was the main funnel through which men, ships, planes, and materiel flowed. Nineteen forty-five would be the year of Hitler's death and the turning of America's force onto Japan.

I was born early on the morning of January 7, 1945 in a medical clinic in Alameda, the peninsula town south of Oakland connected by a short tunnel. During wartime, hospital rooms were scarce, and soldiers were given priority. Three days later, the attending physician issued my birth certificate—with a typo. My name, on paper, was "Benjaman Fong Torres."

* * *

One evening in late 1946, in the front parlor at 206 Eighth Street, my father drew a chair up to where a record-cutting machine was sitting on the floor, near the Zenith console radio. Before tape recorders, people could make their own records, etched onto plastic-coated metal discs. Our parents had taught us to sing Chinese songs and, when they pestered us enough, one or the other of us would break out in song—at the neighborhood grocery store or pharmacy, at a village cousin's party, and, at least once, on the passenger liner to China. At home, Sarah and I happily shrieked into the recording machine's microphone, while Barry shied away.

But the recorder served another purpose. Our *Po-Po*—our grandmother on our mother's side—didn't know how to read, so my father decided to send her recorded messages, which she would be able to listen to at a store in the village.

On a blank disc spinning at seventy-eight revolutions per minute, my father placed a tone arm with a recording needle onto the outer edge of the disc and began to speak.

"Ah Po! Ah Po!" he called out to Grandmother. "Do you know who this is? I am your unpious son-in-law, Fong Kwok Shang.

"Today, our family is still separated. I don't know when we shall see each other again. Having abandoned our beautiful motherland and being separated by mountains and oceans, we live like orphans overseas."

For all the anxiety of dislocation, however, my father was anxious to impress on *Po-Po* that her daughter had not done wrong in marrying him. He allowed himself a bit of uncharacteristic braggadocio. "Compared to my brothers and sister—I don't want to brag—but I think I am doing quite well," my father said.

That was so, he said, because he and my mother were living very frugally. He reported that they now had four children, and told of dividing his time between family and work.

"In all conscience, I don't think I have done enough for the family," he said, with the humility expected of him. "But everyone in the family is very kindhearted. I believe this good environment is due to you, grandmother, and to your upbringing of the family. I owe you a great deal of gratitude, and I don't know how to repay you. Thank you from the bottom of my heart."

My father then called Sarah, Barry, and me to the microphones to sing for Grandma. As always, Sarah and I were the loudest; Barry let out a few yelps and retreated.

Father then labeled the disc and placed another blank onto the turntable.

This one would be for relatives in his village and in Manila. To them, my father was far less brash.

"From the day I left Manila," he began, "many winters and summers; months and years have gone by. It has been twenty years long. During these twenty years, Little Brother has gone through a great deal.

"My business is not going forward. There is nothing to brag about. I am still my old self. My future looks bleak. I feel so shameful for myself. Fortunately, I am healthy."

As if to assure his family that he knew he was not the only one who'd had hard times, he launched into a summary, from his perspective, of recent world events.

"Ten years ago, Japan launched the bloody invasion against our motherland without any reason. Our compatriots suffered a lot from the inhuman actions by the Japanese. For that, the Japanese had shown their utmost ugliness in front of the world. They were out of their minds. They wanted to conquer the entire world and rule it under their fists."

The Japanese, my father said, caused hardship for family members both in the Philippines and in China.

"But," he said, "God has answered our prayers. Our motherland has been liberated. The invaders have surrendered. You are recovering from your wounds. I wish uncles, aunts, and brothers peace and health, and may your business opportunities resume, now that you have escaped the tiger's mouth."

My father continued with his downbeat assessment of his own

fortunes. "Here in America, after the war, business is not as good as before," he said. "The situation has changed. There are more problems between workers and management. Workers want wage increases. Strikes are everywhere. Take our restaurant, a small business. Business has dropped to one-third compared to the past. My income is just enough to feed my family. Fortunately, everyone is fine.

"I wish my uncles, aunts, and brothers a prosperous future and good health. This is your Little Brother's wish."

My father was overly modest. Only seven years since marrying, he and my mother had a family of four children. Business was down at the New Eastern, but they were doing well enough to send money back to China and the Philippines and to afford a car, a washing machine, and a radio.

He was not a wealthy man, and he had not scaled America's Golden Mountains. But with a home, a family, and a business of his own, he could say that he was continuing the climb.

By 1948, letters were no longer enough.

In the fall, before the arrival of the last child, my mother made what she feared would be her last trip to China.

She had been thinking of her homeland ever since leaving it eight years before, and she felt discomfort almost every night—particularly at evening's end. She watched as my father threw out leftover food, and she thought about people starving in China. It was a great deal more than a cliché we'd be hearing for years to come, as she prodded us to finish our meals and, no matter how stuffed we were, to "eat some more."

In her dreams, all of China was suffering in the aftermath of the war. But her worst dreams were that her mother had died of hunger. With postal service from China so erratic, she often spent weeks worrying about her family. Soon after the war, she got a letter from them. *Po-Po*—grandmother, as we knew her—was fine. But, the family wrote, she was sixty years old, and she wanted to see my mother while she was still healthy. A few years before, her father had died, and my mother, who got the word by mail, could not risk going to the village.

Mother was torn. She didn't want to leave her family, and yet she couldn't deny her mother. With the Communists pressing southward after taking Henan Province, time was running short.

So that Father wouldn't be left with four kids to watch, she took Sarah and me with her. We traveled to Hong Kong on the *U.S.S. President.* The trip, lasting almost three weeks, left my mother seasick and weakened. I remember shopping with her in Kowloon, where she was visiting people from her village. At one point, visiting the son of a cousin, she fell down the ladder leading up to his loft. After her recovery, we continued on to Canton, the largest city closest to her village. We took a five-hour train ride to Hoi Ping.

Even at age three, I knew we were in a foreign land. It was home to our mother, and Sarah and I were made to feel as if we belonged. But there was no denying my senses. The countryside reeked of the pungency of animals and of a land with no sewage system. The villagers were used to it, but Sarah and I constantly made faces to each other. "This place stinks," she'd say, pinching her nose.

Sarah watched in horror as *Po-Po*, who practiced folk medicine, treated visitors in the front room of her house. One man came in with sores on his leg, and *Po-Po* proceeded to scrape at them with a knife. Then she tied strings around the sores and lit them. While the patient only flinched, Sarah ran screaming out of the house.

Out in the streets, we fought the smells with food. I loved steamed taro, a potatolike vegetable, and, in Canton and Hong Kong, found egg custard tarts sweeter than any I'd had at home. Sarah had more sophisticated tastes. She asked for the shark's fin soup she'd tasted at Chinese banquets, and she wanted roast pigeon. *"Ai-ya,"* my grandmother said, shaking her head at the thought of such luxuries. With the civil war going on just to the north, food was in short supply, and my mother would skip meals to spare food for the rest of us.

By the end of 1948, the Communists were moving steadily toward Canton, and my uncle urged my mother to flee.

We had been in Asia five months, and my mother knew it was time to go. No one knew what the consequences might be for Chinese visitors from America if the Communists overtook the village. We were Americans by birth, but our mother had not become a citizen, and, in her heart, she would always be Chinese. But she also knew that her family was now in California. We sailed from Hong Kong to the Philippine Islands in January, and, after a quick visit with my father's family, took a Pan Am prop plane to Honolulu and on to San Francisco.

When our father asked us about China, Sarah reported that everybody hugged Mother in greeting, and that Mother had cried when she first saw *Po-Po*. She politely refrained from saying how much the countryside stank.

Father asked what I thought of China. "The streets are all dirt," I said in Chinese. "When you walk, you step into mud."

By fall, almost all of China was in the hands of the Communist party, and on October 1, Mao Zedong established the People's Republic of China, declaring: "The Chinese people have stood up."

To Americans, it was Red China. Our parents pronounced *gung-chon-ong*—Communists—with a bitterness born of worry over the people they left behind.

·· 4 ··

BROTHERS

AND

SISTERS

I did not know what a wedding was. At age six in the fall of 1951, all I knew was that I was going to be involved in a big one.

One of Grace Fung's sons was getting married, and somehow, among Grace and her husband Jack and my parents, it was decided that I'd make a perfect ringbearer.

I could tell it was a big deal by the way my parents spoke to me. My father always spoke firmly, but with an agreeable laugh, while my mother offered the gentle touch, a softness leavened by the understanding that in our house, she handled most of the discipline. Now, as they told me of my responsibilities, I sensed that I was about to do something grown-up. This wasn't just going to school, or joining my siblings in a simple chore, or singing a song at the neighborhood grocery. This was stand-alone time.

"Fung Moo and Fung Bok are our good, good friends," my mother said. "It's a big wedding, several hundreds of people. You'll have to practice and make sure you do it right. You don't want to *seet-meen*—lose face."

No, I wouldn't want to ... *what?*

"How can I lose my face?" I asked.

She laughed.

"Losing face means disgrace, loss of respect for your family. So you must be good."

We went shopping at Roos Brothers, a downtown store that, to my amazement, stocked only men's clothing. We'd always gone to big department stores or to Pay Less for clothes—to wherever the sales were.

At Roos Brothers, my parents picked out a rental tuxedo for me. Now I knew for certain that this was a big deal. It was a vanilla white, double-breasted tux with pleated black pants and patent leather shoes.

I remember the sensations of trying on the formal wear, of standing in front of the tall mirrors, of the clerks checking the fit. I looked so different. This was more adult than almost anything I'd seen my own father wear. With this on, I knew that I could never lose my face.

My job, as I learned at the rehearsals, was simple: to hold an embroidered pink satin pillow bearing the wedding rings and to march quietly down the aisle to a point between the bride and groom—Nancy and Wayman—and the minister. There, I'd keep the rings within reach of the minister, and when the pillow was empty, I'd take a step back.

I was thrilled. It was my first chance to perform in front of a big crowd of strangers, and I couldn't wait for September 16 to come.

To accommodate a party of more than three hundred, the Fungs decided to have the ceremonies and banquet in *Dai Fow*—"Big Town," as the Chinese referred to San Francisco—and on the appointed Sunday afternoon, 360 people filled the pews of the San Francisco Presbyterian Church on Stockton Street.

To me, the wedding was one big show, with grown-up men in tuxedoes just like mine, eight bridesmaids in chiffon dresses of various pastel colors, and the organist now playing the music I'd heard so many times at rehearsals. I felt row after row of eyes on me as I walked slowly down the aisle with the ring. It was, I would later learn, a typical Chinese-American wedding, the exchange of vows taking place in a Western church, in English, followed by a big Chinese banquet laden with food and rituals from the Far East.

The *yum-choy*—the banquet—was at Sun Hung Heung, a stately old restaurant in Chinatown. I wasn't allowed to stay up for all of it, but it was my first glimpse of the festivity with which the Chinese celebrated special occasions. The dining room was twice the size of our own at the New Eastern. Like ours, the walls were paneled in dark wood, but here they were decorated with panels of red and gold banners wishing the bride and groom good luck and fortune. Family members, friends, and representatives of family associations made short speeches, most of them in Cantonese. And a roomful of big round tables held a feast of dishes I would come to know well at banquets in the years ahead. There was the fanciest soup in existence, made of shark fin, representing power and prosperity; a parade of poultry dishes—chicken, squab, and a crispy roast duck with steamed buns you could peel into flat pieces to sandwich around slices of duck. There were oblong dishes of huge black mushrooms with oyster sauce, of diced chicken with cashew nuts, of steamed whole fish, all to be washed down with tea, orange soda, or every Chinese kid's favorite: Belfast sparkling cider. Some of the adults, mostly the men, would drink a pungent rice whiskey called *Mm-ga-pei*, a taste most Chinese children never grew to acquire.

While my parents joined in the toasting, staying well into the evening, I slept in a room in the back.

Then it was back to normal life at our two homes, the flat on Eighth Street and the New Eastern Cafe.

* * *

Oakland was a dull gray in contrast to San Francisco's cosmopolitan colors, and our Chinatown had none of the San Francisco Chinatown's glamour or tourist-drawing power. But, for kids, there was excitement enough.

Just across Webster Street, at Seventh, was a corner shop with all the latest comic books: Red Ryder and Little Beaver, Batman, Lone Ranger, Gene Autry—hanging along a wire on clothespins. At Eighth, there was the Man Sing Wo, a small shop where older Chinatown residents picked up Chinese newspapers from both San Francisco and abroad, along with cigarettes, cigars, salted plums, and watermelon seeds. They could while away hours reading, smoking, and chatting. Kids ventured in for candy— Chinese and American—and for soda pops, which stood in water bottleneck high in a big red Coca-Cola cooler. Older kids played pinball, providing a syncopated background for the men's chatter.

We found far less interesting the shops that dealt with our restaurant; the barnyard smells of the poultry store where chickens were stacked up in cages; the butchers and seafood stores; the wet-concrete-floored bean sprout store where we picked up five-pound sacks of sprouts to lug back to the New Eastern.

But there were also the *dim sum* restaurants, where we could get sweet pastries and *cha-siu bow*—steamed buns encasing chopped barbecued pork. Some early mornings, I'd tag along with my father to the corner coffee shop, only steps from the New Eastern, where he'd have a cup of coffee and a slice of custard pie. I'd go with him and sit with a sponge cupcake and a rare glass of milk—not part of the Chinese diet at home— while he had his moment of relaxation before the workday began.

We got our hair cut by a woman who always seemed to be sixty years old. We called her *Git Moo*, "moo" being the word attached to the name of an older woman. Younger women were addressed as *seen-nye*. Git Moo was the widow of Fong Git, who opened his barber shop in 1906. By the time we came along, Git Moo was running the shop by herself.

We hated getting haircuts, sitting on a wooden plank placed over the chair arms so that Git Moo, her own hair short and netted, her shoulders stooped, and her movements slow and deliberate, could reach our heads. She made our visits as short and sweet as she could. She'd cut our hair, collect our seventy-five cents, then shuffle through a curtain leading to a back room and emerge with lollipops for us.

The undisputed leader of our pack was my sister Sarah, the first born, the first coddled, and the first to be subjected to the customs of the Chinese family. She was expected to do everything: to help at the restaurant, to take care of her little brothers and sister, and excel in school. She soon began to rebel.

Sometimes, my mother once said, she wondered if somebody at the hospital switched babies on her. Sarah was so ill-tempered. She'd kick little sister Shirley out of their room during the night if she made a noise or tugged their blanket. Shirley wound up in the kitchen pantry, where she slept on a cot amid foods and supplies.

Sarah was a central part of a circle of five girls who hung together at Lincoln School, just blocks away from Chinatown. They picked each other up every morning. There were Gerry and Maeley, who picked up Lucy, proceeded on to Jackson Street to get Darlene, and the four would collect Sarah for the final two blocks to Lincoln.

After school, they'd go to Maeley's house to listen to music and gossip about the boys in school and do homework, or meet at Lincoln Park and play paddleball, softball, and basketball, even organizing a basketball team that Sarah named the Royalettes.

They were all Chinatown girls, all of them from lower- to middle-class families, all of them locked into the chop suey of Chinese culture and tradition—except for Maeley.

Maeley's parents were Chinese opera singers who were living

and performing in San Francisco when a fire broke out at their theater, destroying the costumes. Her father left for Hong Kong, ostensibly to help acquire a replacement wardrobe, and never returned. It turned out that he had a girlfriend in Hong Kong.

Maeley, who was four when her father disappeared, was placed in a foster home until she was ten, when her mother, having found a new male companion, took her daughter back into her life, a life that was neither Chinese nor American. Her mother slept in during the day, then left to play mah-jongg with friends, leaving Maeley to fend for herself.

Sarah, meantime, was at the New Eastern. She helped wrap won-tons, and as soon as she was deemed responsible enough, she was looking after Barry and me in the rice room. The babies, Shirley and Burton, whiled away their time in the adjacent room.

Sarah struggled to learn English. Like so many Lincoln School students, she'd heard mostly Cantonese at home, and entered school with no knowledge of English. Until about the fourth grade, she couldn't read the books she was given at Lincoln. Once she learned, she excelled, getting better grades than her friends and emerging as the brightest of them all.

Barry was the Man. Having been the first-born boy, Barry held a status none of the rest of us could ever aspire to. In China, girls were worthless, nothing but future wives and slaves of some man, good for little more than bearing children. And they were deemed good at that only if they bore boys.

Males would carry on the family name. They would work and support not only their own family but their parents and grandparents as well. They were the familial elite. And among all the boys in the family, none enjoyed a higher ranking—and none had more expected of him—than the Number One Son.

Barry knew none of this as a kid. He tore through life, doing well in school when he was interested, goofing off when he wasn't.

From the beginning—in first grade at Lincoln—he was graded

"average" in both scholarship and conduct. When he was in fourth grade, his teacher noted that he had difficulties with enunciation and ascribed it to his coming from a Chinese-speaking family. But he noted that Barry was very bright, a quick learner with an inquisitive mind for art.

At home, inquisitiveness led to destruction. At age five, he took screwdrivers and pliers to toys, radios, and even Mother's sewing machine. "I can put it back together!" he'd say when he was discovered with the remnants of something that used to work. *"Ai-ya!"* Mother cried. "It took forever to save up to get this, and now . . ." "I just want to know how it works!" Barry would scream through his spankings.

Mother never forgot what Barry did at the New Eastern. One evening, he managed to punch a hole into the wall between the rice room and the adjacent sleeping room. He tried to patch the hole with newspapers. Frustrated with his efforts, he then set a match to the papers. My screams brought Mother running, and she put out the fire.

"Who did this?" she asked Barry.

He looked over at me. "Ben," he said.

She looked at the remains of the newspaper in the fresh hole in the wall. She looked at me. I was all of five years old.

"You lie!" she said. *"Ky-Doy!"* And Barry, the "bad boy," was in for a spanking.

From the time he entered Lincoln School, Barry's best friend was a boy from a broken home. William Fung's parents separated when he was two, and neither father nor mother particularly wanted responsibility for him. That chore fell to his grandmother, who took him into her apartment in Chinatown, just around the block from us.

They got close because they were placed close to each other. In school, Bill and Barry often stood in line together because of the proximity of their last names.

Bill considered himself handicapped, as his grandmother spoke only Chinese. Barry, too, heard little English before going to Lincoln School and, like so many Chinatown kids, played catch-up in the first several years of school. But while Barry spoke with a stammer and a noticeable Chinese accent for years, he never felt the traumas Bill did.

One day, in the first grade, Bill's teacher asked all the kids to name their favorite pie. Bill knew what he wanted to say—custard—but didn't know how to say it. In Chinese, the pie was identified by its main ingredient, and Bill had learned the English word for it. So, when his turn came, he mustered up all his bravery. "Egg," he said. "Egg pie."

The classroom filled with giggles. It would be a long time before Bill spoke up again.

I sat happily in the middle of my family, with an older sister, older brother, younger sister and younger brother. I was perfectly positioned. I wasn't expected to be the most responsible, and I wouldn't be spoiled, or be the last in line for handed-down clothes.

If Sarah was the social one and Barry the *ky-doy*, I was the performer. My stint as a ring-bearer for the Fungs had made me feel special, and I liked being in the spotlight.

This is not a particularly Chinese trait. We're supposed to be reserved. But at age eight, all I knew was that when I heard the radio, I wanted to get in there with all those tiny little people who were telling jokes and making music. Our Zenith console stood four feet high, which was taller than I was. My little-people theory seemed entirely plausible—until I saw a table radio.

I liked the nods and applause we'd get when we'd sing for friends in Chinatown, and I was the first in line whenever we used our record-cutting machine. But the first song I sang in public was an American pop tune with an Italian accent.

Barry was almost eleven, I was nine, and we were attending Lincoln School. The school ranged from kindergarten to eighth grade in two imposing gray buildings. First-generation Chinese parents drew comfort from the fact that, at Lincoln, ninety-five percent of the students were Chinese.

Every year or so, the school would stage a talent show, and Barry and I wanted to impress a third-grade teacher we'd both had. Her name was Alma Eybel, known to everyone, of course, as "Miss Eyeball." She was fast on the draw with a wooden ruler. But she had a weakness for music, and, many years before we got there, she had introduced a miniature xylophone, which she called "song bells," to her students.

Miss Eybel had the responsibility of putting on the talent show and kept her eyes peeled for potential participants. She'd already gotten Sarah and her pal Maeley to sign up to sing "Anything You Can Do," from the Broadway musical *Annie Get Your Gun*. Now, Miss Eybel was after Barry and me. She knew me as a boy who was known to yelp out a song—in English or Chinese—now and then. Barry was a bright and eager student, but he had some difficulties with English, and he was not a performer.

Still, it was important that we do what Miss Eyeball asked. So we decided to team up. We chose a song off the radio—"That's Amore" sung by Dean Martin—and, after school, we'd practice. With Sarah's help, we worked up a bit of choreography, patterned loosely on what we'd seen of Gene Kelly, Frank Sinatra, and Fred Astaire on television.

On the big night, we climbed onto the stage at Lincoln School. In the glare of the spotlight, Barry and I couldn't see any of the three hundred people in the audience. What they saw were two very nervous little boys at the microphone. And one of them was dressed very strangely.

Just before the show, a teacher had draped me with a Mexican serape—for a bit of that international flair required for a song like "That's Amore."

I began the song:

> *In Napoli, where love is king*
> *When boy meets girl*
> *Here's what they sing . . .*

And then, in approximate unison, Barry and I joined voices:

When the moon hits your eye like a big pizza pie
That's amore!
When the world seems to shine like you've had too much wine
That's amore!

Here, hoping that we wouldn't get ensnarled in my serape, we did a tentative little softshoe and continued:

Bells will ring ting-a-ling-a-ling, ting-a-ling-a-ling
and you'll sing, "Vita bella!"

We sang about a "pasta fazool"; we made reference to a "gay tarantella," which I thought was a happy spider. We didn't know what we were singing, and we didn't care. Barry was just happy that he'd survived and that Miss Eyeball was pleased. I was happy to be on stage.

As the fourth child and the second girl, Shirley was in an unenviable position. She had neither the responsibilities of the first born nor the leeway of the last. Following the first two boys in the family, the two who'd be out there in those white-collar professions that every Chinese parent wanted for their kids, Shirley had less expected of her. When she heard stories about herself as an infant, she wondered how much she'd been wanted.

One such story took place just after she'd been born in November 1946. At that time, Chinatown was still doing good business in the aftermath of the war. With Chinese New Year just beyond winter's horizon, Mother decided to leave Shirley in the care of a sitter through New Year. For the first several months of her life, then, Shirley lived in Alameda, in the same house where I had been born. The clinic had been converted into a nursery.

Mother visited once a week, and each time she noticed that

Shirley was crying—loudly. By January, a month before New Year, the sitter refused to keep her, saying Shirley's bawling was disturbing the other children. Mother took her home.

Not long afterwards, a worker at the nursery mixed up a supply of baby formula with Clorox. All the babies, my mother heard, had died of poisoning. She looked at Shirley in her crib and told Father: "She must have been crying so much because she didn't want to die."

With the arrival of Burton in April 1949, shortly after our China visit, we had a family of seven crammed into a two-bedroom, one-bathroom flat. Sarah and Shirley shared one large room until Shirley's move into the pantry. Mother and Father had the dining room, which, once again, had the baby crib set up in it. A door from our parents' room led into Barry's and my bedroom.

I was naturally closer to Barry than to any other sibling. We were bound, more than anything else, by the restaurant. Every day, we sat together at a round table in the back of the dining room, peeling the ends and spines off pea pods, pulling the legs and shells off frozen prawns, folding won-tons, and peeling water chestnuts. We studied in the rice room, and we played throughout the back areas of the restaurant. We came to understand that we were a working-class family, and we knew what we didn't have. But we also enjoyed what we did.

In the early fifties, when Uncle Miltie helped make television a mass medium, we didn't have a set. Sarah watched TV and gobbled up reels of *Flash Gordon* serials at her friend Loretta's house, but my first look at the new medium was upstairs from the New Eastern, at the Ying On Benevolent Association *tong*, or meeting hall.

At the *tong* above our restaurant, the association sometimes entertained members and friends with Chinese musical recitals. If I stayed in back of the room and kept quiet, I could watch. It was a slice of China: the stringed instruments, flutes, and tiny drums of an opera orchestra; the audience in their high-backed rosewood chairs; the clouds of smoke from pipes, cigars, and cigarettes.

But I found the music too strident to take for long stretches. Far more appealing was the TV set perched atop a cabinet.

The association members were avid boxing fans, but on weekends, they'd let us watch westerns—Wild Bill Hickok, the Range Rider, the Cisco Kid, and, of course, the Lone Ranger—and comedy, most of it on the *Colgate Comedy Hour* with Dean Martin and Jerry Lewis, Eddie Cantor, Abbott and Costello, and Jimmy Durante.

Watching the cowboy shows, we'd want to reenact scenes. We had holsters and cap pistols, but we made many of our own toys and costumes. A yellow kerchief was all it took to be part of the heroic U.S. Cavalry. After a Chinese swordfight movie, we'd attack a fruit crate for wooden slats, which we'd turn into swords. To play basketball at the restaurant, we'd wrap the red netting from an onion sack around a barrel hoop, which Father would nail onto the backyard fence. Tired of how easily the hoop fell, we'd stick up an open-ended cardboard box. To catch the rubber baseballs we threw back and forth, we'd fashion "mitts" out of paper bags.

We saw American movies on weekends at the nearby T&D Theater, which kids called "the Tough & Dirty." It was a grand old movie house where we watched cowboy heroes, monsters from outer space, spectacles like *20,000 Leagues Under the Sea*, and the first experiments in 3-D. We saw the Chinese movies on Thursdays, when the New Eastern was closed and we'd go with our parents to *Dai Fow*—San Francisco. We always knew we'd arrived when we could smell the coffee beans being roasted at the Hills Brothers plant under the San Francisco end of the Bay Bridge.

We saw plenty of anti-Communist films, but none of the messages sank in. We'd make our toy swords to recreate the fight scenes, and I'd make fun of the opera singers, mimicking their atonal sounds with nonsense words approximating Cantonese. My father would join in, waving his long-handled wok utensils like sabres, and we'd go back and forth until my mother, laughing, shushed us all.

Beneath the nonsense, our parents had a mission in life: to instill Chinese culture in us.

While Japanese-Americans, stung by their experiences in internment camps during World War II, were more determined than ever to assimilate into the American mainstream, first-generation Chinese had no such goals. They were *Chinese*. That's how they thought, and that's what they read, wrote, and spoke.

Their children, they would grudgingly allow, were Americans as well as Chinese. Ideally, they would succeed—the boys as doctors, dentists, or lawyers; the girls as wives of doctors, dentists, or lawyers. Still, they'd be Chinese at the core.

And so, as each of us turned eight, Sarah, Barry, and I found our school days lengthened by several hours in Chinese school at the nearby Chinese Community Center, a modern, two-story building with a gymnasium and courtyard and a tiled pagoda facade. A perfect statement of Chinese-American symbiosis.

Here, teachers taught language, calligraphy, culture, and history and, not incidentally, manners. We stood when the teacher entered the room and paid him more attention than any teacher at Lincoln. For a lot of the students, Chinese school was mainly a chance to see other kids, and they didn't take it seriously. Some of Sarah's friends regularly cut classes to go to Chinatown, buy *cha-siu bow*—steamed pork buns—saunter into their classroom late, and proceed to eat.

But our parents were serious. So every afternoon, we'd go home, pick up our Chinese stuff—thin paperback lesson books, calligraphy books, pens, pencils, and ink—in a cigar box, and go off to Chinese school, working for a 甲—the equivalent of a grade of A.

We sat attentively through lectures about Sun Yat-sen, and we learned calligraphy by copying characters into books with pages of squares in vertical rows. We learned to hold a Chinese brush pen straight up, to dip it into black ink soaked in cotton balls in little bottles. We traced large characters onto tissue paper. I had little trouble transferring my interest in drawing to calligraphy. I did all right in Chinese school, but my heart was elsewhere.

After I'd graduated, one of my teachers told my mother that he'd often catch me reading an English book I'd slipped in front of my Chinese lessons. However, when he called on me, I somehow had the right answer. It was rote learning, and none of it stayed with me for long.

At home, we found ourselves facing a foreign language within the Chinese language. Our parents spoke the *tze-yup* dialect of Cantonese, the dialect of their native Hoi Ping region and three other districts west of the Canton River delta in China. (*Tze-yup* means "four districts.") In Chinese school, the teachers spoke— and tried teaching us—*sam yup*—a dialect spoken in three *(sam)* districts north of the *tze-yup* districts. In the early fifties, Mandarin was nowhere near becoming China's national language, but our teachers were wedging in some basic Mandarin phonetics—*baw-paw-maw-faw . . . der-ter-ler-mer . . .*

We hated all this gibberish. Here we were, kids groping with English, and we were also getting two or three distinct dialects of the Chinese tongue drummed into us. We had to split our time in the rice room between pencils and Chinese brush pens.

Growing up, I was the same as everyone else. That is, I dreaded being different. But we were, and we were reminded of it every day—not just in school, but at the restaurant and at the dinner table, where we had greens of one sort or another— *bok choy* (Chinese greens), *gai choy* (mustard greens), or *gai lon* (Chinese broccoli)—with sliced beef, pork, chicken, or *lop cheung*—Chinese sausage. Everything was "Chinese." Sometimes, we'd have roast duck—Chinese-style, of course—or a wonderful hot egg custard studded with *lop cheung*, or dig into a patty of minced pork, made crunchy with diced water chestnuts, on top of which sat a slice of salted fish or some pickled greens. Salted fish, like bitter melon and thousand-year-old eggs, was a food that took us years to get used to. We had it so often that Sarah got to thinking of it as a low-rent, poor people's food. But, as Dad told us once, there were always people poorer than us.

There was a man, he said, who wanted to have some salted fish but couldn't afford it, "So he smelled his foot instead."

Fortunately, my parents could also work wonders with more traditional seafood, and we'd have whole rock cod or bass, steamed and ladled with soy sauce and peanut oil combined with green onions. In season, we'd have steamed crabs, and, long before I heard of calamari, we had sautéed squid on the table.

We looked aghast at some of the more exotic foods laid out before us. Sarah liked chicken feet, but most of us blanched at the feet of either chickens or pigs, and we were relieved that Dad happened to enjoy fish heads, duck heads, even the occasional head of lettuce. We'd make faces while he wolfed down what we thought were a crab's "brains"—its mysterious, egglike liquids—after we'd taken most of the meatiest claws.

Whatever we had, we had it with steamed rice. There was rice at every meal, and if we'd reached the bottom of the rice pot, we might end a meal by pouring hot water into the pot, scraping the hardened shell of rice that had formed, and enjoying a most unique meal-ending "soup."

We never had dessert, and we never had what I came to think of as particularly American foods: lamb, veal, salads, cheese, olives.

And I always wondered: Did any other family—even Chinese—use newspapers as tablecloths? We'd remove our bowls and dishes, then wrap all the bones and other discardables into a newspaper pouch and toss it in the garbage. It makes sense now, but it seemed odd at the time.

Except for nights when the New Eastern was closed, we didn't eat together. Mom and Dad were always getting up to do something in the kitchen. When one or more of us were sick and had to stay at home, Dad would prepare and place dinner into a portable stack of metal containers, which Mom or Sarah would bring home.

Having all this great Chinese food did one thing for us: It gave us a longing for American food. Once in a long while, we'd get slices of grilled T-bone steak, and Dad made a wonderful beef stew, with large chunks of carrots, potatoes—an unknown in the Chinese diet—and tasty hints of five-star anise in the sauce.

But our most American dinner came once a year—at Thanksgiving.

American holidays came as a shock to my parents. Two months after her arrival in Oakland, my mother was home one evening when her doorbell rang. She pulled back the curtain on the front door window and found herself confronted by two children—one a ghost, the other a witch. Even though they were clearly children, they frightened Mom, and she hurried to the telephone to call Grace Fung.

"What is this?" she asked. "Children in make-believe clothes at my front door!"

Grace told my mother about Halloween. For good measure, she also explained Thanksgiving and Christmas.

Growing up, we had costumes for Halloween parades at school and went trick or treating. At Thanksgiving, we had roast beef, mashed potatoes, apple pie, and just a little turkey, because our parents thought turkey caused *gneet-hay*, a Chinese affliction that translates into "hot air" but for which we never learned an English equivalent. Many American foods, we were told, caused *gneet-hay*.

But while we had tricks and treats and Thanksgiving and Christmas, we also had Chinese New Year every February, or whenever the first day of each Lunar Year arrived. To us, the Chinese calendar was confusing, with New Year—and Mom's and Dad's birthdays—falling on different dates every year.

The Chinese also make New Year a two-week-long affair, and I never did figure out the difference between *Hon Neen* (which seemed to precede the actual New Year) and *Hoy Neen* (which meant "open year" and, presumably, the beginning of the new year). At some point, we knew that we'd receive *hoong bow*—little red envelopes containing a coin, given by adults to children to reward them for good manners and to wish them good luck.

I knew that, no matter how far from home, the children were expected to gather for dinner on those days in a show of family unity. Every year, our parents would put out their round, lacquered, wood platter—called by some a "tray of togetherness" and by others a "tray of prosperity"—with eight compartments for a variety of sweets—candied melon (for health), sugared coconut strips (togetherness), kumquat (prosperity), lichee nuts (strong family ties), melon seeds (dyed red to symbolize happiness), lotus seeds (many children), and longan (many good sons).

All over the house, there'd be bowls and platters piled high with oranges and tangerines, which meant good luck and wealth, and wherever Chinese visited during the two weeks of New Year celebration, they would bring gifts of fruit and go through an exercise of manners that befuddled us.

The hosts would chide the visitors for bringing oranges.

"Oh, not necessary," they would say, knowing full well that the gift was almost mandatory in Chinese tradition.

The guests would insist; the hosts would relent. Then, at the end of the visit, the hosts would pile the guests up with oranges and tangerines.

"Oh, no, no," the departing guests would protest, fully prepared to accept the exchange of fruit—which they would bring to their next hosts.

At dinner, every course, as with every aspect of the New Year celebration, was laden with symbolism and purpose. We had to have chicken, simply steamed and presented whole, indicating completeness. The same reasoning applied to fish, roast suckling pig with thick, crunchy skin and an even thicker layer of fat, and, as a yin-yang balance, a vegetarian dish called "Buddha's monk stew," composed of Chinese vermicelli (noodles, uncut, symbolize long life), fermented bean curd, cloud ears, tiger lily flowers, and gingko nuts.

Before dinner, we'd set off firecrackers outside the house—to ward off evil spirits—and create an echo of what for most Chinese was the highlight of New Year's: the parade through Chinatown, San Francisco, with its block-long golden dragon. We rarely made it over to *Dai Fow*, but contented ourselves with Oakland's street celebrations. On Webster and surrounding streets, teams of young lion dancers from judo and karate schools made the rounds of business establishments and family associations, which hired the lions to chase off bad influences with their supernatural powers. While neighbors and passersby gathered to watch, they performed amidst gongs, drums, and exploding firecrackers, and, at show's end, climbed high, ignoring lit fireworks at their feet, to snatch a string of *hoong bow*—red envelopes containing dollar bills—payment to the lions for warding off the demons.

I was fascinated by the lion's head, with the blinding primary colors, the bulging, bejeweled, fur-browed eyes and the pom poms springing out of its forehead. The lead dancer would hoist it over his head, thrust and jerk it up and about, and flap its extended tongue and white-whiskered lower jaw, dancing acrobatically with two other men who worked under a long, multicolored fabric train behind him, forming the body of the lion.

Back at the New Eastern, I'd take a cardboard box that had held eggs and, with paper, water colors, crayons, string, and fabrics Mother had left over from her garment work, fashion my own lion's head, complete with a flapping lower lip. Barry and Shirley were happy to pound on garbage can lids or a Quaker Oats box while I pranced around the backyard.

Our parents were delighted that we would embrace Chinese New Year with such enthusiasm.

In American school, we rarely talked about our rituals. We were already different enough. Even at lunchtime, when many children would line up for hot lunches of macaroni and cheese or hot dogs, our bagged lunches identified us as Chinese. Our parents made sandwiches of chicken, Spam, or, more often, *cha sui*—barbecued pork.

I was reminded of my Chineseness even in the comic books I'd escape to. I remember the Blackhawks, a paramilitary team that never fought the Nazis without their mascot, "Chop Chop," a round little Chinese cook wielding a Chinese knife. He was about half the size of the rest of the team. While all the others wore rugged blue uniforms, Chop Chop was outfitted in a green and yellow smock, and his face was a bright orange-yellow.

I remember feeling embarrassed at how Chop Chop stood out, the way he looked, the way he talked. How I wished he—and I—didn't require a different color ink in the comics.

·· 5 ··

THE GAMBLER

At age ten, in 1955, I fell in love with baseball. At that time, Oakland's team was in the Pacific Coast League, which ranked high among the minor leagues and had ball clubs in Los Angeles, Seattle, San Diego, and San Francisco.

I loved the sound of the game that came out of the radio. And I loved following the daily shifts in the standings, in the averages of pitchers and batters. The Oakland Oaks were a miserable ballclub with a history of poor seasons and commensurately poor attendance figures. In 1905, for a game against the Portland Beavers, the Oaks drew one paying customer. Legend has it that the public address announcer opened his microphone and said: "Good evening, Sir." I always wondered why he even needed a mike.

I had just reached the point of memorizing the names of all

the Oaks when the owner sold the team, which became the Mounties and moved to Vancouver.

During that sad last season, every chance I got I'd huddle at the radio by the cash register in front of the dining room and listen to Bud Foster and Bill Law call the play-by-play.

The fact that I had time to listen to entire innings between cash register rings was bad news for my father. Chinatown had become quieter, and business at the New Eastern had slowed.

For Chinese-Americans in general, things were getting better. World War II had cemented China's relationship with the United States, and in 1943, the Exclusion Act was repealed. The next year, the California State Legislature repealed a constitutional provision forbidding the state to employ Chinese. And in 1948, the United States Supreme Court ruled as unconstitutional the neighborhood covenants that had restricted Chinese, blacks, and other minorities from buying property. Free to pursue housing throughout the community, Chinese-Americans began moving out of Chinatown.

Another factor was the outlawing of *pak kop piu*, a lottery game that was for decades one of the economic backbones of Chinatown.

Pak kop piu dated back to the 1870s and was the basis for the casino game Keno. Players, using Chinese pens and ink, marked up to ten of eighty Chinese characters on a ticket. If five or more of their characters matched the twenty drawn each day, they won. After each twice-daily drawing, results were posted, and winners would take friends out to dinner. Big winners often celebrated by hosting huge banquets.

All of this was illegal, and the lottery houses had to deal not only with the police—who were naturally paid off—but robbers and each other. They formed mutual-aid societies that provided member houses with protection, but not all houses belonged to the same societies, and misunderstandings led, at least once, to a gambling house version of a tong war.

In the thirties, seventeen lotteries operated in Oakland's Chinatown, and by the fifties, the number had grown to forty, most of them behind or in the basements of stores around Eighth and Webster. Right around the New Eastern Cafe.

Since restaurants profited handsomely from the lotteries, it made sense that they were among the businesses most interested in helping shield the lottery. We were among the dozens of businesses that distributed tickets and took in money, and the tickets became such a part of our lives that Sarah, for one, memorized all eighty characters. She was one of the younger lottery runners, making the rounds of stores and restaurants to pick up marked tickets and delivering them to an adult, who would take them into the lottery house.

But in 1954, a new federal anti-gambling law shut down the lotteries, and, without the nightclubs and movie theaters that San Francisco had to draw visitors in the evening, Oakland's Chinatown became a ghost town.

When business slowed, my father began listening to a couple of friends he'd known from a neighboring village in China. They had a restaurant in Reno, Nevada, and although they had closed it, they were telling my father that if he took it over, he'd make a fortune.

"We lost a little money," one of them said, "but we had too many people. You are talented; you can do the work of three people. That way, you make money."

That sounded reasonable to my father. He was nothing if not a hard worker. He was brimming with energy, willing to try anything.

My father saw Reno as a perfect opportunity to move on. It was like another shot at the lottery. If he won, he'd be able to set up his family in grand style. If he lost—well, he could always find work at a restaurant.

My mother didn't believe the men. "Why would they close the restaurant unless it had lost a great deal of money?" she asked. A closed restaurant, she thought, was tougher to restart than one that simply had a transition of ownership.

"They'll cheat you," she said. But my father knew these men. They were older than him—nearly old enough to retire, in fact—and would have no reason to cheat him.

"There's nothing here in Oakland," he said. "I want my own restaurant." He'd been his own man for nearly ten years. Why change that now? So, when his village friends presented him with a lease agreement written in Chinese, he signed.

Suddenly, he was the proprietor of Ming's Cafe, which adjoined a hotel in downtown Reno, just two streets over from Virginia Street, the town's main casino and hotel strip.

In a sense, he was doing what he and so many fellow Chinese had done before. He was leaving home—this time in America—to go off in search of a gold mine. He would make money and send it home, eventually coming home himself, the good and worthy provider.

We had no warning. Just, one day: "*Ba-Ba* is going to Reno. Barry's going with him."

Barry had just begun his second year at Westlake Junior High School. Most of the time, our parents would have put his schooling first, but this was a special case. Our father was going away, and he wanted both company and help.

At Westlake, Barry was still buddies with William Fung, even though they were now taking different classes. They had a common interest in the military, in guns and rifles; World War II comic books and movies; model jet fighters. They both enjoyed destroying things.

They'd finish putting together a model plane—say, an F9FX Cougar, one of the first-generation fighter jets of the war—then stand back and admire their work.

"So, what do you think, Fungus?" Barry would ask.

"Same thing you're thinking, Fish," Bill would reply.

"Let's see how this guy does in combat," Barry would say. Bill would pull a string of firecrackers out of his bomber jacket and they'd stuff them into the cockpit. Then they'd light matches to the fuses and hurl the plane at a wall. If it wasn't destroyed, they wanted to know why. They'd repeat the process until the jet was shredded.

One day, in a hallway at Westlake, Barry opened fire on Bill with a water pistol. Bill waited a few days, then showed up at our flat, where he challenged my brother to a showdown. From our bedroom window, Barry dropped a water balloon onto Fungus, who ran off, but returned with a neighbor's garden hose, flooding our floor.

Our mother, who'd always eyed Bill with suspicion, heard the commotion and came running. When she saw the mess, she knew what had happened. She opened the window again and called after the fleeing Fungus: *"Ai-ya! Ky-doy!"* she shouted. "Get out of here!" Exasperated, she turned to Barry. "Useless thing!" she said with a sigh. She was talking about Bill.

When Reno came along, the idea of separating her son from Bill's bad influence appealed to her. She'd be losing Barry for a while, but maybe Reno would do him some good.

In 1955, my father took over Ming's Cafe. He and Barry moved into a hotel room above the restaurant and bar. My father was fifty-two now and intent on succeeding. It didn't matter where he did it. But for Barry, Reno was a shock to the system. Soon after he arrived, Reno went into one of the coldest winters in its history, and Barry found himself confronting the first snow, hail, and bitter cold he'd ever experienced. He was thrilled and, on the phone, challenged us to snowball fights as soon as we could visit.

In Oakland, at the New Eastern Cafe, Barry had done his share of chores. Now, he'd have to do more. In Reno, he was Dad's only reliable ear and help. Regardless of his own language limitations, he'd have to help translate for our father, double-check the books, and serve as an extra pair of eyes on the employees.

On his first Monday in town, Barry was enrolled at nearby Northside Junior High School. The town's schools were integrated, but there were very few Chinese in Reno in the mid-fifties. Still, Barry fit in fine and managed average grades.

My father had other things on his mind. Business never picked up the way the village men had promised. He'd reduced the payroll by doing most of the work himself, but the ravaging winter weather kept customers away.

In Oakland, Mother got a job as a seamstress at a Chinatown garment factory and sent most of her earnings to him so that he could buy food and supplies and keep Ming's afloat.

The rest of the family visited once, and I remember feeling like I was in a foreign land. The snow was the first we'd ever seen, and Barry and I spent hours hurling snowballs at each other.

Then, the dark, romantic world of cocktail lounges, of martini glasses and glittering trays of olives and cherries, of "Cherry Pink and Apple Blossom White" on the jukebox, was a new phenomenon for us. It was the stuff of *Casablanca*.

Ming's was really nothing more than a Chinese restaurant, but to me it was the slickest spot on earth. It was a place that seemed to have been built for another song on the box: Sinatra's "Learning the Blues," about empty tables and deserted dance floors.

We left Reno with no idea when we might see Dad and Barry again. But we knew it wouldn't be any time soon, and I felt sad. I missed Barry at home, and now I'd have this image of him in a glamorous nightclub so far away from Chinatown.

6

LIFE WITHOUT

FATHER

There wasn't exactly a vacuum around 206 Eighth Street without our father and Barry. Sarah didn't even miss Dad, since he was so often in the kitchen when she was in the rice room, and still at the restaurant when she was home. And when he was home on weekend mornings, before opening the restaurant, she'd be out.

Of course, we missed them, but we also appreciated the elbow room around the apartment. We all settled into a different rhythm while they were away.

Evenings, when school work—both American and Chinese—was done, we'd do our household chores. As soon as we were able, we ironed our own clothes and cleaned our own rooms. Then we could gather in the living room to watch the Admiral television set my father had purchased, in a burst of optimism, just before taking off for Reno.

It was a handsome console in blond wood, a lovely showcase item even when it wasn't turned on. We were amazingly agreeable on what we'd watch: situation comedies and game and quiz shows. Our regular fare included the cunning Bob Cummings, the wisecracking Eve Arden in *Our Miss Brooks*, sweet Spring Byington in *December Bride*, goofy Red Skelton, the perfect family of Ozzie and Harriet Nelson, and Mom's favorites, Lucille Ball and Jerry Lewis. Maybe it was the broadness of their comedy. Whatever it was, my mother said, "It helps me understand English." She even swore that the louder the shows, the more effective the language lessons.

Mother first tried to learn English around 1945, attending evening classes at Lincoln School, where she sat in a room of mostly Chinese immigrants, with a few from the Philippines and Mexico as well. She was inspired by a woman who'd been a shipmate on her trip from Hong Kong to America.

"My friend wanted to learn English so she would be able to talk with her children," Mother said. "But after a few classes, I decided it would be better to teach my children how to speak Chinese."

China regards itself the Middle Kingdom, a center of the universe superior to all around it. It calls itself *Joong Gok*—central state. In much the same way, my parents felt they didn't need English to survive. They'd lived their entire lives in a China away from China. Everyone they cared about spoke their tongue. So why struggle to learn a strange new one?

We saw no use for Cantonese, other than to appease our parents. We had enough on our hands, learning what to us was the most complicated language in the world, the one we'd be speaking and writing all our lives.

We picked up enough Cantonese by osmosis at home and in Chinatown to get across basic thoughts, and, I guess, our parents picked up some English through Jerry Lewis and Lucy. But without an effective common language, a wall arose between parents and children. Yes, we could talk and understand most of what the other was saying. But shadings, detail, nuances, turns of phrase ... all of those, and much more, would be blocked by the omnipresent wall.

Over the years, the kids would encourage my mother to go back to evening school, but she resisted. English was far too complicated a language for her to learn. Besides, she had to take care of us and work in our restaurants, as well as do work at home for garment factories. Every night, it seemed, Mother stayed busy at her Singer, which she set up in the front foyer of the apartment. Soon, the area began to resemble an annex to the factory, its tables piled high with fabric, sewing patterns, and clothes in various stages of completion. To save money, she knitted sweaters for us, and we took turns holding the skeins of yarn out for her to roll into balls. These were the peaceful moments with Mother, when she'd talk about how hard Father was working, how many sacrifices they were making for the family.

"You must work hard, too," she said, and I knew to expect stories about China, and what the Communists were doing to our family in the village, and how important it was for us to do well, so that we could help provide for them.

This was the Chinese way. In American families, parents might dote on their children. In Chinese culture, filial piety was the highest ideal. The children had an obligation to support their parents. In China, a nuclear family included grandparents and in-laws, and the elders held equal rights to discipline the children.

Our grandmother, of course, was in China. Except for a worn black and white photograph of her, we knew nothing about *Po-Po* or our cousins, aunts, and uncles in Chek Hom or Gow Bay Hong.

But by our parents' constant references to them, we knew we didn't have the kind of family we saw on television. We had obligations: to work hard, so that we could send money back to the village, to work cooperatively, and, above all, to be respectful.

We were not to talk back. If we dared to say anything about friends at school being able to go more places or do more things than we did, our mother would admonish us about Americans.

"They don't care about family," she said, meaning that no race cared about family the way the Chinese did. In China, she said, grandparents were members of the household—and honored ones, too. "Chinese take care of one another," she said. "Americans take care of themselves."

Mom had by now met a number of Sarah's friends—most of them Chinese—and she didn't like any of them. When she heard gossip about them or their parents, she'd pass it along to Sarah as more reasons not to associate with them. And she didn't understand why they wasted their time playing basketball. "Girls don't do that," she said.

Mom would invariably invoke the name of a child in another Chinese family and tell Sarah how good he or she was. Why couldn't we be more like them? Sarah would turn away and roll her eyes. Her mother's main problem, she decided, was that she didn't like anyone or anything that took time away from studies or work at the restaurant.

Sarah and her friends continued to meet at Maeley's. Now, with the birth of rock and roll, the girls were learning to do the Bop. They wanted to keep up with changing fashions, but none of them had money, and their clothes were mostly homemade. They did know, however, to roll their bobby sox down over their buck shoes.

Maeley was going through more disruptions at home. A new man had entered her mother's life, and she had agreed to remarry, but Maeley's prospective new stepfather arrived in San Francisco with a surprise: his first wife. He announced that he wanted to live with both her and Maeley's mother, who would, in effect, be a concubine. Maeley's mother rejected that idea, and he agreed to let go of the first wife and to live with her in the house he had set up in San Francisco. That left only the question of what to do with her daughter. Maeley, comfortable with her friends at

Tech, chose to stay put. She wound up in the house in Oakland—
with the rejected first wife.

Maeley and the woman rarely spoke, and Maeley clung even
closer to Sarah and their friends.

With the Oakland Oaks having moved to Vancouver, I became
a fan of the Vancouver Mounties, but it wasn't easy rooting for
a team none of my friends cared about. I still followed baseball,
and when October rolled around in '54, '55, and '56, it was
amazing how sick I'd get and how, to my dismay, I had to be
home just as the World Series was being broadcast.

But music was becoming my real passion. On the radio, I'd
been hearing an endless stream of ballads aimed at adults. "Why
Don't You Believe Me?" by Joni James, "A Guy Is a Guy" by
Doris Day, "Lady of Spain" by Eddie Fisher, and "Don't Let the
Stars Get in Your Eyes" by Perry Como were the big hits,
along with novelties like Rosemary Clooney's "Come On-a My
House" and Patti Page's "How Much Is That Doggie in the
Window?"

And, I confess, I loved it. I was not aware of rhythm and blues,
whose artists paved the way for rock and roll. I knew R&B and
country tunes only as they were covered by pop artists. "Your
Cheatin' Heart," for me, was Joni James', not Hank Williams',
and "Sh-Boom" was by the Crew Cuts and not by the Chords.

But it was only when Elvis Presley came along that I took
note of how important the singer was. Elvis knocked me out,
and I didn't care that it was mostly girls who were going crazy.
Watching him on *Stage Show*, the variety half-hour hosted by the
Dorsey Brothers Saturday nights in early 1956, and later on *The
Ed Sullivan Show*, I was struck not only by his electric energy
but by his carefree sense of humor in the face of television's
Establishment. He had nerve, and it pulsated through his every
snarl and swivel. I bought every record he put out and every
magazine that had him on the cover.

Suddenly, radio, which had seemed ready to roll over and play dead with the advent of television, took on a new life, and so did a whole generation of young people.

My mother, who heard through friends at the garment factory about these new, intertwining threats to society, what the Americans were calling "rock and roll" and "juvenile delinquency," didn't have to hear much of Elvis or Little Richard around the house. Sarah did most of her bopping at friends' houses, and I listened to the radio and my records late at night. Anyway, she was distracted by a more mundane problem I had: a troublesome leg rash that had bothered me for a couple of years, and that my mother thought I got in China. Nothing we got at the drugstore, nothing our family doctor recommended seemed to work on the rash, which covered both legs from feet to knees.

We went to the local herbalist, a flamboyant character named Fong Wan, for cures. Fong, dressed in his customary suit and tie, peered at my troubled legs. "We must get rid of poison!" he declared, stabbing his finger in the air. He prescribed a formula of fourteen herbs imported from China. There was an herb known as "cow's knee" and a rhubarb that would purge the toxins from my system. There were barks, berries, seeds, and roots; ginseng, menthol, and peppermint leaves that went into a brew to make one wince. Fong Wan tried to soothe me with the old Chinese proverb, "Good medicine is bitter to the taste," but truisms were of little comfort when I was confronted with his concoction.

Even a trick common in Chinese households—taking handfuls of golden raisins along with the medicines—didn't help.

Fong Wan advertised himself as the world's greatest herbalist, but in my case, the greatest wouldn't be enough. It would be several years later, when I was in the ninth grade, before Grace Fung suggested something that worked instantly: good old calamine lotion. My parents were too relieved by the solution to be embarrassed about all the Chinese medicines they had wasted on me. In fact, they—and we—kept on taking assorted pebbles, pills, herbs, balms, and ointments for whatever ailed us.

Despite the rash, which I supposed was curable, and my small stature, which I feared was not, I pursued sports. At age eleven, I joined a summer baseball team sponsored by Lincoln School's recreation department. Then, having barely lifted a bat for the Red Dragons, I tackled basketball.

It was a fantasy propelled by the impression the sport had on me. I talked to a few friends, the tallest of them being a black kid named Ronald Coleman, about forming a team. I had no vision of what this team would *do*, but he didn't seem concerned. I hit the sporting goods stores and got equipment catalogs. I drooled over the jerseys and shorts, designed logos, priced everything out, and reported to Ronald, whom I'd named captain.

"We don't got that kind of money," he said.

"Maybe we can save up," I said.

Ronald knew better. "Let's go shoot some baskets," he suggested.

At home, our parents implied that we'd do well to make friends mostly with Chinese. They had bad names for white and black people—they were *bok guey* and *hok guey*, "white demons" and "black demons."

Once, when she used *bok guey* to describe a perfectly nice man we'd dealt with, I asked her why she called black and white people demons, devils, ghosts.

"I don't know," she said, surprised to be asked. "We've always called them that. People were calling them that when I got here."

And the Japanese—those vandals of China—were beneath contempt. It didn't matter that Japanese-Americans had nothing to do with Japan's actions.

We were oblivious to such biases. Although Lincoln was mostly Chinese, there were other races there. My sister and her gang had black and Hispanic friends, and my friends included a Japanese girl, Sherry; my basketball buddy, Ronald; and, for a memorable year, a troublemaker named Leo Mercado.

Leo was big, with curly blond locks and a thick, friendly voice that could turn tough with other kids, or belligerent toward authority.

Like Sarah's pal Maeley and Barry's buddy Bill Fung, Leo came from a broken home; his father deserted him before he knew what a father was. He, his sister, and their mother lived in a set of projects called Auditorium Village, a few blocks east of Chinatown, on the southern tip of Lake Merritt.

As Chinese New Year of 1956 drew near, one of us came up with the idea of selling firecrackers. I'd procure the fireworks; he'd do most of the selling.

No problem. We scraped together whatever money we had, and I got the explosives. Fireworks weren't easy to find, but they were legal. Each morning, I'd haul a sack of the red packages, ranging from tiny firecrackers bundled together by their fuses, to the regular, two-inch numbers, to a few specialty items like cherry bombs. If I knew of kids who were interested in buying, I'd take a supply. Otherwise, Leo took the parcel and went about business.

Chinese New Year was shaping up nicely when the bubble burst.

I was at Lincoln Park when Mr. Pichotto, my teacher, asked me to accompany him to the principal's office.

I shook the entire way. I knew we—or at least I—had been busted.

The principal came right to the point.

"Do you want to tell me about the firecrackers?" he asked.

"What firecrackers?"

"The ones you and Leo have been selling?"

Ah, yes . . . *those* firecrackers. Apparently, two things had happened. A fellow student had told a teacher that we were peddling fireworks. Coincidentally, Leo was giving a prospective client a sample of a rare specialty item, the slightly more expensive and profoundly more explosive cherry bomb. It was noticed.

For my parents, and particularly for my mother, my bust was a personal humiliation. To them, our citizenship grades were just as important as our scholastic marks. Getting caught and reprimanded was *seet-meen* (losing face) of the worst sort. And the whole affair was particularly galling to them because only a couple of years before, I'd been outside the restaurant playing with firecrackers. I had lit a fuse and held the firecracker an instant too long. I suffered only a burnt thumb, but my parents had hoped that I'd be scared forever by explosives. *"Ai-ya,"* my mother moaned, worried that I was headed down some ruinous road Barry, the first son and the first *ky-doy*, the original "bad boy," had paved. She forbade me from ever seeing Leo Mercado again.

Without a bad influence like Leo around, I wound up making my mother proud in the school year of 1956. I entered the annual *Oakland Tribune* citywide spelling contest, and won the Lincoln School championship. I got a junior dictionary for my efforts, but what I prized the most about the competition was another moment in the spotlight.

Ming's Cafe barely survived the winter, and my father looked forward to spring. His waiters told him that once people took care of their income taxes, they'd be flocking in.

But on April 15, the owner of the building visited and told him that he owed back rent for several months. If he didn't pay, he'd shut down the restaurant.

"I paid in advance for this business," said my father. "I have a contract."

The contract was in Cantonese, and the owner, a white man, would have none of it. He had his own legal contract with the previous operators, he said. It was transferable to future operators, and according to his deal, my father owed him not only back rent but back payroll taxes.

My father called my mother. It was over. He and Barry packed up, and before the end of April, the month that was supposed to bring them their jackpot, they were back in Oakland.

* * *

For a while, our family life went back to normalcy. My father got a job as one of the head cooks at the original Trader Vic's restaurant in Emeryville, and we saw more of him than we had in years. In summer, we were off on our usual short vacations. We'd go to Penngrove, a small town in Sonoma County an hour's drive north of us, where Grace and Jack Fung had an egg farm, and where Sarah, their goddaughter, had extended visits when school was out. We also made our annual day trip to Stockton, in the San Joaquin Valley. We always managed to schedule this for the hottest day of summer, and we'd swelter our way through hundred-degree days never heard of in Oakland.

In Stockton, we visited with the family of a man named Bing Wong and his wife, a woman whose maiden name, Soo Hoo, was the same as my mother's. They were not related, but one of my mother's shipmates—the same one who inspired her to take her first English language classes—knew the Stockton Soo Hoo and insisted that they meet. Once they did, they became friends and began taking turns visiting each other's homes. By happenstance, they had children at about the same times, and as each family grew to a total of seven, the visits at our apartment got to be uncomfortably cramped. Also, it was agreed by all of us that Mrs. Wong made the best picnic food. And so it was that our summer visits became strictly Stockton affairs, full of sun, food, and play. Our matched groups of kids all got along and ventured out to the parks around town, allowing our parents to visit quietly.

In the fall, I entered Westlake Junior High, two miles north of our apartment and a world away from Lincoln. Chinese had made up more than nine of ten students at Lincoln. At Westlake, in my class of two hundred, only one in six was Chinese. The majority was white, and we had a good number of blacks and Hispanics as well.

Lincoln was peaceful. Westlake was coming off several years of racial tensions that had led to some noisy disturbances. A new principal, brought in the year before, had restored peace.

Lincoln had been only a few blocks away from home. Westlake was daunting. It took a steep uphill walk to reach this vast campus of industrial shops, gyms, outdoor playground and fields, and its centerpiece: a Spanish-style, T-shaped building.

It helped that Barry, now in ninth grade, was at the same school. Although we naturally had our separate circles of friends, he offered advice about teachers, showed me short cuts around the school, and suggested that whenever I was confronted by a student demanding "Gimme nickel"—a not uncommon occurrence—I give up the money.

"That's how you stay out of trouble," he said.

After school, Barry and I worked together delivering the *Oakland Tribune* around the neighborhood. The paper routes gave us daily admission tickets into the wide wide world of people who weren't necessarily Chinese.

Most of the route was a matter of flinging a paper at a customer's front door. But some of the doors were inside big apartment buildings, and entering them was like having my senses involuntarily expanded. I smelled the musk of decades-old buildings; the odors of long-lived lives; the aroma of meals from worlds I'd never known.

We only matched senses to faces once a month, when we had to collect. Most of the subscribers paid promptly, but there were always procrastinators and a few who played hide-and-seek with our $3.50 a month, of which I would get fifty cents.

With them, it was a strange sort of sparring; a kid, not yet a teenager, trying to get a grownup to pay for a month of papers they'd had delivered to their front steps daily.

"I don't have it."

"Oh." A downward look. "Tomorrow?"

"How about Friday?"

"Think you could have it Wednesday? I need to pay up."

"All right." Reluctantly. "We'll see."

That meant they wouldn't even be home Wednesday. Newspaper work can turn you into a cynic.

For all the grief, there was nothing like counting up the month's take—before the *Tribune* got its majority share.

But the best part of the job had to do with time, not money. Sunday mornings, we had to get up before dawn and walk down to the Lyon building by the Tribune Tower downtown to fetch our fifty hefty papers each. On rainy Sundays, Dad would take us in his car for the deliveries. But clear Sundays—without Dad around—were the best. At seven in the morning, after delivering the papers, we had a breather from home and the restaurant.

We'd hit DeLauer's newsstand on Twelfth Street to look at the comics, and Barry would teach me how to hide a couple under my shirt. Barry was a gifted shoplifter. Depending on the situation, he could be careful—"Never take more than one or two things"—or brazen. In the summer, after our route, we'd walk up Thirteenth Street to the Western Notion and Novelty Company, a warehouse of fun and games. While Barry checked out model airplanes, BB rifles, and bow-and-arrow sets, I was at the rack of practical jokes, making heavy decisions about joy buzzers and flies in ice cubes. It was in the toy stores that Barry would either win gold medals or get arrested. For the sheer challenge of it, he'd walk off with kites and BB rifles while, eyes wide, I'd follow behind, giddy with the anticipation of sirens chasing after us at any moment.

"Nothing to it," he'd say, ditching the items he had no use for or couldn't possibly explain to our parents.

One day, his luck ran out. He was caught with an archery set hidden (mostly) under his jacket. Because he was only thirteen, the store manager called home and asked to speak to our mother. She was at the restaurant, and Sarah answered. As soon as the caller said he was from a toy store, she was alert.

"Yes, I'm his mother," she said. "What seems to be the problem?"

Listening to the store owner, Sarah sounded horrified. "Send him home at once," she said, summoning up her most commanding voice. "I will take care of him." She apologized for the store's inconvenience and assured the caller that, if Barry were fortunate enough to survive the punishment she had planned for him, he would never steal again.

And then she hung up and started laughing. All the way home, Barry would be expecting a whipping, only to get home to be greeted by a sister who, once again, had one up on him.

At night, when we were supposed to be asleep, Barry and I read our comics by flashlight under the covers. When transistor radios were first sold, we treasured the one we got. But I also managed to get a pocket radio, in the shape of a rocket, that required clipping a wired antenna to an outside line. I'd string it out our second-floor bedroom window to the clothesline and listen to music through a plastic earpiece. It was barely low-fi, but I didn't care.

When rock and roll took off and 45 rpm records came into vogue, we were left behind. We couldn't afford a new phonograph player. Barry decided to make one himself. He got a children's 78 rpm model at a thrift shop and honed the capstan down until the speed decreased to the speed of rock and roll. Then he mounted it onto a cigar box.

"So smart," my mother said when she saw the cigar box phonograph. "If only you'd make good use of it."

I, personally, couldn't think of a better use for Barry's smarts. I was glad to have him back from Reno. As close as we were, we didn't seem to have much time together. In his short life, it seemed that one thing or another would conspire to keep us apart.

7

ROUTE 66

It sounded like the longest pee ever taken. Lying in my bed, listening with wonder, I'd time it, counting the seconds off in my head. Thirty seconds. Amazing! And on it would go—forty-five, fifty, a full minute.

The subject of my admiration was Lee Sing, one of the cooks at the Ding How restaurant in Amarillo, Texas. As Lee relieved himself in the nearby bathroom, I thought that I was learning all about growing up. Let's see: You got bigger, which meant your penis would increase in size. And, naturally, you'd pee much longer.

At age twelve, I was *very* sophisticated.

* * *

My father, restless working for others, had taken another offer. A Chinese Texan, whom I always knew as "Mr. Joe," was building a restaurant in Amarillo, along Route 66, the fabled highway that stretched like a twisted grin between Santa Monica and Chicago. Joe would run the restaurant while my father would be one of three partner-cooks. He assured my father that it was a no-lose deal. The partners would share in the profits of the restaurant, and if the business somehow lost money, Joe would absorb the loss.

My father accepted the deal, and he wanted me to go with him.

I didn't like the idea of being uprooted, leaving school and friends. But I had no choice. As bad a boy as my parents thought Barry was, he'd gone off to Reno and proven himself to my father. I felt like some of the clothes I wore: a hand-me-down, a boy who'd never be quite as big, as strong, as his older brother. This was my chance to prove myself worthy. I began to feel better about leaving.

One spring night, Sarah sat me down in the kitchen at our flat. She was sixteen, and she seemed envious that first Barry, and now I, had managed some kind of a getaway. "You're so lucky," she said. "No more Chinatown. You can do what you want." Sarah was a junior in high school, and all around her were Chinese boys being pressured toward college and white-collar careers.

We took a train to Texas in the summer of 1957. My father and I rarely talked, and I buried myself in the latest issue of *Mad* magazine. I'd recently discovered its inspired mix of goofiness and anarchy, and had a stack of issues with me.

As we crossed Nevada, on our way into Arizona, my father turned to me.

"Twelve years old," he said. "You're a big boy." I looked up, a little sheepishly, from my *Mad*.

"Barry was twelve when he went to Reno," my dad was saying. "In old times, I was twelve when I stopped school to work with my father." I put down my magazine. It occurred to me how rarely we ever talked. It wasn't just the language thing. At home, Mom had done most of the talking to the children. Now, Dad was offering a bit of his history.

When he was twelve, he said, he was given the choice of continuing school, which he had attended for four years, or helping his father, a sundries salesman, make his rounds, carrying goods by shoulder to outlying villages and towns. Even if he continued schooling, there was no way out for him. So he decided to help his father, walking as much as forty miles a day.

And now, I was twelve and headed for the Texas Panhandle.

It was spring when we arrived, but summer had beaten us there. We had to get used to temperatures surpassing one hundred by late morning. It was like Stockton, with no escape back to the saner climes of the Bay area. I couldn't wait for the building to go up—even a wall—just so there'd be a bit of shade. But despite the conditions, I got a daily kick watching a restaurant being built from the ground up, and to know it was being constructed from the sacks of cement, and the piles of cinderblocks and bricks, and the planks of lumber, and the buckets of tar and plaster scattered throughout the property.

The Ding How would be unlike any Chinese restaurant I'd ever seen. In Chinatown, buildings were old and flush against each other. Here, we were on open land, in what felt like the desert. Here, workers were putting up a sprawling ranch house of a restaurant, a contemporary white brick building topped and offset with Oriental touches—red awnings and a circular moon gate of polished, deep red bricks.

My father was a natural calligrapher who made strong, bold strokes with his brush pen, and he found his skill put to use right away. He wrote out the Chinese characters reading *Ding How*— "very good"—that would be transferred onto a marbled pattern on the entrance floor.

Watching the walls go up, I shared my father's optimism about the Ding How. But I also shared the reservations he had about the majority owner.

He was bigger and brasher than most Chinese men I'd ever met. He liked to wear large-brimmed hats, suits, and sunglasses. Once, before the Texas venture, he and his wife picnicked with our family by Lake Merritt in Oakland, and in every snapshot from that day, he stands aloof, looking off into some unknown distance.

While the Ding How was being built, we were put up at his house in Amarillo. It looked like the home of a man who'd done well for himself and his family, and it gave me hope that, someday, we'd live in a house just like this one.

But when the Ding How was set to open, we moved from the Joes' into a bungalow at the rear of the parking lot behind the restaurant. Besides my father and me, the two other cook-partners—Lee Sing and a man we would call "Little Joe"—would be living there.

It was little better than slave quarters, this low-slung, two-room shack with a bathroom entered only through my father's and my bedroom. We had no more furniture than in a jail cell; there was neither heating nor air conditioning, and the climate attracted an unending swarm of worms, which I swept off the front doorway several times a day.

Walking to and from the restaurant in the darkness of night, I had to be careful about not stepping on grasshoppers and crickets.

Ding How was designed for the tourists rolling through on Route 66. On the wide red awnings to the left and right of the front door were two neon signs: CHOP SUEY and CHOW MEIN. This was not a restaurant that was going to challenge diners. Chop suey wasn't even a Chinese dish when it was concocted in the mid-1800s in San Francisco for hungry gold miners. It was a dish a Chinese cook had slapped together from available vegetables and meat. *Chop suey* meant "bits and pieces," or a miscellany, and only its popularity among westerners forced it onto menus in Chinese restaurants. Chinese themselves never ate chop suey. (Chow mein is another matter. We love that stuff.)

To give Ding How's visitors a sense of the Orient, our wait-resses, none of them Asian, wore red satin blouses with mandarin collars, and black slacks. Big Joe, dressed to look the wealthy Texan, played host. At the cashier's stand, a glassed-in counter displayed souvenirs for sale: ivory chopsticks, back-scratchers, plastic Chinese soup spoons, folding fans, and wisdom hats. By the counter there stood a rack of postcards, both naughty and nice. We sold a little book of risqué sayings attributed to Confu-cius, but written by a comedy writer, most likely not Chinese.

In a top-drawer restaurant like Ding How, there was no place for a kid like me. Big Joe had no interest in a low-overhead, family ambience. I was kept backstage, in the kitchen, doing occasional chores.

That was fine by me. It left me plenty of time in the bungalow, studying, reading my *Mad* magazines, drawing cartoons, watch-ing Little Joe's TV set, and listening to the radio. I absorbed stars like Marvin Rainwater, Marty Robbins, and Gene Austin, as well as Top 40. But in my musical universe, there was still no one like Elvis.

In the heat and dust of summertime in the Panhandle, I began exploring my surroundings and got my first whiff of freedom.

Across the highway, I could indulge in one of my favorite American foods—chili and beans—and play an early electronic version of shuffleboard. On nights off from the restaurant, Lee Sing, he of the long peeing sessions, would sometimes take me to the local auditorium to take in some professional wrestling.

When summer turned to fall, I had to think about school. I had no idea where I'd be going. Amarillo in 1957 had segregated schools, and Mary, the head waitress at the restaurant, had to call the Amarillo school district office to tell them about this Chinese boy, and to ask whether I'd go to the regular school, Horace Mann Junior High, just up Route 66 on Buchanan Street, or across town to the Negroes' school, George Washington Carver.

Someone in the office determined that I would attend Horace Mann.

I was shocked by my sudden immersion into segregation, and by my lack of choice in the matter. I didn't care which school I'd go to. I'd mixed with all colors over the years. Besides, wherever I went, I'd be the only Chinese.

I enjoyed walking to school. I'd hike along Route 66, past motels, truck-stop diners, bars and gas stations, a trailer park, and a bowling alley, to Buchanan Street. A left turn, a couple more blocks, and I'd be at Horace Mann.

It was a strange first few days, dealing with the wild shift in racial ratios. At Westlake, one in six kids had yellow skin. At Horace Mann, it was one in 433. Taken as a group, the students at Horace Mann were a portrait of youth before juvenile delinquency.

My classmates accepted me as just another new kid in town. They invited me to join them at the after-school hangout a block or so away from campus, where kids drank root beer floats and listened to rock and roll and rhythm and blues on the jukebox. Inside the jukebox, there were no racial borders, no segregation. The coolest sounds were being made by Elvis and Jerry Lee and Buddy Holly, but also by Little Richard and Chuck Berry. The kids would bop to Laverne Baker one minute and to cowboys like Johnny Cash or Marty Robbins the next. Rock and roll was an equalizer. And for me, it was more than a way to have fun or to feel like part of the crowd. It was a way to feel Americanized.

For my English elective, I chose speech and drama. Without having been told, I knew that I had what was known as a Chinese accent. Some sounds in English don't exist in Cantonese, and vice versa. Chinese words stand on their own as pictograph symbols; there is no alphabet. Cantonese, then, can sound choppy. And so, too, would our English. I had trouble differentiating among various *ch* and *sh* sounds, and bridging words smoothly. In childhood, in Chinatown, it was neither good nor bad; it was just the way we were. In Texas, I decided to try and sound, as well as be, more "American."

* * *

I remember the shock I felt in physical education class when Coach Kile, a handsome young man, looked at me early in the semester, clapped his hands, and yelled, "Let's go, Chop Chop!"

For a kid who was longing to belong, it was a devastating blow. Trying only to fit in, I had been singled out; I was that round little yellow-skinned guy in the comic book. I was the Ching-Chong Chinaman. I had to be; after all, it was a teacher who was saying so.

And, of course, I was utterly powerless to fight back.

I ran with the rest of the boys in PE, taking solace in the fact that none of them took to calling me names. In speech class, I listened hard and learned to mimic Texas accents, to speak, as Shakespeare wrote, "trippingly on the tongue," to camouflage, in any way I could, the verbal vestiges of my Chinatown upbringing.

I tried to be cool. The passport to cooldom in 1957 was rock and roll. So, in the bungalow, in front of a mirror, I lip-synched to Elvis Presley songs.

One night, a banquet at the Ding How featured a band fronted by a cool-looking singer named Royce—slicked-back Elvis hair with a spit curl up front, flashy red jacket and black slacks. Royce sang rockabilly: Gene Vincent & His Blue Caps' "Lotta Lovin'," Buddy Knox's "Party Doll," and, of course, Elvis. For weeks, I couldn't get "You're Right, I'm Left, She's Gone" out of my mind. I'd run back to the bungalow for some more practice.

Once or twice, I got invited to parties, but I never went. It wasn't that I couldn't, although my father was opposed to my going out without a chaperone—like, for instance, Lee Sing. But I'd never attended a party with schoolmates before.

Life in Oakland had not prepared me for the wide open possibilities of the Panhandle of Texas. Now that I had a measure of freedom, I wasn't sure how to be free.

I had one schoolmate over. His name was Jackie Hines, and

he came from a broken home. After school, he'd ride over on his bicycle and we'd hang out around the still-empty rear parking lot. He gave me my first bike lessons, even letting me use a spare bike he had at home.

One day, we were both riding around behind the Ding How, making circles in the concrete, when he jumped off, sat down against one of the five posts that held up the front roof of our bungalow, and waved me over.

I slowed my bike, using another of the posts to bring me to a dead stop, dismounted, and joined him on the ground.

"I found out something," he said.

"What?"

"It's about *sex*."

"So?" I was trying to be nonchalant, but he knew better.

"You already know how it's done?"

"Well . . . not *exactly*," I said, meaning I didn't know the first thing. He could have told me Santa bought babies, and I would have said, "So?"

Jackie then told me that a girl had told him how sex worked. "It usually happens in a bathroom," he said.

I became somewhat more alert. *This* was news.

"And then they take off their clothes, and he puts it in her."

"It," I didn't have to ask about. But where did *it* go?

Jackie shrugged. "Somewhere around the stomach, where the baby comes out."

I refrained from bringing up this wild rumor I'd heard—something about a stork—and I asked him a few more questions. What did kissing have to do with it? Was it fun? What's the deal with babies being part of it?

Jackie had no easy answers. The girl's information, after all, was based on sex being a phenomenon that took place in a restroom. Still, I knew more now than I ever had before.

At age twelve, I still had no interest in sex. At least not in knowing the morbid details. Back at Lincoln School, kids had burst out laughing after trapping victims in what was supposed to be a dirty joke.

You agreed to answer "Bendix"—the name of an appliance manufacturer—to every question posed.

"What kind of washing machine do you have?" they'd ask.

"Bendix."

"Where does your father work?"

"Bendix."

"What does your mother do?"

"Bendix."

The kids would roar. And I didn't have a clue.

It didn't occur to our parents to talk with us about sex. That wasn't the Chinese way. When Sarah had to confront her first period, she did it without our mother's involvement. She learned about sex through films shown in home economics. When Shirley expressed her first interest in going out on a date, she heard Mom's summary judgment: *"Hoy see how."* Translation: "A waste of time."

Having an older brother like Barry, I wasn't totally ignorant about sexual matters. Thanks to the magazines he acquired on our Sunday morning outings, I knew what naked women looked like. They had breasts, a muted gray zone where boys had penises, and they were usually playing volleyball.

But in Texas, my feelings about girls intensified. Given more time to myself than I had at home, I'd sit and watch TV. Besides Wally Cleaver going off on his first dates while an awed Beaver watched, there'd be these intensely romantic old movies late at night. Tender, unrequited love inevitably got requited. And I'd be like Beaver, watching and pining away for just one leftover shard of those magical feelings.

In real life, at Horace Mann, kids were going steady, exchanging ID bracelets and St. Christopher's medals to display their devotion to their one and only. It was love, eighth-grade-style, and I wanted some.

On nights when there were school dances or parties I couldn't

attend, when I'd finished work and repaired across the rear parking lot to the bungalow, I'd turn on the radio and move around
the concrete floor the way I saw kids doing on the local bandstand
show. I didn't go as far as to dance with a broom, but I did think
about Holly Clark.

She wasn't as cute as Milly Porter, who I imagined could step
straight out of *Father Knows Best*, or as pretty as Marsha Giffin,
who had the upturned nose and dimples of a model. Holly had
naturally wavy brunette hair and a friendly face, and she wore
neat blouses and crisply pleated skirts. But I liked her most
because she laughed at my jokes and cartoons. And she didn't
have a steady boyfriend.

And so, in the clumsy, adolescent, hiding-behind-jokes way I
would adopt for much of my life, I attached myself to her, giving
her a personalized ID bracelet—that's what all the other kids
were doing—and deluding myself into thinking that we were, in
some way, a couple.

Once or twice, I walked Holly home after school. At the front
door of her family's house on Ridgemere Drive, I'd peek in
through the front door, into her quiet, pin-neat, middle-class
living room, and think: "This is the way it should be."

When the school year ended, she was off to a vacation with
her family, and we never talked again.

For all the bold steps I took into uncharted territory in Texas,
I still felt conspicuously small. Even for a person of average size,
that's a common feeling in Texas. But when Coach Kile had
called me "Chop Chop," I took it not only as a racial stab but
also as a reminder that I was short.

And so, at the Ding How, I'd go into the men's room, where
there was an overhead pipe. I'd get up on the toilet, reach up,
and hang from the pipes, thinking I could stretch myself taller.
I'd read the Charles Atlas ads in the back of comic books and
think about sending away for muscles. I never did, and stayed
puny.

Still, my sister Sarah had been right. I grew up in Texas, and my time there was pivotal. It was my first experience away from Chinatown, from Chinese peers, and from the family. Suddenly, on the eve of my teens, I had a respite from the matched set of expectations with which Chinese children are born. We were told early on that we had to study hard and become either a doctor, dentist, lawyer, or, if we weren't quite up to snuff, maybe an engineer.

We were going to do what our parents could not, they told us. While they had to struggle to earn a living and to raise their family, we would be the ones who would take full advantage of the opportunities offered by the Golden Mountains. We would make our fortunes by wearing white collars. Good children all, we would then repay our parents, helping to take care of them in their old age.

I had no such interests, and in Texas, away from such talk, I could fantasize about rock and roll stardom, about being on the radio, about drawing cartoons and writing jokes, or, failing such glamour jobs, commercial art. Since grade school, I'd known that I could draw—both Barry and I seemed to have inherited some of our father's artistic skills—and I got some cartoons into the *Oakland Tribune*, which published kids' stories and drawings in the Sunday paper.

Nosing around one day in the chief partner's office at the Ding How, I discovered the typewriter and, within a month or so of toying around, was hunting and pecking through most of my homework. In spring, using the typewriter and a rubber stamp kit, I even put together a personal magazine with stories and parodies I'd written. I let one or two friends see it, so that I could claim that the magazine had had some circulation beyond a couple of kindly Ding How waitresses.

The Ding How, from all appearances, was a solid success. Residents and travelers passing through Amarillo kept the restaurant full the first several months, and even when winter brought a lull, there seemed to be enough business to keep a crew of six waitresses constantly busy.

But my father never saw the profits. The main partner, the man whose brainchild the Ding How was, the one who put together the crew of partner-cooks, plowed the initial profits back into the restaurant. That was acceptable. But, after a while, my father was convinced that not all receipts were being properly registered, that at least one partner was pocketing a disproportionate share of the proceeds.

He confronted the others, and they, for various personal and business reasons, stood together.

"You got me here from Oakland, and now you cheat me!" my father shouted one day in Big Joe's office. Caught up in anger, he lost his voice and began to choke. I ran and fetched a glass of water so that he could continue his argument. But, three to one, it was hopeless.

I, his thirteen-year-old son, could do little. One night, knowing how frustrated my dad was while he was toiling through a dinner rush, I wandered out to the parking lot in front of the restaurant and stared at the elaborate sign of neon and light bulbs that rose thirty feet high to beckon Route 66 travelers into the restaurant. After checking to be certain that no one was in the lot, I threw rocks at the sign until I knocked out one or two light bulbs.

There, I thought, dashing toward the side alley to the back. That ought to teach them.

A few more arguments later, my father had had enough, and we were back on the railroad tracks, on our way home.

·· 8 ··

WORKING

FOR A

LIVING

Back in Oakland for my last year of junior high, I joked around in class and in the hallways, using humor—most of it stolen from *Mad* magazine—to get back into the social mainstream. I wrote for the school paper, and, when a teacher suggested that I should run for student body president, I inserted into my campaign speech a topical joke about a popular boy in school, and won.

I ran student council meetings according to *Robert's Rules of Order*, and I also set up a records-at-noon program to pipe hit sounds outdoors every Friday at lunchtime.

When I had to think about what I might want to do in life, something steered me toward newspapers. Through English class, I entered an essay contest on the topic "What My Education Means to Me." I wrote about being interested in journalism and

drawing, and particularly about becoming a newspaper colum-
nist. "I want to see myself behind a typewriter, pounding out a
story for a newspaper," I wrote.

Another budding writer was Ann Wai.

Ann was from China, by way of Hong Kong. She'd settled
into North Oakland and transferred to Westlake a year before
to take an English class the school offered for foreign students.

Ann stood out immediately. She didn't look like a Chinatown
girl. Her skin was fairer, her face wider. She liked to adorn her
hair with a bow. A lot of boys, just beginning to notice girls,
were knocked out.

We met in Mrs. Brinker's English class, which she took in
addition to her special class. It took me only a couple of months
to work up the nerve to ask her out for an after-school soda. We
took the bus downtown to Kress, a clone of Woolworth's.

Just sitting next to her at the fountain, I felt triumphant. Sure,
it was daylight, but I was actually out with a girl. This was no
half-fantasy, the way it'd been with Holly Clark in Texas.

While Ann scanned the menu, I ordered a root beer soda. The
clerk nodded. "I see you're taking your sister out," he said.
"What would she like?"

I couldn't believe it. Ann and I looked *nothing* alike. She was
my *date*, and now, this ... soda *jerk* had ruined it. Ann stayed
cool.

"We're friends," she said, laughing. After she ordered, she told
me why we'd been mistaken.

"You're very young," she said, meaning not only that I was
young at fourteen, but that I looked even younger.

Ann, in contrast, was old. She was sixteen. We were in the
same grade because she had been advised to repeat ninth grade
so that she could continue to work on her already very good
English.

I continued to stew. That didn't seem reason enough to have
a guy strip me of my status as a dater.

Ann kept the conversation going, asking about me and thanking me for befriending her and helping her, here and there, with her English.

Born in China, she had spent a few years in Hong Kong, had come over in 1955 to San Leandro, a suburb of Oakland. She spoke no English until her arrival in America. Now, she lived right near Oakland Technical High School. Would I like to see her house?

I adored her house—not for anything about it, but because I was in a *girl's* house. There was no one home, and Ann flicked on a radio and breezed through a perfunctory tour. We talked about our classes, and I mentioned the compulsory dance classes I was taking at Westlake, where we two-stepped and box-stepped our way through the easily measured rhythms of such hits of the day as Elvis Presley's "Too Much" and Johnnie Ray's "Just Walkin' in the Rain."

Ann, busy with her English studies, was excused from the lessons. "Can you show me how to dance?" she asked.

In class, we had been taught how to ask a girl to dance and how to say "thank you" afterwards. Still, I wasn't ready for this.

Dancing with Ann was nothing like lurching, eyes to the floor, counting one-two-three-four in a gym in the midst of a roomful of stumbling adolescents. Or like practicing at home with Sarah or Shirley. This was like something out of the movies. Much clumsier, but also much more adult and romantic.

Of course, even as I held her, I had my feet draw out a box and prayed hard that my imaginary container would stay off of her feet.

That was my date with Ann. She sensed that I had a crush on her, and she knew better than to encourage me. By inviting me to her house, she'd expressed her fondness for me. But, at the same time, she had reminded me that she was living near Oakland Tech. My parents were looking for a house outside of Chinatown, meaning I might not be following Sarah, Barry—and Ann—to Tech. At that age, in those times, different schools meant different worlds. We would most likely not be seeing each other again after Westlake.

Barry was now a junior at Oakland Technical High School. While I'd been away in Texas, Barry switched from his newspaper route to a job at Moon's Chinese Kitchen, a small, six-table, mostly take-out place in Emeryville, in the black ghetto between Berkeley and Oakland.

Moon's owner, a Mr. Tso, had met our father soon after Dad's arrival in Oakland. He and his wife, who oversaw the restaurant with their son, Bong, hired Barry to take delivery orders on the phone and pack them in the kitchen.

With Reno, the newspaper route, and now Moon's, Barry never had time to socialize. In school, he was still tight with Bill Fung, and although Barry had begun to notice girls and had an easy time talking with them in school, neither he nor Fungus was ready to go out on dates. Besides, after school, while Bill might go bowling with Herbert and Gilbert Wong, Barry had to set off to Moon's Chinese Kitchen.

In his first semester at Tech, Barry met Norma Yee. They had a Spanish class together. One day, the teacher said something that struck them as *estupido*. Norma rolled her eyes, Barry nodded, and they clicked.

Norma Yee was bright, pleasant, and friendly, with an easy laugh and a self-deprecating manner. They began talking and found common ground. Like Barry, Norma had to work after school. Her family ran a grocery store halfway between Tech and downtown Oakland. Norma had a boyfriend, Kevin, who was much older than she—he was already at the University of California at Berkeley—and Barry and she soon settled into a *Go-Go-Mui-Mui*, a big brother–little sister relationship.

In Chinese families, siblings do not use names with each other. An older brother is (switching now to our own, *tze-yup* dialect) "Goo-Goo," an older sister is "Day-Day." A younger brother is called "Di-Di"; and a younger sister is "Moy-Moy."

As Norma's Go-Go, Barry would dispense advice to her, even though she was five months older than him. But when, in the course of one of their talks, Norma told Barry: "God, you're so much wiser than me," Barry could only agree.

Barry was all over Norma about Kevin. "Going around with him is a serious mistake," he said. "He's off to college, and that's just another world. You're just going to get left behind."

When she and Kevin broke up, Barry was on her case about her social prospects, and played Professor Higgins to her Eliza Doolittle.

One day, he gave her a quick once-over and pronounced: "You need to be careful, Norma. You're looking kind of dowdy these days."

If Norma protested, he'd push on: "You're not like the other girls in my circle of friends, so come on, let's polish it up a little. Do something about your hair."

For all of Barry's generosity in critiquing Norma, it was she who had a boyfriend, while he had no girlfriend. As spring surrendered itself to summer, and juniors were thinking about their upcoming prom, neither Barry nor Bill had a clue about who they might take. All they knew was that the Junior Prom was an important date, the first significant social event for the Class of '60.

Fungus wound up with something short of a dream date: the sister of a friend.

Barry, on the other hand, took a lovely girl who was still going to junior high school. It was Ann Wai.

I had introduced them a few weeks before, when Ann was at our house to borrow a book from me. Now, they were off to his prom.

Ann knew that I liked her, and although she'd accepted Barry's invitation as if it were just a casual date, she knew I was upset.

Before the prom, she came to me. "I'm sorry," she said. "To me, it's just a date."

It was the same for Barry.

"It's no big deal," he said.

To me, of course, it was. I didn't know that Ann considered me too young for her. All I knew was that I'd had a soda date, and Barry was taking her to a dressed-up, big-deal high school prom.

It was a slap in the face, a stinging reminder that I would always be Barry's little brother, following in his footsteps. I had with the *Tribune* route, and I had when I went out of town with our father. Upon graduation from Westlake, I was going to join Barry at Moon's Chinese Kitchen.

And, one spring day, I followed him into trouble with the law.

I was at Pay Less, a sprawling discount department store. I was in the records department when I decided to take a few 45 rpm singles. Beyond that mistake, I broke one of the few rules in the Barry Fong-Torres manual: I got greedy. I took maybe eight records, slipping half of them under a coat and the other half between a couple of textbooks I was carrying. It may be that the store detectives, watching from a perch above the main floor, had seen me swiping the first record. No matter. As I made my way out of the store, a man in a sport coat and slacks stopped me.

"Just a second, young man," he said.

He didn't have to say another word. I simply turned around and accompanied him back into the store. He ushered me to the back and up a flight of stairs, where I saw the secret spying room for the first time.

"We saw you taking some records," the man said.

I fished them all out and handed them over. I felt embarrassed—especially when one of the records turned out to be "My Happiness," a schmaltzy tune sung by Connie Francis.

There was no point trying to lie my way out of it. "Gee," I could have said, shades of the Beaver, "this record must've fallen between my books." But the four under my coat would be tougher to explain.

The man asked for some identification. Being fourteen, I didn't have much. I went through my wallet and gave him a couple of student body cards from Westlake.

He studied one, then another. He looked puzzled. "Charlie Brown?" Jeez. Typical of my humor, I'd signed one of the cards with the name of a cartoon character—one who, appropriately enough, was on the dim and hapless side.

The detective looked at the other card.

"Is this right? You're the student body president?" By now, he had reason to question anything I'd placed before him.

I felt like Charlie Brown at his most sheepish, when his mouth is just one squiggly line. I nodded.

"Well, you should know better," he said.

"I know. I'm sorry."

"Well," he said, "we'll let you go this time. But we're keeping your name—your *real* name—on file. So we don't want to see you up here again."

"You won't, sir," I said, as polite as I could be in my panicked state.

I thanked him and fled. I didn't return to Pay Less for several months.

As I had after the firecracker-selling incident, I balanced my criminal behavior with a good performance in school, completing my term of office without a hitch and winning another school spelling championship to add to the one from Lincoln School. In the citywide competition, I slipped up on a word I'd never heard: "fatigue."

In the summer, I joined Barry at Moon's where he, at sixteen, had taken on part-time duties as a waiter. Taking telephone orders and packing them up for the delivery boys, I felt like I was in my first real job. I'd worked for the family; I'd delivered newspapers; I'd spent after-school hours assisting a sightless newsstand vendor at the Oakland Post Office. But this was different. I had a supervisor, adult co-workers, and customers to deal with. I had to wear a beige linen jacket, which I thought was neat. I got used to eating dinner with the other employees, who got low-budget diets of oxtail stew and sliced beef tongue. On tongue nights, I'd beg to have anything else—even prefab patties of Egg Foo Yung.

One weekend afternoon, I was taking yet another order of shrimp fried rice and fried prawns on the telephone. Reading back the order to the customer—"Now, that's one order of shrimp fried . . ."—my voice cracked, and when I pieced it back together, it had slipped a notch. At age fourteen, I had reached adolescence—in a Chinese restaurant.

After a couple of years of messing around, Barry got serious about getting into the prestigious University of California in Berkeley, which, to Chinese parents, was synonymous with a successful future.

Barry finished up at Tech with a scholastic flourish. At Moon's, he hurried through his work so that he could wedge in time on the books. The owner's wife didn't like either of us using her time to study, but, for Barry, it paid off.

Sarah was the first true rebel of the family. After graduating from high school with excellent grades, she entered U.C. Berkeley, where she harbored dreams of becoming a chemist who'd discover an element that would be named after her. Instead, she discovered the Beat scene, jazz, and boys.

If Sarah, who'd been good at home and in school, could suddenly turn on my parents like some pickled salted plum, what could they expect from the rest of us?

Shirley, a year and a half younger than me, would bear the brunt of their paranoia. As Sarah slipped away from their control, they tightened their vise on Shirley; she was watched more carefully, judged more harshly.

Where Sarah was dry, cynical, satirical, and skeptical, Shirley was her flip side: affable, innocent, open. Yet no matter what she did—hard work, good grades, and even, years later, actual Chinese boys as dates—it wasn't enough. She would spend most of her youth and young adulthood trying to please her parents, and never quite succeeding.

As tough as my parents were on Shirley, they pampered Burton, who was born in 1949. He had been unexpected, and he caused my mother endless guilt. If she had known she was pregnant, she said, she would not have gone to China to visit grandmother. In Hong Kong, she had fallen down a ladder, and she didn't get enough nutrition in the village. She felt that all this resulted in Burton's being smaller than average.

Other times, my mother would point to the accident at Lake Tahoe, where the family took occasional holidays. Our parents would disappear into the casinos—Dad to play Keno, Mom to play blackjack or the slots—while we whiled away hours with games in the recreation center. For a family that had no knowledge or interest in the outdoors, that had little skill in talking with one another, and that wanted primarily to get away from the drudgery of the restaurant, these vacations were fine.

In 1960, Shirley and Burton made the trip with our parents; Barry and I stayed behind, with Sarah as our guardian. While Mom and Dad were in town, Shirley and Burton lolled by the motel pool. None of us knew how to swim, and Shirley limited herself to paddling around in the shallow end.

Suddenly, she saw Burton falling into the other end of the pool. She screamed for help. Within moments, two men ran out of the motel, jumped in, and pulled Burton out. They took him sixty miles to the Washoe Hospital in Reno, where he was examined, pronounced all right, and released. Back in Oakland, Burton went to our family doctor in Chinatown; again, he was declared fine.

But the incident never stopped troubling our mother. As Burton struggled in school and at home, as it became clear that he was having difficulties reading, writing, and speaking, Mom would point to the incident in Tahoe—or her fall in Hong Kong—as the reason.

And Shirley felt a finger pointing at her as well. Few words were spoken, but she could sense the blame being directed her way.

Growing up with Burton, we never knew what was wrong. All we knew was that our parents spoiled him. While we were required to hit the books and bring home good report cards, Burton was relieved of that pressure. So when he came up short in reading, writing, and talking, we wrote it off to the special treatment he'd received. Besides, he was a hard worker at the restaurant, and that seemed to please our parents. In Burton, they had no rebel. And when one or the other of us would yell at him to do his homework, and he wanted to continue peeling prawns or watching television, Mom and Dad were on his side.

·· 9 ··

A NEW

HOUSE

In summer of 1959, we moved out of Chinatown.

Just seven years before, the restrictions barring people of minority races from owning property in various parts of Oakland had been lifted, and the Chinese of Oakland had fanned out. This marked another of the differences between the Chinatowns of Oakland and San Francisco. Across the bridge in *Dai Fow*, Chinatown was its own state, a community so defined and powerful, so protective of its citizens that they often found it both unnecessary and difficult to leave. In Oakland, people who lived in Chinatown were anxious to get out. Sure, they felt welcome and comfortable there, but, like Oakland itself, it was lifeless compared to San Francisco. As soon as they were allowed to, and could afford to move to another neighborhood, they packed up.

To a Chinatown family, East Oakland was another world. It began across Lake Merritt and stretched southward and eastward, over hills and mountains and quiet streets with fine homes. East Oakland people seemed to be better dressed, to have better cars, to speak perfect English. I never imagined we'd live there.

If he'd had his way, my father would have preferred to start another restaurant venture, but my mother controlled the family's finances. Once, she recalled, an elderly man had advised: "First, get your home, and then establish your business." The man had also told my father: "You can't hold onto your money. Let your wife keep the money for you."

My mother was adamant that, with the family growing bigger and the flat at 206 Eighth Street not getting any larger, we would have a new home. Scrimping and saving, and adding whatever she made from her work as a seamstress and whatever we kids could chip in from our jobs, she saved up $2,500, which she figured would be enough for a down payment. Then she announced to us that we were buying a new house.

All we had to do was find one. Sarah, Shirley, and I watched the real estate ads, taking note that many of them took pains to add "All Welcome." Our parents went out on days off to see the possibilities. After several weeks of futility—the houses were either too small or, if large enough, too expensive—the children's interest waned. We all wanted to move, but it seemed impossible.

One evening, Mother called Shirley aside. She had the *Tribune* with her, opened to the classified ads. "You teach me to read," she told Shirley. "I'll find a house myself."

Shirley went through several listings with her, telling her, as best she could, what "rumpus," "tiled bath," "stucco," "patio," and "double garage" meant. In her English lessons in citizenship classes, Mother had learned mostly about presidents, senators and congressmen, and, finding little of use, let the language slide. Now, she could ferret out homes with her new skills, and, one day, this ad caught her newly trained eye:

"*No Carfare, Mom!* Oakland High, McChesney Jr. High, churches, shopping, only minutes away, walking. 3 bedrooms. A buy at $14,000, try $2,500 down." It was more than she wanted to spend. But we had the down payment, and, she told herself, "If it's near school, we can save on transportation."

She and Shirley arranged to see the house. When the realtor stopped in front of 1221 East 33rd Street, my mother peered out the car window at a small, white stucco house. Neighboring homes, one at the corner and several across the street, were noticeably larger. Our parents didn't know it, but they were in a neighborhood that had come to be known as "China Hill," because of its popularity with well-heeled Chinese-American families.

There were no Chinese neighbors in sight, but the house appealed to Mom right away. For one thing, it stood alone. Whereas on Eighth Street we were welded to the apartment next door, this house had a driveway along the right side, and it led to a large garage in back. At the rear of the house, a previous owner had built an upstairs bedroom. And although three bedrooms didn't seem to be enough for a family of seven, there was a solution. The garage could be converted into a bedroom.

My parents bought the house for $12,500, and in the summer of 1959, we moved in. So much had happened in the year since Dad and I had returned from Texas. Besides graduating from Westlake, I was finally done with Chinese school. And now we were moving to a new neighborhood.

We spent much of the season working on the house. It needed cleaning and painting, and, most exciting for Barry and me, it needed a new bedroom.

The garage could hold two cars, and it had an adjacent shed at the rear. We could have turned it into a spacious home within a home for ourselves. But we chose instead to share the shed as a bedroom and turn the large front area into a combination study room and family room. And if we ever had a party, it'd be the perfect place.

Dad bought plasterboards and lumber for moldings; he sketched out possible tile patterns for the floor and we chose our favorites, then shopped for the tiles. We didn't install heat or a bathroom. At night, when nature called, we'd have to dash across the short expanse of the backyard and into the basement laundry room, where there was a half-bath.

As we fixed up the house that summer, I soaked up the music of the times—"Kansas City" by Wilbert Harrison, a song of fresh starts and optimism, as well as lust; "A Fool Such as I" and its flip side, "I Need Your Love Tonight" from Elvis, issued while he was still in the Army; the softly harmonic Fleetwoods' "Come Softly to Me"; the falsettoed Impalas' "Sorry, I Ran All the Way Home"; a novelty tune from the popular TV series *77 Sunset Strip* called "Kookie, Kookie (Lend Me Your Comb)"; and a tear-jerker called "Tragedy."

While we got our new home together, a famine hit all of China. Mao's government had made a bold attempt at instant modernization with what he called the "Great Leap Forward" of 1958. But grain yields from the communes were overinflated, and agricultural production fell far short of estimates. At the same time, China used millions of people and tons of wood and coal to produce useless iron and steel. The economy went out of control, and thirty million people would die of famine-related causes.

We settled happily into our modest neighborhood in East Oakland. Our new neighbors—all white, middle-class families— seemed friendly. The couple across the street hired me to water their garden while they were away on vacation. I felt as American as Dennis the Menace.

Every day and night, it seemed, our parents reminded us how lucky we were, and how we had to eat all our food and save our money.

·· 10 ··

THE PINK

PRISON

High school was scary. Not just because it was *high school*, the last years of required education, but also because I was on my own as I ventured onto the campus of Oakland High. Unlike before, I wasn't following Sarah and Barry, with their presence and advice to help.

The school itself looked imposing. It had a nickname, the "Pink Prison," and it fit. The three-story building resembled a gothic castle, with peaked, fluted columns spaced along the front of the structure. The paint job was fading, but yes, it was pink.

Oakland in the early sixties was becoming a racial melting pot, and in my class of 663 students, almost a quarter were minorities.

We had seventy-eight blacks, twenty-one Hispanics, and forty-five Asians.

Many of the kids gravitated to where they were most comfortable, so there was de facto separation of racial groups. My first year there, minority students occupied only seven of eighty-nine student government positions.

That's the way it was in 1960. With the inauguration of a vigorous young Democrat as President, and the first civil rights protests taking place in the South, change may have been in the air, but we didn't sense it. We lived day to day with the status quo. That meant no minorities on television commercials or series, except as maids and servants—or, of course, villains.

With no proper role models, many of us accepted, some more grudgingly than others, that we faced low ceilings.

I did not socialize exclusively with Asians at Westlake, and I was not about to do that at Oakland High. As I got to know the school, I got the feeling that there were no closed doors on campus. You just had to knock. Anyone could try out for anything, and as the semesters rolled on, more and more ethnic minorities began to appear as bylines in the paper, as actors in school plays, as student body officers. I began writing for the school paper and, in ROTC, found a partner in comedy, a new friend named Alvin Kostors.

Like me, Al loved *Mad* magazine and Steve Allen's TV show, and, as a result, sprinkled non sequiturs—"One grunch and an eggplant over there"—into his speech. Like me, he was fascinated by radio. In early 1960, rock and roll was stunted. Elvis was still awaiting his discharge from the Army, and the charts were cluttered with prefab teen idols like Fabian and Frankie Avalon, and with novelty records and story-songs: "Running Bear," "El Paso," and syrupy instrumentals by squares like Percy Faith and Lawrence Welk. The best music on the air was by rhythm and blues artists—Ray Charles, the Drifters, the Olympics, Ike and Tina Turner, Sam Cooke, and Aaron Neville.

Al and I were loyal to Oakland's new Top 40 station, KEWB—"Color Radio Channel 91," they called it, at a time when color television was still a novelty—and I managed to get a job there in the fall as a weekend assistant to one of the newscasters. I showed up Saturday mornings and read the feeds from the wire services, then relayed college football scores to the newscaster, Jack Morris, updating them as necessary through the afternoon. I floated every Saturday to the Bermuda Building, where KEWB had its studios. Just getting past the guard—because I was, after all, an *employee*—would have been payment enough for me.

While I was settling into the Pink Prison, Sarah was giving up on her dream of becoming a world-renowned chemist. Unable to cut into animals, she refused to take any life science courses. After considering and rejecting a change of majors, she left college after two years and got a job with the phone company.

On New Year's Eve, she attended a party in a Chinatown basement and met Dave Watkins, a twenty-six-year-old artist. The party crowd was half-Asian, half-Caucasian, and that was fine by Dave. Since the mid-fifties, he'd had close Chinese friends, and he played mah-jongg at one pal's house in North Beach, adjacent to Chinatown.

While Sarah and Dave began to go out, Barry, in his first months in college, had fallen in love. Her name was Sandy, and they had met at a dance put on by the Chinese Students Club at Cal. Both were new and struggling to fit in at Berkeley.

Sandy's family was well-to-do; her father was a doctor, and her family had moved years ago from San Francisco's Chinatown to the Outer Richmond district, where a few Chinese families had begun to move. She racked up good grades in high school and had her family predicting big things for her. In fact, her grandmother loudly made it known that she was setting aside money to help Sandy open up shop in Chinatown when she'd become a physician.

In her biology class at Cal, Sandy discovered that she had absolutely no affinity for the sciences, and she was distraught. Suddenly, the girl who would be a doctor was rudderless.

Barry had just barely made it into Cal. But, as he had since junior high, he split his time in Berkeley between studies and work. With our father between restaurant ventures again and cooking at Trader Vic's, he got a job there as a dishwasher. He'd barely gotten away with parceling out his time that way in high school. At the university, he found himself in immediate danger of dropping out.

Barry and Sandy shared their classroom miseries. They became nearly inseparable, hitting the library to study, going out for coffee breaks at the Bear's Lair, occasionally splurging for sweets at Edy's Fountain. She visited our house once for dinner, and afterwards, they offered to do the dishes—by themselves. From the living room, all we could hear was laughter. It was obvious that Barry had found a girlfriend.

While my sister and brother were finding romance, I made my way into the spotlight at Oakland High. I wrote a humor column for the school paper, but it was on stage that I came to life. I ran the student assemblies, opening them up with monologues—*A funny thing happened to me on my way to school this morning; unfortunately, my writers haven't decided what it was yet*—and loading them up with guest appearances by local disc jockeys. In the school cafeteria, I occasionally set up a sound system and spun records, and I began getting hired to be a DJ myself at dances for various youth groups. I was quite the multimedia kid.

I couldn't get enough attention. Even in physical education, while most of the boys wore gray sweatshirts with our regulation blue shorts, my sweatshirt stood out. Inspired by Maynard Krebs, the beatnik character in the *Dobie Gillis* television series, I'd torn off the sleeves, and then drawn cartoons and slogans on it. On top of that, I'd put on a necktie.

In more conventional clothing, I attended classes and managed mostly B's. But for a good part of the semester, there was another distraction. Soon after the school year began, my parents purchased a restaurant in Hayward, a small town seventeen miles east of Oakland. It was your basic joint, a small, storefront window and a long, rectangular room with green vinyl-covered booths along the right side, a counter of ten or twelve seats along the left, a few tables along the rear, and the kitchen beyond. The moderately high ceilings held the fluorescent lighting requisite in all Chinese restaurants, so that customers felt like they were under police interrogation throughout their meal.

We all pitched in to get the restaurant going. I came up with the name, the Bamboo Hut, and we found bamboo matting to drape alongside the cash register. I drew the Bamboo Hut logo for the menu and painted it onto the front window with brown and gold paint. For our grand opening in early December, we suggested giveaways of Polynesian appetizers—items my father had made at Trader Vic's—and souvenir chopsticks. With his approval, I worked out a four-weekend advertising campaign with the local paper, including one ad that boasted simply about our "Monstrous Neon Sign," and that culminated at year's end with a four-course prime rib dinner for $1.35.

It worked. We pushed the other Chinese restaurants in town aside for several months. But the Bamboo Hut forced us to adjust our lives. We were the entire staff, and we worked Christmas Day, New Year's Eve, and New Year's Day. We—Shirley, who was a sophomore at Oakland High, Burton, who'd entered McChesney Junior High, and I—jumped onto buses after school every day except Thursday, when we were closed. We worked until ten every weeknight, and an extra hour on weekends, when we put in full days of work. Barry was employed at Trader Vic's, but he'd show up to spell Shirley or me on occasional weekends.

Soon, the restaurant became an unwelcome routine, as we realized that we were being cheated out of the time we could be spending doing what normal kids did—watching TV, hanging out with friends, cultivating hobbies and special interests, and having dinner and doing homework at set times. The teenagers' lifeline—the telephone—was off-limits to us; we had to leave it free for take-out orders. And we were working for nothing but tips, which, as with everything in Hayward, were sparse. Our customers came to the Bamboo Hut for the reason so many people went to Chinese restaurants: for cheap eats. Tipping was a foreign concept to most of them. There were families who rang up bills of maybe fifteen dollars, and from them we could expect two dollars. But they came far too few times.

More regular was a man in his seventies who dressed all in beige, with suspenders holding up his big old khaki pants. He'd clamber in, lower himself onto a stool at the counter—after a while, he had one stool he favored—and issue his order in a roar, through gravel-lined pipes: "SOME APPLE PIE."

For the first several months that we saw this man, that's all he ever said. He stunned us when summer rolled around and, perched on his seat, he bellowed: "SOME APPLE PIE . . . AND ICE CREAM!"

It was a breakthrough in our relationship.

From the time the Bamboo Hut opened until the end of January, I planned Oakland High assemblies at the rear table of the Bamboo Hut dining room, between tables, chores, and studies.

Once we got home—usually around eleven o'clock—the *real* work began. That's where I could cram for tests and write my newspaper pieces for the school paper and for a new neighborhood weekly.

None of this impressed my parents. They wanted me to do only two things: get the best grades possible and help out at the Bamboo Hut. The time for socializing would be after graduation—from *college*, that is. I owed it to the family to be at the restaurant. "That's how it is with Chinese," my parents said.

Just before the Bamboo Hut opened, Mom had taken another shot at learning some English, in hopeful preparation for becoming a United States citizen. Four evenings a week, she attended night classes at Oakland High, where she found encouragement learning from a teacher who was a native of Shanghai. At home, we'd help quiz her about George Washington, the Executive Branch, and Dwight Eisenhower.

In a steady hand, she copied conversational sentences into her spiraled notebook:

A: Watching TV helps my English. Does it help you?

B: Yes, it does, but it also gets me into trouble.

A: What do you mean? How can it get you into trouble?

B: Once I start watching I just go on and on. And I even stay up for the late, late show. I don't get my work done and I hate to get up the next morning.

Mom underlined "stay up" and "get up," so that she could learn the difference between them.

With the opening of the Bamboo Hut, she gave up the classes. Once again, she'd pick up most of her English from television.

At Oakland High, most of my classmates had no idea that I disappeared after school into another life. I finagled just enough time off from the restaurant to show up at selected events—usually to act as DJ or MC—that it appeared that I was social. Few noticed that I never had a girlfriend.

Denied a typical "American" life, I created a fantasy world in my monologues and columns, in which I was a central figure, laughing at myself as well as others. If I couldn't be a man about campus, and attend dances, football games, parties, and outdoor excursions, I'd write about those who were there and participate vicariously. Actually, I was pretty happy. And senior year gave me hope that, despite being Chinese, I might have a chance at a job behind a typewriter or a microphone.

My best friends in my senior year weren't kids in student government. They were two new arrivals, Candace Barnes and Tom Gericke. Candace first heard me on the radio. Through my football season weekend job at KEWB, I'd met the all-night DJ, Michael Jackson, and had invited him to be a guest at my first assembly. In turn, he had me on for an interview about high school. In school, Candace introduced herself, and I liked her immediately. She was thin, with an olive complexion, a goofy smile, and a sharp wit. She spoke with a slight accent—she was from New Jersey—and when I first met her, I said, "Candy? What's your *real* name?"

"Melvin," she said.

In my self-appointed role of friend to all, I watched out for her at our senior picnic, introducing her to everyone I knew; I took her backstage to see assemblies from a different perspective, and to the radio station. At the few parties I attended, we'd do a ridiculous version of the Twist (the only version I knew). And we had quiet talks in the library about the possibilities of life. By midyear, we were buddies, and in January, she organized a surprise birthday party for me. Tactful as usual, I breezed through the door and asked, "Where's the cake?"

Tom Gericke transferred from a Catholic school. He was so outgoing that one social club rejected him as a pledge for being "overly friendly." But with his good humor, he made plenty of other friends.

Once we knew that we had common interests in radio and records, we were best friends, whiling away lunch hours together, talking about making it big with any of hundreds of ideas. On sunny days, we would lie on the sloping lawn facing Park Boulevard. When buddies inquired what we were doing, Tom would say, "We're tanning our teeth."

Tom was with me one day in Oakland's Chinatown. In one store, I spoke some Cantonese to a clerk. Tom was shocked. He'd known me for months, but had never thought of me as belonging to any particular race. "It was fascinating," he told me later. "It exposed me to another side of you."

In May of 1962, at our Spring Carnival, I chanced onto a "marriage booth," in which, for fifteen cents, any couple could go through a mock wedding. Before the end of the day, I had four wives, three of whom I actually knew.

In the real world, I had few dates and no romance.

The closest I came to such a thrill was with April, a doe-eyed Chinese girl with golden skin and a soft voice. To me, she was the cutest girl on campus.

But I always thought of her as the girlfriend of Clifton, who'd been student body vice president when I was doing the assemblies.

With her being taken, which relieved me of any pressures, I had an easy time with her, joking over lunch in the clubroom, a classroom near the cafeteria favored by student government types.

Over lunch, she'd tell me bits and pieces about herself. I thought of her as one of the most Americanized Chinese girls in school, but she told me that her parents had thought of sending her to Chinese school, even though they lived in East Oakland. And while she didn't have a family business to keep her away from a social life, her parents were always on her to study, to get good grades.

In the spring, April was a pom pom girl, and she looked more fetching than ever, dancing to "The Twist" and "Runaround Sue" in her full-skirted blue and white gingham outfit. When she invited me to a party at her house a couple of nights after Valentine's Day, I went. There, she hinted that she was free for a school dance a week or two later. I maneuvered my way out of work at the Bamboo Hut, and we had a date.

Finally, I was at a dance where I wasn't an MC, DJ, or reporter. We did the pony, one of the big dances of the day, along with the mashed potato, and the twist. After I walked her home, we didn't date again.

It wasn't that I didn't want to; I just didn't know what to make of girls. I lacked the most basic social skills. It mattered nothing that I was the kid at the mike; a girl—a special girl—was far scarier than a spotlight blinding you from seeing an auditorium full of people with their eyes on you.

Besides, I'd rationalize, I had no time for dates.

And so, on and off for the rest of the semester, April and I went on what we called an "ignoring campaign," telling each other, "You don't matter as much to me as you think you do."

It worked well enough that April, who'd stopped seeing Clifton when she and I had begun hanging out together, agreed to go with him to the Senior Ball.

I was sunk. The Senior Ball, after all, was the acid test of a high school student's life. I couldn't bring just any date. Instinctively, I had to think Chinese. In our class, there were thirteen Chinese girls; I knew six of them, but the only ones I knew well were accounted for.

Fortunately, I also knew a couple of Chinese girls in the junior class, including Laura, who was bright, attractive, and active in school affairs.

Laura seemed shocked by my invitation. We didn't know each other that well, but she graciously accepted. The prom began at the school, then swung to the Oakland area's poshest hotel, the Claremont, in Berkeley.

There, I would like to say, we danced the night away in the Garden Room, enjoyed various entertainment, partook of the buffet breakfast, and spun out of the Claremont drunk with teenaged joy. The truth is that Laura got sick, and I squired her home well before dawn. She went to great lengths to assure me that I hadn't caused her indisposition. Nonetheless, my Senior Ball experience seemed to sum up my social life at Oakland High rather neatly.

·· 11 ··

SUMMERTIME

BLUES

A couple of friends told me that San Francisco State College had a good radio/TV department, and that was enough for me. I didn't care about following Sarah and Barry into Cal. S.F. State had a number of virtues. First was its location in San Francisco, just a bridge apart and yet a world away from Oakland. Besides a highly regarded, well-connected radio/television/film department, it had a robust daily newspaper serving a student body that numbered over 16,000. And it was going to have among its freshmen several of my high school friends, including Tom Gericke. My mind was made up.

Beyond the exams required for entrance to the college, the toughest one for me came after I'd been admitted: I had to prove that I could swim. Most Chinese can't. Sure, Mao Zedong swam down the Yellow River when he was in his seventies, but for most of us, swimming just isn't part of our upbringing. Since I'd managed to skip most of my physical education classes at Oakland High School by busying myself with student government activities, I'd finessed my way through them without ever hitting the pool.

Now, I had to. Otherwise, I'd have to take a swimming class. In the locker room, after signing in and getting our towels, Tom changed into his swim trunks. I had brought a pair, thinking I'd wade in the water and fake my way through. But, as I watched the instructors watching the incoming students in the pool, all such hopes vanished. I stalled, watching as students emerged from the pool. They'd fetch their towel, then one of the coaches would hand them a slip of paper. They proceeded into the locker room, where they handed in the slip and got checked off.

I sauntered over to the checkout cage and got a look at the slip of paper the swimmers were submitting. I couldn't believe it. They were simply torn squares of lined notebook paper, with a handwritten "P" on it.

I slipped back to my locker, fetched my bag, and did what I had to do. I went to the showers. Then, dripping wet, I went to my locker, fished out a notebook, duplicated a pass, grabbed a towel, reported to the cage and, huffing and puffing, turned over my "P." The attendant didn't even look at it.

I had passed. I had followed in my parents' footsteps and gained entry by way of a false paper.

At Cal, Barry and Sandy, each other's first lovers, began to drift apart at the end of their sophomore year. They came from two different worlds, and Barry never quite got used to Sandy's upper-middle-class status. She had the freedom to travel at will; Barry didn't.

By her junior year, Sandy was dating another young man. Barry, meantime, had found his career path. After two years at U.C. Berkeley, students are required to declare their majors. Barry decided on criminology. The courses he'd taken in social science and U.S. history had impressed him; lecturers like Eugene Burdick and Peter Odergaard had him questioning textbook history, government lines, and the status quo.

One night, after getting home from the Bamboo Hut, where my mother had spoken about how she wished I'd be more realistic about my career ambitions, I asked Barry about his. How was it that the *ky-doy* of the family, my shoplifting mentor, was going to be a crime-fighter? What about the pressures from Mom and Dad?

He shrugged. "I don't think I'm gonna go that traditional Chinese route," he said. "It takes too long to be a doctor or lawyer. Anyway, I'm more interested in people than the law." Used to getting average grades, he'd gotten an "A" in an introduction to criminology course in his sophomore year. He was inspired. He began working with U.C.'s YMCA, in a program modeled on Big Brothers in which adults met one-on-one with youngsters who'd been identified as "predelinquents."

He found the subject of Chinese delinquency fascinating. "Lookit this," he said one evening, looking up from a magazine article he was reading for a paper. "The Chinese have the lowest crime and delinquency rates of all ethnic groups. I wonder why that is?"

"Because they haven't checked your record yet," I said.

He shot me the middle finger.

"Well, I've got some ideas," he said. "Filial piety."

"What's that?"

"The idea that's been ingrained in us—even in you—that the child must not shame his parents or family name with his conduct."

I nodded. I'd certainly heard that song before.

"Racial piety." Barry didn't bother waiting for me to ask him for a definition. "The Chinese race should not be disgraced in the eyes of the Americans."

"Wait a minute. I thought we *are* Americans."

"Yeah, but they," he said, nodding toward the main house, meaning our parents, "don't think so." He picked up a pen. "And one more thing: lack of time—we're just too goddamned busy to get into trouble."

With my mind already wandering back to the homework I had to do, I understood.

"But if you work at it, you can probably find some time," I said.

Barry didn't laugh. "That's another thing. Not all kids are like us . . ."

"Thank God."

". . . So there are going to be problems in the future. The next generation'll probably be more Americanized than we are. Maybe they won't have restaurants and groceries they have to work at, or maybe they'll refuse to go to Chinese school. And there'll be more delinquency. At least that's what I think."

"Here's what I think," I said. "You're getting pretty serious in your old age."

Sarah and Dave Watkins had been dating a couple of years by now, and he'd met our parents.

At first, the quiet young man didn't appear to be any kind of threat, and my mother greeted him in the customary, polite Chinese way. "Have you eaten?" she asked when he first came to 1221 East 33rd Street to pick Sarah up for a date.

By bringing him home, Sarah had made a statement, and our parents didn't like hearing it. They had hoped that Sarah could find a nice Chinese boy. But, by now, they were resigned to Sarah going her own way, and when she told them that she'd known Dave for over two years, they braced themselves for the worst. Mom's sole comment to Sarah about Dave was that he had "lazy eyes." (As with many first-generation Chinese, our mother believed in face reading as a means of reading a person's fate. The eyes, it was said, helped indicate a person's nature and character. Fortunately for us, Mom never read our faces. Or, if she did, she never told us her findings.)

The rest of us had no problems with Dave. We didn't project

into the long-term. To us, Dave was just another guy Sarah saw. Barry and I liked the fact that he was an artist; we were both sketchers, Barry favoring pen-and-ink drawings of whatever he saw around him, and me doing cartoons and caricatures. Dave, in turn, was fascinated by my being such a Top 40 radio nut, with racks of 45 rpm singles and stacks of Top 40 surveys from the local radio stations.

Being a year or two older than Sarah, Dave seemed to me to be from some other generation. He was far too mature to be hanging around, talking with me for long stretches. But in art and music, we found common ground.

Dave wasn't sure how our parents felt about him. He found my mom an outwardly gracious mystery, and he was fascinated with our dad, who appeared to be a lively character, distanced from him only by a language barrier.

Dave's mother, Ethel, had no problem with her son seeing Sarah. "I've always said, 'live and let live,' " she told Dave.

Sarah hung with a crowd in Chinatown that included Gene Meigs, a jazz pianist with connections to Tom Thorndike, who ran a small record label named Carousel. In April of 1963, one of the best-selling albums in the country was *The First Family*, a comedy record featuring Vaughn Meader portraying President Kennedy. It had taken off the previous winter and never seemed to stop selling.

One evening, Sarah was with Meigs at China Smith's, a Chinatown cocktail lounge, when Meigs mentioned an idea for a teen version of *The First Family*. It'd be a takeoff on JFK, to the tune of a pop hit.

All he needed was someone to write and perform the song. Sarah knew that I wrote parodies of songs and that I did a JFK impression. I auditioned for Meigs by phone, wrote a couple of songs, recorded them in San Francisco with a mixture of professional musicians and musically inclined schoolmates, and by summer Carousel had issued "Hey Jackie," based on the Paul

and Paula hit "Hey Paula," and "Young Brothers," which I wrote
to the tune of Paul and Paula's "Young Lovers."

I remember calculating, on the bus from Oakland to San Francisco for the recording session, what my royalties would be if
"Hey Jackie" sold, oh, say, a million copies. Five thousand dollars
was an overwhelming amount of money. And that didn't include
what I'd get for writing the new lyrics. I'd be set for life. Just like
Elvis, I'd buy my mom a house and car. So what if she didn't
drive? She'd think of me as a good son, even though I hadn't
become a doctor.

The record didn't sell. I would have to stay in school and get
a job someday after all.

I continued to hone and show off my JFK impression until one
morning in November. Economics class had just broken up, and
Tom and I were walking toward the cafeteria when a student—
a stranger to us—wandered over and said, loudly: "Did you
hear? The President's been shot." We noticed knots of people
talking near the quad. I saw looks of concern. No one could quite
believe it was true.

As they were for most Americans, the next few hours and days
were foggy, teary blurs. At San Francisco State, I joined a group
of students in the coffee shop, where we listened to the news on
the radio. When the announcer said that the President had been
declared dead, I remember the cash registers falling silent, and
the entire room standing for the playing of the National Anthem.
With all classes cancelled, we went home for the weekend.

I had no interest in politics and didn't know what we'd lost.
About all I knew about Kennedy was that he was the youngest
president since Teddy Roosevelt; that he'd broken a barrier as
the first Roman Catholic elected president; that he had a beautiful
wife and family; that he supported physical fitness programs and
created the Peace Corps; that he sided with Negroes and faced
down the Soviets.

And now his life had been taken, his family turned into mourners. Like many Americans, I was distraught for reasons that I
didn't know. In Hayward that weekend, as we watched the diz-

zying events in the aftermath of the assassination on a portable TV set, I found it impossible to discuss it with my parents.

To them, it was simply *"koy yai"*—so bad. Seeing a shot of the Kennedy children at the funeral, my mother said she felt *"yeem goong,"* a phrase for which there is no direct translation into English, but which I always took to be a combination of shame and pity.

I had an outlet for my grief. Since my senior year at Oakland High, I'd been writing a column for a neighborhood paper, the *Oakland Times*. I wrote an essay about Kennedy, but I really didn't know what to say, and I felt some relief when, as the weeks passed into months, I returned to my usual format of short items, many of them scrounged up from the many hours spent in Hayward.

For most young people, summer meant fun, time off from school, time to go away on vacation. For us, it meant full-time work. We started work a half an hour before the restaurant opened, at noon, and stayed until ten at night, eleven on weekends, and longer if customers were lingering.

The worst times were between lunch and dinner. Although there was no business to speak of, we had to be there, doing chores or reading. We defiantly played ball games and music on the radio during all hours, reasoning to our parents that it was entertaining for the customers. Without the radio, all we would have had would be the clatter in the kitchen and the drone of refrigerators and coolers, the buzz of fluorescent lights—the soundtrack of the dullness of our lives.

It was a dreary time, and I came to despise this job I'd never asked for, and was never paid for. It was a performance I hated, this task of waiting on and serving customers, reciting and explaining Chinese dishes, carrying them out, clearing and busing dishes.

Once in a while, a customer would get to us. It could be the way he snapped off an order or complained about a dish, addressing us as if we were peons. I'd talk back or mix a little Chinese hot mustard (which is to say *very* hot) into his coffee. Most of the time, that would have improved the brew.

We made a habit of making a pot of coffee at the start of the day, and then simply adding water to it through the rest of the day. There was so little call for coffee, and it naturally grew stronger and darker as it sat over the heat that it never seemed to get more pale no matter how much we diluted it. Not being coffee drinkers ourselves, we had no idea how horrid it was.

On occasion, the general breed of our customers would get to Barry. One evening, a man who was a regular at the neighboring bar dropped in, reeking of grease, sweat, and the odors of the street. Barry took a whiff, leaned into the man's face, and cooed: "May I ask what cologne you're wearing?"

Another night, a stricken-looking Shirley whispered to me that a customer had said he wanted to go to bed with her. I relayed the man's request to my father, who grabbed a meat cleaver and ran out to the front room, chasing the customer out of the restaurant. *"Ky-Ai!"* he raged. "Bastard!"

But such moments were all too rare, and when boredom and frustration brought out our mean streaks, we'd round up any cockroaches that had strayed into the kitchen or dining room and, rationalizing that we were trying to help the Bamboo Hut live up to health codes, tossed the roaches onto the hot griddle. If Mom was resting in the basement, Dad would join us at the stove, saying he'd save the fried roaches for the next time a particularly despised customer came in.

To relieve the tedium of the slowest of nights, we'd wage *ah-jehng* (war) on a neighboring Chinese restaurant, Canton Chop Suey. Burton or Shirley would go out as spies and report on how many customers they had. They soon knew to return with undercounts, just to make our parents feel better.

Sometimes, I wished we'd just surrender.

Some summer days, when I'd tired of pitching a rubber ball against a concrete wall in back of the restaurant, I'd go to the library down the street. I worked on building my vocabulary. I

checked out albums of classical music and Rodgers and Hammerstein show tunes. I also wanted to play music, but, unable to
afford a guitar or piano, I banged away on a set of bongos Sarah
had given me the previous Christmas. I absorbed the humor of
Max Shulman and Ogden Nash. And I still read *Mad*.

I had decided what I wanted to be: everything. I was still
modeling myself after Steve Allen.

There were no Asian role models out there in the early sixties.
The only Chinese on radio was Herb Wong, a part-time disc
jockey on a local jazz station, and the only contemporary Chinese
byline I'd seen belonged to Frank Chin, who edited Cal's humor
magazine. On television and in the movies, Chinese images were
freakish—Fu Manchu—or cartoonish—Charlie Chan and his
Number One Son.

I wondered, sometimes, whether it wouldn't be safer and far,
far easier to go and study commercial art. But I heard too many
songs I felt I could write or sing; I had made people laugh, and
that, too, was music to my ears.

In retrospect, I blame my father for my career goals. In our
family, Mother was the disciplinarian at home, but at the restaurant, where we spent far more time, Father was the boss, the
breadwinner, and, to our delight, the entertainer. I enjoyed watching him in the kitchen, working in front of a row of woks,
wielding his utensils like a conductor's baton, but with a jazz
musician's touch for improvisation. In and out of the kitchen, he
sang, mimicked, and made glib, extemporaneous speeches. One
Christmas morning at home, watching us trying on endless new
shirts, robes, and dresses, he disappeared into the bedroom and
pranced back out in one of Mom's dresses, properly accessorized
with a handbag, a scarf around his head, and a song in his heart.

One New Year's Eve at the Bamboo Hut, made deadly dull
by the fact that we had no business, he marched out of the kitchen
waving his wok spatula like a sword and singing a line from a
Chinese opera—in a woman's voice, as male actors often did in
the opera. I waded in immediately, pushing my voice into falsetto
and singing a phrase I'd heard many times on radio broadcasts

of Chinese operas. I broke into a speech, made up entirely of mock-Chinese words, sprinkled with an occasional actual word—often a menu item—and went into sound effects of cymbals and bamboo sticks being struck together.

My parents were amazed, and while Mom laughed, Dad would respond with more operatic posturings. We hardly noticed that a new year had arrived, and that business was dwindling.

•• 12 ••

A Summer

Song

My first romance was, appropriately, a late summer love. I met Janie Lee in July of 1964 at a dance staged by a U.C. Berkeley Chinese club that hired me to be emcee and deejay.

I was nineteen; she was seventeen and a friend of a friend. The minute we were introduced, I liked her. We had a dance, but I broke off to get back to the microphone, and promised to get back to her. By the time I did, she was making her departure. I got up enough nerve to ask for her number. I learned that she lived in Hayward, just a couple of roads up from the Bamboo Hut.

And then I stalled. A month passed before I called about a date. Even then, it was a double date. We'd be going—with Barry and his date—to a performance of *Flower Drum Song*, Rodgers and Hammerstein's musical of the novel by C. Y. Lee about clashes between Chinese and American culture, between generations, between immigrants and native-born Chinese-Americans, between tradition-bound parents who still believed in matchmaking, and independent, modern-thinking kids who thought they were Americans.

The evening was something short of a date. I wanted Barry around, this being my first time and all, but I felt like one of the characters in *Flower Drum Song*—torn between reliance on family and determination to stand on my own.

With Barry driving and with him and his date around all evening, Janie and I felt extremely young, lost in their shadows. But we had just enough moments—eye contact, a shared laugh, an agreement on a point—to make a connection.

At evening's end, she had a reminder for me.

"We still haven't had that dance yet," she said, putting on a pout.

"We will," I promised.

We set up another date just a couple of days later. After arranging for Shirley to cover for me at the Bamboo Hut, we caught a matinee of *A Hard Day's Night*, and then, to get our dance in, went to her house. Janie's taste was for middle-of-the-road: Andy Williams, the Lettermen, and such. Mine was Top 40, encompassing everything from sap to rock.

Even as we danced that afternoon at her house, we weren't sure what was happening. She liked me because, compared with most of the Chinese boys she'd known, I was outgoing—she first saw me at a microphone. We soon learned that neither of us had had a romance before or, of course, had uttered "I love you" to anyone else. We didn't say those words to each other until late that fast-fading summer. She came by the Bamboo Hut one day to visit and said hello to my parents.

They weren't happy with anything that might interfere with my work at the Bamboo Hut. I was nineteen, and my mother said it was still a little early to be going out with girls. But my parents were grateful that she was at least Chinese, and they were pleasant to her.

A few days later, we spent an afternoon together in Oakland's Chinatown, pretending that we didn't want to be seen by certain friends and friends of our families, who'd be sure to report on us. By now, we were holding hands. I gave her albums and things that would remind her what a swell guy I was—such as clippings of my columns. Despite that, she agreed to see me again.

We went to a party one late August night and fell in love. There was more dancing than talking, but, having had our promised dance two weeks before, we spent most of our time sitting and making goo-goo eyes at each other. I don't remember a thing we said, but I know our goodnight took us almost half an hour.

Janie was going away to college in Central California in mid-September, so, as much as my work schedule allowed, we squeezed out time to be together. We had to improvise for places for our innocent petting sessions. Her house was okay, until one of her brothers inevitably and noisily trooped in. We picnicked at Lake Merritt, drove up to U.C. Berkeley to use the music rooms to play "A Summer Song" and kiss; we went to S.F. State, where I was getting preregistered, and snuck into the music department, where she'd play the kind of piano I was longing to learn.

A few days later, she was set to leave for school, and I went to her house to help her pack. We did our work to the music of the Beatles and Andy Williams. Her mother hovered around and helped; she was friendly to me, but I felt terrible. Of course, Janie would be visiting home, and her school was only a hundred miles from Oakland. But I knew that, with her departure, our relationship would be changed. A busy semester awaited both of us; it was inevitable that we'd be distracted.

In the kitchen for a moment of privacy, we kissed each other goodbye—twice—and she gave me a photograph of herself. I refrained from giving her more clippings of my columns; instead, in a fit of optimism, I gave her a box of stationery.

The first letters told of how much she missed and loved me. By October, Janie was wondering, since we couldn't see each other regularly, whether it'd be okay for us to see other people.

A surprise visit to her school fanned the flame, but in November, she withdrew an invitation to homecoming at her college, saying her studies would keep her occupied. By December, there was a frost on her correspondence. She was getting too busy to write; if she was coming home, she wasn't sure when we could see each other. When I complained that ours was no longer much of a relationship, she wrote back to end it, gently, saying that maybe it was just a summer love.

She was right. I thought we'd been crazy about each other, but I was so desperate for some idea of what love felt like that when someone like Janie came along, willing to playact with me, I jumped.

Our summer love spanned only a month, but for me, it was a sweet indoctrination into a new world of attachment.

·· 1 3 ··

COLLEGE DAYS

AND NIGHTS

In the fall of 1964, on the eve of my junior year at S.F. State, I quit my *Oakland Times* column. Bill Masterson, the publisher, was a gray-haired Republican who could have been a more broad-shouldered Eddie Albert—the Albert of the stern-father roles. Masterson didn't like my references to his party's presidential candidate as "Barry Goldbomber," and when he knocked out half of a column about Goldwater, I left.

At S.F. State, I joined the *Golden Gater*, the campus daily, and KRTG, the radio station.

Even for a college station, KRTG was a dim-watted, closed-circuit operation, receivable only by dormitory residents who had an adapter attached to their AM radios. The format was a schizoid mix of Top 40, pop, jazz, and folk.

I auditioned and got an air shift from six-thirty to eight on Wednesday mornings. Since I had no car and still commuted by bus from Oakland, I had a problem. Tom Gericke, who was also on KRTG and lived in the dorm, had a solution. He got the guys on his floor to let me use a supply room Tuesday nights. Each week, I snuck into the room and slept on an Army cot. In the morning, I'd sneak past the floor attendant and make it to the studio.

KRTG had no audience, but it didn't matter. As I'd learn at the school paper, the main—the only—thing that counted was to get out and do it, to be on the air, make mistakes and work through them, and feel the rush of fear. Besides, as long as I could hear myself, I had an audience.

Through the radio/TV department, I became the host and writer of a public affairs show about comedy on KFOG, a local FM station, and I auditioned to be one of twelve students who'd get to host "Records at Random," a live, one-hour Sunday night show on KSFO, the most popular station in town. I won a slot and told my parents at the Bamboo Hut.

"Oh," said my mother, "so you can't work that night?" Then: "Are you getting paid?" Later, she would add that it was nice that I'd been selected to be on radio. Still, she asked, "Why study radio? Chinese can't get a job in radio!"

But it appeared that this one could. In fact, the only time I was reminded that I was Chinese was when the student program director, in one of his evaluations of my work, told me, "You're not pronouncing your final *l*'s, and you're not differentiating between soft and hard *ch* and *sh* sounds."

To him, it was just a little extra homework. To me, it meant trimming away the last verbal traces of those formative years in Chinatown.

For years, the *Gater* had built a solid reputation by reflecting the evolution of S.F. State from a quiet, even bland, school to the most liberal state college in California. The radicalization of

State began with the House Un-American Activities Committee hearings in San Francisco in May of 1960.

HUAC, an arm of Congress, was in town "to gather information with respect to the general operation of the Communist conspiracy," according to one congressman. But to its critics, it was an extension of the fanaticism of McCarthyism, in which anyone left of center was branded a pinko, a Commie. Abbie Hoffman, a student at Cal, called the proceedings a "public pillorying ... one of the great anticommie road shows designed to beef up the Cold War, get some teachers fired, and warn the nation about the ever-present Red Menace."

Dozens of students, from both U.C. Berkeley and S.F. State, gathered outside City Hall and began chanting in protest of the proceedings. When they entered the building and clogged up the corridors, seeking admission into the hearings, police turned powerful firehoses on them, sending men and women sliding down the grand wide rotunda steps. Those who weren't tumbling down fast enough were pushed, clubbed, and kicked.

The confrontation between these riot-geared cops and clean-cut young citizens who at one point sang "The Star-Spangled Banner" in the hearing room only steeled the demonstrators' resolve and drew recruits to their small army.

S.F. State students would figure prominently in a long string of protests: against nuclear war, capital punishment, and racism, with the Vietnam War and the draft a few years down the line. The *Gater* reported it all, and, being human, its writers couldn't help but reflect the passion of the movement.

By the time I came along, the *Gater*, as personified by its editors, had some of the feistiness of its most activist readers. It no longer accepted the status quo.

In my time with the newspaper, I watched the world change.

In that first fall semester, LeMar, which stood for "legalize marijuana," tried to establish a club on campus. A group of students, including three members of the *Gater* staff, spent part of the summer with civil rights workers in Mississippi. Time and again, we went to the Speaker's Platform on the campus quad, where anyone could say anything.

It was a remarkable structure, that small, twelve-by-eighteen-foot redwood stage. It sat at a corner of the sloping campus green, and at lunchtime, students naturally sat on nearby benches or on the lawn. If someone was talking—whether a candidate for the Senate or for homecoming queen, a Black Nationalist or a JFK assassination conspiracy theorist—people would wander over and listen while they ate. Who can guess how many young minds were molded, changed, or even blown by the wide world of ideas and notions aired from the platform?

In fall of 1964, one of the most riveting subjects of discussion on the platform was the very idea of freedom of speech. At Berkeley, the administration was clamping down. Forty State students joined in a Free Speech Movement rally in Berkeley, riding in on a bus carrying a banner reading SF STATE OPPOSES POLICE BRUTALITY.

That fall, we had our first hippie candidate for Homecoming Queen, a green-eyed blonde named Donna, who said she liked "flowers and grass," and that she wanted to ride to the Homecoming Ball on her motor scooter.

And we received a visit from Richard Alpert, a professor who had done research on LSD with Dr. Timothy Leary at Harvard. Alpert advised the three hundred students who attended his talk that "If you want to learn to use your heads, go out of your minds."

We watched and reported all of this with a mix of detachment, cynicism, and empathy. We were having it drilled into us that we were aiming for unbiased, objective journalism, but we were also taught not to believe most of what we were told and to particularly watch out for puff pieces from public-relations types, both on and off campus. Always on the lookout for good stories, we naturally allied with those who made themselves worthy subjects, whether by words or action.

And yet we struggled to maintain a line between the activists, the antagonists, the new hipsters and adventurers. We could go down South and write emotional pieces about police oppression; march alongside war protesters and quote their despair; describe the emerging hip scene and its makers and repeat all of their groovy talk.

But we had to keep a distance.

Or did we?

By January of 1965, I was getting some major assignments, and in the spring, I went from a story a week to just about one a day, even though I was still working at the Bamboo Hut almost every evening.

It was in May that year that I became a liberal. The city editor had assigned me to write about one of the events in "Freedom Week," a celebration of civil rights. Students were invited to take a shortened version of Mississippi's actual registration test—the one given to blacks.

I sauntered into the testing room, a 3.2 grade point average under my belt, and slunk out in disbelief. Of eighty-five students who tried the simple-looking, eight-question test, eighty-three failed, and I was one of them.

The people portraying Mississippi registration workers, modeling themselves after actual workers, had instructed us to, among other things, "fill out the form completely."

I did, but, unless I was white, I probably didn't. Under "birthdate," I'd used a "1" for January. That, the worker said, was an abbreviation. I hadn't been "complete." When I copied a fourteen-word section of the Constitution of Mississippi onto a space of five lines, I didn't use all five lines. Incomplete.

The message was clear. In Mississippi, you couldn't be both black and a voter.

For the story, I had become—or was being treated like—a black person. I was no more black than any of the Gater staffers who'd gone to Mississippi to report on civil rights, or any of the many college students who demonstrated in solidarity with blacks at downtown hotels.

But I didn't need to be black to understand how they were

being mistreated. Long before television aired footage of southern cops hosing down Negroes who'd dared to challenge segregation, I had been taught that blacks were not only different but somehow inferior. It wasn't just at home, where our parents spoke of blacks as untrustworthy and called them "demons," as they referred to people of any race other than Chinese.

When Barry and I were at Moon's Chinese Kitchen in Emeryville, two of the delivery men were Bill and Carroll, both young blacks. We all got along fine, but Moon Moo habitually referred to blacks—who made up the majority of our customers—as *"see-yow gwai"*—or "soy-sauce devils," *gwai* (*guey* in my family's dialect) also meaning demons.

It never made any sense. In school, we'd worked and played with people of all races. We, as Chinese, perceived ourselves as outsiders and wanted harmony with the mainstream; who were we to be passing judgment on or excluding others for the colors of their skin?

But, growing up, we knew that we'd be asking for trouble from the older generation if we were to fraternize too closely with certain ethnic groups. The Japanese—owing to Chinese history—were the worst of all. Next, blacks. Then, any number of fellow minorities and, finally, white demons.

And so it was that, aside from language barriers, my sisters, brothers, and I rarely talked to our parents about our friends. At school, while maintaining a distance taught to us in journalism classes, I leaned toward the impressionable, the idealistic students of all colors who were linking arms to question the status quo.

For the 1965–1966 school year, I became city editor, in charge of assigning stories. I received a grant of eighty dollars a month.

It was enough money to move away from Oakland. Once I explained to my parents that the job required my presence daily, at all hours, but that I'd still be able to work at the Bamboo Hut on weekends, they agreed. Barry, Shirley, and Burton all still lived at home, and while Barry, who graduated from Cal in 1964 and was working towards a master's, was still at Trader Vic's, Shirley and Burton took over most of the work in Hayward.

I moved into a house in the Sunset District, near campus, with two old high school buddies, Dan Mazmanian and Tom Skinner.

With those two, the house was always well stocked with cheap beer and jug wine. While both Dan and Tom, who'd already lived in several apartments in their first three years at State, had learned to cook, I knew mostly how to eat. I didn't even want to know how to cook. That was my father's thing, and I'd just escaped the twin kitchens of life with the family.

But I contributed. Because I was going home weekends, I invariably returned with restaurant food—a stack of frozen veal cutlets, a handful of rib-eye steaks, cans of vegetables. Whatever it was, it came in handy to a group of college boys.

Soon after we moved in, I got a letter from Candace Barnes, my buddy from high school. She was moving to town from New York, and could she store some stuff with me until she got settled?

She arrived in October, more worldly than I'd ever remembered her, and, within a couple of visits, had us smoking marijuana. Candace was way ahead of us. For one thing, she'd already tried LSD. She asked Tom if he could score some dope. Tom had some friends at work—a parcel delivery company—who provided him with a few joints, and one November evening, we all sat together in the living room.

"Now, if you start laughing, that means you like it," she said. A part of me—the staunchly conservative part that kept me away from cigarettes and liquor until the weight of peer group pressure made me cave in—wanted not to like it. But we all laughed, Tom the loudest. Dan and I mostly coughed while we waited to see God. I would learn later—after a good deal more experimentation with *cannabis sativa*—that I had a strong resistance to both alcohol and drugs.

I also lagged behind in another of life's great highs: romance. Dan had a sweetheart he saw regularly, and Tom had begun seeing Candace regularly on weekends. I had love songs on my record player.

It was pathetic. I hadn't dated since breaking up with Janie, my summer love of 1964, that winter, and there was no beginning in sight. I had no experience to speak of in approaching or dating women. At the same time, I was embarrassed that, being a college student and, beyond that, an editor at the daily paper, I was such a social virgin, and that unease didn't help matters.

I didn't blame the lost opportunities in high school years, the evenings devoted to work. I told myself I was being selective. In the back of my mind, I wanted to avoid any potential problems at home by trying to find Chinese girls to date; there were none at the newspaper. So what was I to do?

I'd listen to love songs, and I'd lose myself in work, so that in not having time to pursue a social life, I was giving myself another excuse for not having one.

The first day of November was a slow news day. We'd dealt with them before. This time, we turned to an event I'd covered over the weekend. Readers of our Tuesday paper were greeted with a bold headline across the front page:

A 'SQUARE' RALLY FOR ORAL SEX

A photo showed two S.F. State students at Union Square, the heart of the downtown shopping district, with placards identifying them with the Sexual Freedom League and calling for the legalization of cunnilingus and fellatio.

My story reported that another placard read DOWN ON WOMEN; that the ten demonstrators were confronted by a self-styled preacher clutching a Bible and a tambourine; that a young woman wondered aloud, "What's cunni*ling*-us?"; and that it was a sex act that was technically illegal in California, even between husband and wife.

The article concluded: "Nearby, a lady who'd made a sunshade out of a BLAKE FOR SUPERVISOR campaign strip understated, 'This is the most fascinating place in the world. It has a flavor all its own.'"

It was just a light, human-interest feature. And when I wrote it, that's what I intended. But not to the chancellor of the state college system. He called the school president to demand that both Dave Swanston, the editor, and I be expelled. The president refused, but, to assuage the chancellor, the head of the journalism department had Dave hauled before the Board of Publications, an arm of the student government, and Dave was declared guilty of "overplay." Neither he nor I received any punishment.

At the *Gater*, I wrote a column every Wednesday called "Whatever's Right." It was a gossip column, but, now and then, I sounded off on one pet peeve or another.

By far, my biggest peeve was the draft.

It seemed that, just as life was getting to be fun, we were in danger of being yanked away and sent into some jungle in Southeast Asia, a country whose Communist forces had rebuffed the French and, as North Vietnam, was now fighting the American-backed, anti-Communist regime in South Vietnam.

By spring of 1965, President Johnson had sent the first U.S. troops into Vietnam. There were 27,000 soldiers in the country, and by July, we had our first casualty count: 500 dead. The Selective Service needed more bodies. By year's end, we'd have 170,000 troops in Southeast Asia. And it was up to the local draft boards covering every American town and city to feed the escalating war's machine.

In short, Uncle Sam wanted us. Sometimes, it seemed that the long finger he was shooting out of those famous posters was aimed directly at me and my scrawny neck. Here I was, having just begun my senior year when, two days before Halloween, the local board of the Selective Service System, the one based in Oakland, ordered me to report for a physical examination.

At 7:00 A.M. in late November, I showed up at the Joint Examining and Induction Station in Oakland. About 2:30, I staggered out, squinted at the wintry sunshine, reached for a notebook, and wrote down my experiences for my column.

There was the sergeant who addressed our motley crew: "Awright jennamen, I'm gonna say'is one time only so lissenup and lissenupgood. This'ere's yer intelligence test and yer to answer these questions to the best of yerability. Anyone who deliberately fails this test will find'imself takinit again . . . at seven o'clockin the morning . . . it ain't no fun, jennamen."

A young soldier who reminded me of Sal Mineo told us how to fill out our medical history forms. Leave a few lines blank, he said, "unless you have a nosebleed every twenty-eight days."

The main exam was conducted by two doctors who seemed to be in a race to leave the room first. If they didn't spot something obvious among the three dozen of us—"noticeable defects such as missing fingers or broken legs"—we moved on to the next station. I wanted to bring up any number of health problems I'd had—that rash from China, a recurring hay fever that ran in our family, bouts of arthritis—but the examiners were herding us through.

A couple of weeks later, I got the bad news: I was healthy. At least healthy enough for the Selective Service to judge me "fully acceptable" to the Army. Before year's end, I received my orders to report for induction into the United States Army on January 13, 1966.

It didn't matter that, as the *Gater*'s faculty adviser, Jerry Werthimer, had informed the draft board, I had made "more than normal progress" toward my degree, that I had maintained a "B" average, worked on the campus radio station, was city editor of the newspaper, and was "recognized by administrators, faculty, and students as one of the ten top seniors." Maybe I should add here that the professor was anti-war and might have stretched my wonderfulness a little bit.

Dr. Werthimer ended by noting that the date for induction was the day before final exams for the fall semester began. It was the first time in my life that I was looking forward to finals.

· · 1 4 · ·

GROOVY

KIND OF

LOVE

The draft issue hung a worrisome cloud over what had begun as a most adventuresome semester, the social and political changes driven by a soundtrack that made it clear that we were in a movie we'd never seen before. Over that summer of 1965, pop music had grown up. Bob Dylan, who'd dabbled with electric guitar as far back as 1962, had recorded "Like a Rolling Stone" and performed it, electrically and defiantly, at the Newport Folk Festival. The Byrds had taken his "Mr. Tambourine Man" into the charts and added "folk-rock" to the music lexicon. The Beatles were expanding both their minds and their music; they were listening to everything from Dylan ("You've Got to Hide Your Love Away") to chamber music ("Yesterday") and, like Dylan, were forcing expansions of the parameters of rock and roll re-cordings and what could get radio airplay. And those punks, the

Rolling Stones, were talking for a lot of young people through Mick Jagger's refrain about not getting no "Satisfaction." Along with the artful Simon & Garfunkel and the Laurel Canyon lullaby singers, the Mamas and the Papas, they were changing the sound of Top 40 radio, widening its scope and appeal. Now, KRTG became Top 40, with jingles, time checks, and zany contests. We, the disc jockeys, were encouraged to come across as somewhere between enthusiastic and overly so. I started sounding like what radio people call a "puker"—a jock who talks as if he's about to throw up.

Having learned that the station had no listeners the previous year, KRTG dropped morning broadcasts. Now, we were on between four and ten at night. Tuesdays, I'd finish up at the *Gater* and hike across campus to do my show from seven to sign-off.

At an open house in the radio/TV department, I met a fellow broadcasting student. Mary Keith intrigued me with her beauty, a blend of Donna Reed wholesome and Ursula Andress exotic. But, like me, she was self-conscious. She'd heard that I was a DJ and an editor at the *Gater* and got me talking. Soon, I invited her to visit the newspaper office. She took to the rush of activity there and, within a week or two, attended a *Gater* party with me. We began seeing each other regularly.

She lived in a tiny, ground-level studio apartment off Union Street, and I got a thrill the first time I visited. For one thing, Mary was the first girl I'd become friends with who wasn't living with her parents. And her place was inescapably, immediately intimate. The first thing I ran into was a curtain that hid the bathroom.

Half of the room was taken up by a desk, a couch, and a tiny stove. Behind a partition was her bed. Her decor was absolute college; it was whatever she could score for little or no money, and we acquired much of it together. Both of us were away from home for the first time—she was from Barstow, a small town north of San Bernardino in the Mojave Desert. We leapt into San Francisco with childlike abandon, hitting all the restaurants we could afford and taking souvenir matchbooks and menus from each one. On sorties into Fisherman's Wharf, we'd sneak off with stacks of sourdough bread bags with which Mary papered an entire wall in her apartment. She turned the menus into mobiles by suspending them from the ceiling.

We tooled around town in my first car, a 1960 Ford Falcon, and roared up the steepest streets so that we could send the car flying, only to crash land on level ground.

But, for all the time we spent together, we rarely had a real date. Until another young woman entered my life, and even then, Mary and I spent most of our waking hours together, many of them barely awake.

We spent many nights in that Union Street apartment, doing schoolwork into the morning hours, with me often doing her work.

"Ben, I'm having trouble with this paper on home appliances."

"No problem. Let me take a look."

And I'd be writing about toasters and waffle irons for the next few hours.

One night, just before spring break, I was over with another male admirer of hers, Fred, who worked at a liquor store down the street.

We were both supposed to be helping Mary to type a report, but Fred had just survived a hold-up at the store.

"You know, I think I need a drink before we start work." Before long, he was passed out on the couch while Mary and I stayed up all night, writing and typing.

The next evening, she and I hit a *Gater* party until one in the morning.

On those late nights, our background music flowed from a bedside clock radio I'd given Mary. On radios everywhere, we were hearing songs from the Beatles' album *Rubber Soul*, which marked a new height of sophistication and adventurousness in songwriting, instrumentation, and studio techniques. At one party I attended shortly after the album's long-anticipated release, an entire room was filled with people marveling at the clear stereo separation of vocals from instrumentals on various cuts.

As elliptic and intriguing as songs like "Norwegian Wood (This Bird Has Flown)" were, they spoke to me directly.

Plaintive and wistful, cornily romantic, or impatient and fed up—the songs of *Rubber Soul* were a soundtrack to the story of Mary and me. We had instantly become best friends; we appeared inseparable. She visited not only at the newspaper office but at my radio shows; we had endless sodas together at local fountains. We confided in each other. But something was missing: sex.

She came into my life too fast—I still had no experience— and we moved so quickly into a comfortable relationship that I knew no graceful way to try to shift it to romance. As time passed, I found myself alternately longing for her and being upset with her for not sending me a written invitation to her favors. I allowed myself to think that my being Chinese had something to do with it.

One night, she as much as confessed that it did. "I don't think of us as being an interracial couple. We walk around together and I don't think about it. And then I see other couples, and I think, 'Oh, that's what an interracial couple is.' But I've also thought to myself, 'We'll always just be friends because you're Chinese and my family wouldn't accept it, and life would really be pretty difficult.'"

Before she came to that conclusion, however, we were enough of a couple that I, too, was wondering and worrying about how she'd play with my family.

One early evening, I was sitting with Dave Swanston, the editor of the *Gater*. I'd arrived early at his rambling Victorian flat for a party, and we were shooting hot air before the craziness.

He'd been in a serious relationship with a black woman at State, and he was talking about his mother's reaction to it.

"Yeah," I said. "I think my folks would go crazy too, if they knew who I was seeing."

Dave looked at me, puzzled. He knew who I was seeing; he'd certainly noticed Mary around the office.

"Gee," he thought to himself. "Is Ben also dating a black woman?"

He reached for his drink. "Who're you talking about, if I might ask?"

"Mary, of course," I said.

He thought for a moment. "Oh." He laughed. "I'm sorry. I didn't think of you and her as interracial."

I joined him in laughter. "Yeah, well—just ask my *parents*."

For my twenty-first birthday, in January of 1966, the draft board gave me a postponement of my induction into the Army "until further notice." I had a modest celebration: My roommates fried up a veal cutlet and heated up some creamed corn for me, and we had a round of Fisher's beer, a brand, like Red Mountain wine, beloved by thirsty and thrifty students.

Soon afterwards, I covered a talent show on campus and met Michelle.

I was stunned: Michelle was a Chinese girl in contemporary arts. She was a jazz fan, a modern dancer, a poet. She lived with her big family—parents and five siblings—in an alley apartment, just a walk up a hill from San Francisco's Chinatown.

Michelle's father operated a nearby garment sewing shop; her mother was a housewife who worked at the shop. We understood each other immediately; we were both second-generation Chinese-Americans in large, lower-middle-class families; we had the same feelings toward our parents, the same mix of devotion and rebellion. If there was anything that might keep us apart, it might be that we were both Chinese, and that true independence meant doing what our parents wouldn't want. But we didn't think that way. In me, Michelle saw an Asian guy like none she'd encountered in her life. I wasn't headed into the straight life; I wasn't studying to become an accountant or a white-collar professional. My music wasn't confined to the violin. Before me, she'd never thought of Chinese boys as romantic figures.

She told me as much. "They're all so responsible for their families and so *practical* about what they're going to do with their lives," she said as we sat together on the campus quad. She looked at me and smiled, then laughed self-consciously.

Finally, she had someone she could thoroughly relate to.

For the first time since Janie Lee in Hayward, I felt the kind of romantic spark that had me buying gifts, indulging in long telephone calls, and going on long, slow walks full of chatter and laughter. We'd stroll through Fisherman's Wharf and pick the longest pier to walk onto—just because it'd take the longest time. One night, when we'd outlasted the last Muni trolley, I walked from North Beach across town to my house in the Sunset District, humming a tune Michelle and I had come to call our song: "A Groovy Kind of Love," by a British group, the Mind-benders.

By spring of 1966, Sarah and Dave Watkins had been seeing each other for more than five years, and it was inevitable that they would marry. Dave, the soft-spoken artist, was a stable, mature man; Sarah was a solid combination of free spirit and hard worker, a cynical, good-humored young woman. They had a wide circle of friends from various communities, and the wedding, which was to take place in the spring of 1966 at the Westminster Presbyterian Church in Tiburon, a tiny town across the bay from Mill Valley, promised to be a free-flowing, festive affair, reflective of the times.

It was, but it took place without our parents. Outwardly, they had accepted Sarah and Dave's relationship, but much of what might have been considered a consensual silence owed to the unyielding language barrier between parents and children.

When push came to wedding, Mother cryptically informed Sarah that she and Father would not attend.

"I can't change my feelings," she said.

Sarah argued that, at the least, they could attend, and Dad should take her down the aisle.

"We are not coming," said Mother.

"Then I'll ask Barry," Sarah said.

"That's not right," Mother said, her voice rising.

But to Sarah, it wasn't right that her parents couldn't accept the most important decision she'd made in her life.

Just before the wedding day, April 2, Sarah got a call from Mom.

"Maybe we'll come," she said.

"Don't bother," said Sarah. They'd slapped her and Dave too hard with their initial rejection, and she was not about to have her wedding day spoiled by parents whose deep disapproval couldn't help but pervade the proceedings.

And so it was that while Sarah and Dave exchanged vows, and friends and family gathered, my parents drove to the Bamboo Hut, with Burton in tow, and conducted business as usual.

Still, they had their impact on the wedding. Defying their wishes, Barry, Shirley, and I attended. At first, we thought we'd all have to bring Chinese guests—just in case our parents might someday see the wedding photos. Barry knew a number of both Chinese and Japanese girls at Cal, and brought a lovely young woman from Hong Kong. Michelle wasn't available, so I invited Mary and made a mental note to keep her out of any photographs. Shirley was dating a young Chinese man she'd met at Cal State, but when he dropped in at the Bamboo Hut, Mother had dismissed him for what she considered "sneaky eyes." Shirley, too, had to work to avoid having him appear in any photographs.

As spring rolled around, I decided to apply for the editorship of the paper. I'd have to become a graduate student in order to serve, but that was fine with me. The draft was hovering over me, and if staying in school would keep me out of the service, it was all the more reason to offer myself to the newspaper. At the end of senior year, I was chosen as editor for 1966–1967.

Our graduation ceremonies were at the Cow Palace, a giant building just outside the city limits, in Daly City, that was often used for Roller Derby, dog shows, and rock concerts. I skipped graduation and received my diploma in the mail.

Graduation was further muted by the fact that I'd lost Michelle. She'd met a Caucasian musician and, just before semester's end, began dating him.

I felt crushed—and powerless. I had no experience fighting for a girl's affections. Who was I to try and stop her? Michelle had said she could relate to me because I was a Chinese guy who knew about rock and roll and the arts. Now, she'd found a guy who played music, who could write songs, and perform with her. With me, she'd gone from Chinatown Chinese to an Americanized Chinese. Now, at my expense, she was graduating.

·· 15 ··

ON OUR

OWN

With graduation, the house in the Sunset was breaking up, and I heard from Tom Gericke, my high school buddy. He'd gotten a job at a bank, making training films for employees, and was staying in San Francisco. He'd found a beautiful apartment in Pacific Heights, the fanciest part of town, and asked if I wanted to be roommates with him. Despite some reservations, I agreed.

The main problem was that it had only one bedroom. In our naiveté, we thought we could make it work. There was, after all, a living room, and most of the girls we dated tended to have homes of their own. It'd be like the dorm life to which Tom had become accustomed. Big deal.

The other problem was the rent. It would be ninety dollars each, or twice what I'd been paying with Dan and Tom out in the avenues. As editor of the campus paper, I had decided I should have a car, and had salvaged that 1960 Ford Falcon out of a lot. I would need some money, more than the tips I collected at the Bamboo Hut.

I sent out a raft of résumés to local newspapers and radio stations and wound up going back to the *Oakland Times*, where the publisher had forgotten our arguments and needed a news editor.

The work was deadly dull, but there was one wonderful bonus. Using my position with the paper, I got into Candlestick Park in San Francisco on August 29, 1966, for a Beatles concert.

The Beatles were coping with the backlash from John Lennon's remark that the band was more popular than Jesus, and they were moving away from their mop-top, teenybop image into more complex music, addressing more adult concerns. The result was that, on a typically chilly summer night in San Francisco, they drew only 25,000 fans, well short of a sellout.

Along with a couple dozen other reporters, I had a seat in a press box above and behind home plate. We talked through the four opening acts, and by the time they were finished, it was almost 9:30.

The Beatles, dressed in dark green, double-breasted Edwardian suits, made their trek from the clubhouse to the elevated, caged-in stage set up over second base.

From the press box, we heard a half-hour of adolescent screeching, over which the Beatles raced through a rapid-fire, eleven-song show. I reported that "three separate troops of frenzied kids" hit the outfield grass during the Beatles' performance; that once, between numbers, McCartney saw security cops chasing three kids around the outfield, turned to his mates and asked: "Well, should we just watch this, or go ahead with our own show?" I noted that George Harrison wore white socks. What I did not report was something no one knew that evening: that we had just witnessed the last paid concert the Beatles would ever do.

As fall and the *Gater* editorship approached, the *Oakland Times* publisher asked me to stay on until he could find a replacement.

I started the fall semester at S.F. State, then, darting between newspapers, with the Bamboo Hut, as always, on weekends.

None of us escaped the restaurant. Shirley even chose her college—Cal State at Hayward—partly for the convenience of the commute to the Bamboo Hut. And Barry found time for some weekend shifts while taking his first steps into a career in law enforcement.

Having graduated from U.C. Berkeley, Barry began work toward a master's degree in criminology. He worked as a houseparent for a cottage of fifteen teenaged delinquent or disturbed youths in Oakland. At Cal, he was a research assistant in the School of Criminology. And, on a grant from the National Institute for Mental Health, he organized and ran an experimental coed group counseling program at Marin County Juvenile Hall, using encounter techniques.

Now, as I began my stint as editor, Barry got a job as a deputy probation officer in Fairfield, a small orchard town an hour's drive north of Oakland.

At age twenty-three, Barry could well have been in the military. But his childhood interest in the military and his enrollment in ROTC notwithstanding, he had come to oppose the war in Vietnam.

One day, we were talking about our mutual lack of interest in joining the military.

"Especially when you could get confused for the enemy," said Barry. "We're already being called gooks—you know, 'You all look alike.' "

"I say let them fight their own war."

"Well," said Barry, "they're going to have to fight it without me. I'm going to stay in school until it's over."

I told him about a student who'd been at State for eight years and was still going strong. He smiled. But it was difficult having to juggle graduate work with a full-time job. Still, he seemed to have no choice.

"The pro-war people ask how anyone can protest the war," he said. "What I don't get is how anyone can *fight* this war."

* * *

Shirley had struggled in her first year at Cal State Hayward, but rallied in her second and gained admittance into U.C. Berkeley to major in social science.

This was bad news—at least to Mom. Going to Cal would distance her from the restaurant.

She got strong support from Barry, who helped her through the application and transfer process, but now she had to face Mother with the news. It was not easy. To Mom, a transfer to Cal meant nothing more than Shirley having less time to be in Hayward.

With no financial support forthcoming to offset Cal's far higher tuition, Shirley took on-campus jobs in exchange for boarding. She put herself through her last two years of college, although, on occasion, Dad would call her aside and slip her some money. Ever the dutiful daughter, Shirley continued to commute to the Bamboo Hut.

Barry offered her a tip. He had dated Pauline Wee, who was the Chinese Student Club's Spring Informal Queen. Knowing that winners of the crown got a $150 scholarship along with a tiara and trophy, Barry suggested that Shirley enter, even though she was not a member of CSC.

She did, and Barry and I attended the competition among eight U.C. girls at a hotel in San Francisco. While we cheered her on, Barry felt not a little irony. Shirley was being sponsored by Pi Alpha Phi, the Chinese fraternity. Barry well remembered having pledged the frat a few years before.

"I just want to see what it's all about," Barry said at that time. But when he was rejected, Norma—his *Mui Mui*—was livid. A former boyfriend of hers was in Pi Alpha Phi, and she began hearing fraternity members bragging about blackballing Barry. They had judged him on trivial matters. When Barry told them that he worked—not only at Trader Vic's but also as a busboy at a cafe on campus—they rolled their eyes.

If Barry was upset by the rejection, he didn't show it. He

laughed when he told Norma about it, as if he'd been testing the whole frat-rat process and knew he had no chance. Besides, he never had much use for what he saw as the privileged class—those kids whose parents paid their way through school, with a shiny sports car to boot, while he had to struggle for every dollar.

Now, he'd got the last laugh. Shirley won, and Barry got a date with one of the runners-up.

Absorbed with the *Gater* and KRTG, I spent little time at the flat on Clay Street, and it was just as well, with our one-bedroom situation. I didn't have any dates for the first several months of school, and when Tom did, he could spend time at his date's place. The one-room setup was even enjoyable at times. Whoever woke up first usually began shouting, "Good morning! Good morning! Good morning!" in an approximation of a disc jockey on KFRC, the reigning Top 40 station in town.

On weekends, we occasionally had girls over. They'd invariably take pity on our circumstances—the shared bedroom, the Madras bedspreads doubling as window curtains, the restaurant chairs and the wooden produce crates taken from Chinatown alleys that served as tables—and offer to bring and prepare food for us.

But it was mostly Tom who had dates. I continued to see Mary, but I shied away from *Gater* staffers through the Swanston year and into the early fall. I listened to the lovey-dovier of the music we had in our collection, songs like "Monday, Monday" by the Mamas and the Papas and "Cherish" by the Association. I liked the achingly romantic soundtrack from the achingly romantic film *A Man and a Woman*. It was a great way to start the day. I could feel intense frustration for the next dozen or so hours.

When I finally had sex, it was with Rosalind, a Chinese girl who'd written a letter to the *Gater* denouncing Homecoming. We met at the newspaper office. "I thought you were half-Chinese," she said. "Wow. A Chinese-American editing the paper."

The next social event I knew of was a wedding. I invited her, and she accepted.

Rosalind, who was from Idaho, framed her round face in long black hair, which she often set off with a headband. In my view, all women, with the possible exception of Luci Baines Johnson, looked great with headbands, and when Rosalind showed up at the wedding reception in a *cheong-sam* jacket, heels, and a white headband, I was hooked.

For our second date, we went to a movie, then returned to my apartment on Clay Street. Tom was out, and she wasted no time seducing me. I never let on that it was my first time, working hard to suppress my amazement at every aspect of our night together—not to mention every aspect of her body. I worried that I was gawking at her nakedness too much. I worried that she'd laugh once she saw me without clothes. After all, no girl ever had before.

Now, I finally knew what everyone around me had seemingly known for years. But I couldn't share my exhilaration with Rosalind. It just wouldn't have been hip. So I continued to look at her body until it was time to take her home.

Walking her to her door, I felt a little sad. I knew that I liked, but didn't love, Rosalind. I was grateful—no, relieved—to have had my first time. Still, there was an emptiness to the experience, and I was so slow to ask Rosalind out again that she moved on to other adventures.

Just as I'd come to life with women—well, one woman, anyway—the draft intruded again.

Over the summer, I'd informed the local board that I'd been accepted for a master's degree program at State, that I would be editor of the paper, that I had a B-plus average in my senior year, and had completed my bachelor's work in four years' time, making the kind of "normal progress" of which Uncle Sam was known to approve. The draft board sent back a big, fat "So?" and now, in October, declared me 1-A. Three days after Christmas, I was ordered for induction once again.

Clearly, being a student wasn't working too well. I consulted with friends and applied for status as a conscientious objector. I presented the local board with letters from the president of S.F. State, the chairman of the journalism department—who pointed out that he was himself a World War II veteran whose views clashed with my own—the campus pastor, and my sister Sarah.

On the student-deferment front, the dean of students wrote on my behalf.

The local board didn't even consider the C.O. application—it came in too late, it said, even though I'd filed my first request before it sent my induction notice—and confirmed my date with the Army on January 25, 1967.

I then went over the board's head, writing to the state director of Selective Service, and, on January 24, he ordered a postponement of induction "until further notice."

I breathed one more sigh of relief. But, in early February, I was classified 1-A again.

·· 1 6 ··

ENDINGS

AND

BEGINNINGS

In the San Francisco hippie scene, 1967 began on the fourteenth of January. Two days before, at the Print Mint in the Haight-Ashbury, members of the Haight community, along with Gary Snyder, the poet, and Jerry Rubin, a leader of the anti-war movement, announced plans for an all-day event in Golden Gate Park. It was being called "Pow-Wow, A Gathering of the Tribes for a Human Be-In."

They issued a press release: "Berkeley political activists and the love generation of the Haight-Ashbury will join together with members of the new nation who will be coming from every state in the nation, every tribe of the young (the emerging soul of the nation) to powwow, celebrate, and prophesy the epoch of liberation, love, peace, compassion and unity of mankind . . .

Hang your fear at the door and join the future. If you do not believe, please wipe your eyes and see."

"Wanna check it out?" I asked Mary. We were studying for semester finals, and this Be-In thing was going on from one to five—probably later—on a Saturday.

"Why not?" she shrugged.

We figured we didn't need to wipe our eyes to see. At State and around town, we'd watched as San Francisco had exploded in a succession of amazing scenes. Hippies, the Haight-Ashbury, free love, drugs, and rock and roll had combined with elements of the Beats of the fifties and the political radicals of the sixties, and caused what the mass media would later call a "youthquake." The media, of course, played a role in the phenomenon; its coverage of the Haight—called "The Hashbury" by one newspaper—triggered an influx of new seekers.

They congregated first at events staged wherever the novice producers could book a space: a union facility called Longshoreman's Hall, down by Fisherman's Wharf; California Hall, owned by a Rotary Club; and, finally, two old ballrooms, the Avalon, taken by Chet Helms and the Family Dog, and the Fillmore Auditorium, where a New York transplant, Bill Graham, began staging regular concerts.

The first public gatherings were based, of course, on rock and roll—but this was the grown-up stuff, inspired by Dylan, the Beatles, and the Stones and played by, for the most part, ex-folkies who blended in not only rock and roll but rhythm and blues, straight blues, jazz, folk, country, and other strains—whatever sounded either right or far out. Acid was still legal in 1965, and the music and its environment seemed designed to enhance the experience of psychedelics.

Mary and I would pay our two dollars apiece and walk into nothing less than a new world. On the vast walls behind and alongside the stage, there were light shows in which artists swirled colored oils and gels and projected the patterns, pulsing in time with the music, and sometimes mixing in loops of cartoons and old movies. Here and there, strobe lights made it seem that anyone moving under them was appearing in an old-time movie. Black lights transformed all white objects, from clothing to teeth, into a brilliantly glowing violet. People painted flowers and peace symbols on the floors and on each other's faces. Most of all, people got high and danced, often with no need for partners, all around the room, dancing endlessly because the bands, with stony, surreal names like Chocolate Watchband, Big Brother and the Holding Company, the Grateful Dead, Quicksilver Messenger Service, and Jefferson Airplane, tended toward formless jams.

That's what life had become: a formless jam. And every weekend in 1966, at the ballrooms, at nightclubs, at casual parties, and at free concerts in the parks and the streets, the hippies could see how their scene had grown. But it was a two-headed scene. In Berkeley, the main concern seemed to be politics, and much of what was going on in the Haight seemed trivial. In San Francisco, the acidheads and "flower children" were content, for the most part, to stay blissfully unaware of free speech and civil rights and peace movements. They were practicing peace and love in their own pads, on the streets, and in the ballrooms.

The Human Be-in, its planners decided, would bring the different worlds together in "a union of love and activism."

For young people who were going to the parties, the ballrooms, and the protests, it would be a chance to see just how many of them there were. Musicians had expressed amazement at how many people were showing up at the dance concerts. Now, they had a chance to fill up an entire park.

And for people, young and old, who were curious about these hippies, it was a chance to see what all the fuss was about.

Mary and I dressed in an approximation of what we'd seen at various dances. She wore a flower-print dress, and I put on jeans and an Army shirt that I'd picked up at a thrift shop and thought appropriate, given my battles with the Selective Service system.

Arriving at Golden Gate Park in a midafternoon blessed by sunshine, our trip slowed down by traffic jams of both cars and people, we were stunned. We'd been to dance concerts and protest rallies, but they didn't prepare us for what we encountered.

The Polo Fields, a site selected by an astrologer and a dope dealer, was a meadow the size of six square city blocks, and it was filled with twenty thousand people, many of them college kids, hair still crew-cut, but many, too, with their hair long and wild, wearing tie-dyed shirts and pants, shawls and capes, kerchiefs and top hats, warpaint and cowboy hats. Bold and old seemed to add up to new. They bore bells and cymbals, and held aloft banners, and they carried guitars along with flowers, knapsacks, and blankets.

"What is going *on?*" Mary asked, her eyes wide.

I had no idea. It was what we had seen on campus and around town, and it was what we'd heard about in Berkeley—multiplied by some unknown number and force.

Allen Ginsberg, who was making his own dance from the Beat generation to whatever this was going to be, was dressed in white tunic and pants, like a hospital orderly, with several strands of beads around his neck. He sat on an Indian rug on stage, played finger cymbals, and chanted. "We are all one," he repeated until the phrase became a mantra.

Timothy Leary, with a sprig of daisies tucked behind each ear, suggested that we tune in, turn on, and drop out.

Most of the raps about this "union of love and activism" went unheard, as people spent most of their time absorbing this outrageous new scene that was taking shape before their eyes.

That's what Mary and I did. We wandered around the field taking in the sights, and, looking a long distance toward the stage area, trying to figure out which rock bands were there. The Dead, Quicksilver, Big Brother, and the Airplane all played, and as it was in the ballrooms, this was rock and roll being presented as never before—casual, laissez-faire. The Dead shared the stage with a boy waving a large red banner and with a lovely young woman in a diaphanous dress doing a free-form shimmy. Throughout the field, people got up and, in the midst of dozens sitting around them, danced with abandon.

We sat on the grass and smiled at the people around us. Every few minutes, it seemed, someone would pass around some food, an open jug of wine, or a lit joint of marijuana without discrimination or any hopes of seeing them again. While many took whatever came their way, we declined, having learned from smaller parties elsewhere that brownies were likely to be baked with pot, and that LSD could be mixed into anything from Kool-Aid to turkey sandwiches.

Mary had no interest in drugs, and told me how guys would try to get her under the spell of pot or psychedelics. She didn't mind that I was smoking pot on selected occasions—like, say, when it was around.

But I had never been stoned in Mary's presence, and I was not about to begin this day, when sensations were already more than vivid, and when nothing might be what it appeared to be.

Instead, we left before the Be-In concluded, had dinner, and went to her little apartment to study.

In school, I had my hands full as editor of the *Gater*. But when I got a call one afternoon early in the year from a man named Gordon Lew, and he told me that he had begun a weekly paper in San Francisco's Chinatown—and that it was the first paper to try to address the English-speaking and -reading Chinese-American public—I had to at least meet with him.

We met in Chinatown, in the back of a stationery shop where he was putting his paper together. I liked him instantly. He was Buddha-like, both in physique and countenance. In his early thirties, he was new to journalism. Born in Canton, he came to America in 1952 to attend college in Boston, and moved to San Francisco in 1959. He taught Chinese school in a church, decided to enter the Pacific School of Religion in Berkeley, became an ordained minister, and got a job at the *Chinese Times*, translating stories from English to Chinese. He was immediately hooked, and within two years, he had gathered a few friends together and started up a tabloid-sized paper he named *East West*.

Standing by a table loaded down with stacks of papers, he spoke with a gentle zeal about serving the community, of taking Chinatown journalism into modern times. He modestly showed off the first few issues, and pointed out how, with offset printing, he was able to produce a cleaner, crisper paper than Chinatown had ever seen before. All he needed was some help, and all he had, on the English side, was Ken Wong, a fine writer and reporter who was working at another Chinatown paper and wrote for Gordon only under a pen name. Ken had suggested that Gordon scour local colleges for Asians in journalism departments. That's how he'd found me.

I hadn't given much thought to Chinatown, other than to invade it on occasion for the good, cheap food at several favorite restaurants. I knew nothing of its inner workings, its politics, and the upheavals just beginning. Nor did I know about China, which was going through the Great Cultural Revolution.

I was focused on college and work, and I told Gordon as much. "I can't work for you on a regular basis, but maybe I can do an article now and then—especially if they're about college matters and happen to deal with Chinese."

He was agreeable, and I was soon a regular visitor to the little shop in Chinatown. Once, I rapped out a story there in my usual style, pounding the typewriter keys like a gospel pianist, and Gordon turned to Ken Joe, who edited the Chinese section. "This young man types so fast," he said in Cantonese, "it seems like smoke's coming out of the typewriter."

Fact was, I was a print junkie. I loved getting words and pictures transformed into a newspaper or magazine. I had the *Gater* five days a week, but with *East West*, I was on new turf, with a new set of challenges and possibilities. As I read *East West*, I wanted to know more about Chinatown. And as I began to figure out the divisions in the minicity, I joined in Gordon's quest to make *East West* a forum, a responsible funnel of information and opinion; a way to let the Chinese community know that the times were changing—even in a tradition-gripped enclave like Grant Avenue, San Francisco, California, U.S.A.

* * *

When, in spring, *Time* magazine published the news that the fiber on banana skins, lightly toasted, then smoked, could result in a high, the *Gater* countered with a piece of news a reader sent us: that smoking the crushed, dried leaves of hydrangea—a plant easily found on the campus—could result in a similar effect, although, we warned, toxicologists advised that hydrangea contained a form of cyanide. Hydrangea could be stimulating, the authority said, "but cyanide is also a lethal poison, and smoking very much of it just might take you on your last big trip." Nonetheless, other newspapers and other media ran with our story.

True to *Gater* tradition, we had our adversaries, most notably in student government. But S.F. State in 1967 was not the same as it had been just three or four years before. The college was becoming more than one school. Radicals and adventurers had united to form an "Experimental College," offering courses not likely to be found in any traditional catalog. There were classes called "Surrealism in Everyday Life," "Zen Basketball," and "Introduction to Frisbee." Soon, the *Gater* was not the only newspaper on campus, as the experimental forces created Open Process.

We were being challenged not only on journalistic grounds but on economic ones as well. The *Gater*, after all, derived most of its $50,000 annual budget from the Associated Students, the student government body. With another paper to finance, we were likely to get less money. Things got tense.

And I failed the *Gater*. In the heat of my problems with Selective Service, and on advice from a friendly teacher, I didn't sign up for any classes for the spring semester. I wanted to concentrate on the paper. Besides, I planned to take more graduate courses after my year there.

This wouldn't have been noticed if the newspaper's profile hadn't been so high. We were involved in a heated campus election: One of our own columnists had mounted a satirical run for president—and won, leading to charges that, before filing his candidacy and quitting the *Gater*, he'd used the paper for his own political purposes. The *Gater* itself, critics charged, had influenced the election with its articles criticizing the student government, and I was roasted for coming out against a student-led strike that crippled the college's food service.

When someone leaked word to Leo Young, the journalism department head, that I hadn't registered for classes for the semester, it took him less than a full puff on his pipe before he asked for my resignation. Before stopping to think, I submitted it and ignited a furious reaction around campus.

For one thing, there was no rule in the Board of Publications bylaws requiring the editor to be a registered student. For another, the registrar's office said it considered me enrolled, since all students were allowed an undeclared leave of absence for one semester. And the admissions office said I was considered a "continuing student" until June. Also, it was pointed out, it was the responsibility of the Board of Publications, and not the department chairman, to call for an editor's resignation.

Various factions went nuts over the incident, but the bottom line was that there was, indeed, a school rule that those in student activity positions must carry at least a half-dozen units. I didn't, and I was gone.

The worst consequence of the whole affair was the loss of Mary as my friend. Soon after I resigned, someone told me that it was she who tipped Leo Young off about my nonstudent status.

Naturally, I didn't believe it. My informant said something about Mary dating a *Gater* staffer who was upset over the paper's role in the election and sought to bring me down.

I still didn't believe it. But I became so curious about just who it *was* that I asked Mary about it.

"I hear you know who did it," I said.

Mary looked puzzled. She didn't know what I was talking about.

I was never good at being subtle, and I pressed ahead.

"You should know who did it," I said, pausing just enough to give her a chance to confess before moving on, "because I heard *you* did it."

She couldn't believe it. That I would even think to associate her with such a traitorous act was nothing less than a treachery to our friendship, to our trust in each other. "What would I have to gain from doing something like that?" she asked. The more she protested, the more rigid I got. I'm sure that my frustrations with our relationship and her romances with others had something to do with it. She held her ground until June. By now, my accusations had caused others to look at her with suspicion. Mary left for Barstow, fleeing not only San Francisco but my life. I felt so bad, I didn't know how to feel. It was as if a love affair had hit the rocks; we had that strong a friendship.

Three days after I cleared out my desk, the results of an American Collegiate Press competition came in. The *Gater* received the "All-American" rating, the ACP's highest honor. The judges—professional newspaper people—liked the paper's "good, lively coverage," front-page makeup, editorial creativeness, and excellence in writing, sports, editing, and headlines.

S.F. State would roll on to far more turbulent times after my departure—S. I. Hayakawa and cops on horseback were yet to come—but by then, I was occupied elsewhere. I became a disc jockey.

After college, I was full-tilt into the hippie scene, going to the Matrix, the Fillmore, the Avalon; collecting posters; smoking marijuana and spending long hours staring into the fireplace; and marching in a couple of anti-war protests.

But I wasn't a hippie. In fact, I held one of the straightest jobs one could find in media—playing elevator music on a local radio station.

KFOG was a pioneer among the stereo stations on the FM band in the early sixties. It had settled into an easy-listening format, one that was described, in those times, as "elevator music," akin to Muzak, designed to float inoffensively in the background.

It was the strangest job. I played reels of taped music, hosted by a woman who called herself "Dolly Holiday," on behalf of the sponsor, Holiday Inn. While the tapes played, I typed the next day's program logs and, on occasion, wrote some advertising copy for local restaurants and automobile dealers. Once an hour, I broke in to read a few short news stories from the Associated Press wire machine.

On those six-hour shifts, I found time to work on proposals for the numerous ideas Tom Gericke had conceived for radio and television shows that would exploit the hippie movement. Before there was such a term, we aspired to be hip capitalists.

By now, Tom and I had moved out of our one-bedroom apartment. Just around the block, on Sacramento Street, Tom found a Victorian flat with four bedrooms. The monthly rent was $225. With a couple of roommates, it'd be perfect. We moved in and stretched out. We had no idea what the future had in store for us.

Barry was living in Fairfield, where he'd been hired as a deputy probation officer the previous fall.

Although he'd avoided athletics through most of school, he'd recently taken up skiing and learned to play tennis. One day in May of 1967, he was playing tennis in Fairfield when he spotted a woman on an adjacent court. She was hitting balls by herself, and Barry had noticed ball after ball flying off her racket and over a wall.

"Hi," he said. "I see you're having a little trouble. It could be the way you're holding your racket. If you want, I'll show you." The blonde stiffened. Her name was Kate Michaels; she was a flight attendant, and she was passing a few hours while waiting for a Pan Am flight to leave from Travis Air Field.

"Thanks, I'm fine," she said with a smile that she hoped would not say too much.

"Are you sure?" Barry asked. "Let me show you later."

When Barry finished his game, he returned to Kate. By now, she'd tired of running and fetching her stray balls. Barry gave her a few pointers, and she noticed an immediate improvement.

After the lesson, they went for coffee, where she learned that Barry was a probation officer. She was soon taken by his force, his confidence. Kate was twenty-one and unattached. When Barry asked if she'd like to see him again—perhaps for an evening in San Francisco—she agreed.

To break the monotony at KFOG, I began bringing in my own albums and sneaking the softest ones in, replacing 101 Strings with the Mamas and the Papas; cutting Mancini for Donovan. In the dead of night, with an audience to match, the slight elevating of elevator music went unnoticed.

One August morning, I spent a couple of hours writing a letter to Mary. She had begun teaching school in Barstow, a small California town where her aunt lived. I had come around to believing her innocence in the *Gater* affair. Nursing a hope that we could patch things up, I wrote an obit of our relationship.

She came to town for a visit. She was tentative, still feeling the bruises from my attack. Mary hid it from me, but she'd been depressed all summer. What she couldn't hide was a massive weight gain that she ascribed to laziness. To me, she was as beautiful as ever. As an apology, I gave her a gift typical of my taste: a set of yellow and orange kitchen canisters.

"You shouldn't have," she said with a laugh. I think she really meant it.

At home on Sacramento Street, Tom and I added two roommates: Doug, a television sound engineer we knew from college, and Blair, who'd been a reporter. All of us had professional goals, but at night and on weekends, we partook of the times, hitting the dance concerts, collecting Fillmore and Avalon posters, scoring marijuana by the lid or, sometimes, chipping in on as much as half a brick, and acquiring all the latest albums by the Beatles,

Jimi Hendrix, the Doors. We were a strange crew. We were media freaks, but we refused to watch television. Instead, we played music and Scrabble.

Sometimes, with other dope-smoking friends around, we'd play a game we called "Origins." Sitting in a loose circle in the living room, a joint moving from hand to hand, one of us would utter a name or phrase. Without a break, whoever was "it" would begin to make up its etymology out of whole cloth and thin air thickened by *cannabis sativa*.

"Draft board," Doug would say.

"Ah, yes," I'd respond. "Well, everybody knows that one." A stalling strategy. "That goes back to George Washington's time, when he needed an army." Without knowing what I was going to say next, I'd say it: "His generals would order all civilians to this log cabin." (The word *board* was in my mind.) "They'd show up, see . . . often in the dead of winter. There'd be a strong draft blowing through the room, and those men who could withstand that—who didn't catch cold—would be deemed fit to serve."

A flimsy story, to be sure. But few of us were in a position to challenge it, and, unless another player wanted to challenge the story—by conjuring one of his own—the etymology stood. No points were given, which made sense. The whole exercise was pointless, played only for giddy laughter into the night.

"Brassieres? Sure. Of course, you know about braceros . . . Tennis? Well, the Eskimos used to play this game after they'd come home from fishing. They used a net, which they called a 'nis.' One-nis, two-nis . . ."

Who needed television?

Thanks to Doug's technical wizardry, we had alternatives to television entertainment beyond hand-rolled cigarettes and made-up games. When he learned that streetlights were turned on and off by photoelectric cells, he began controlling them from his bedroom with a simple flashlight. One night, he called Tom and me into his room, which looked out onto Sacramento Street. He pointed out his window, and we saw a color photo of Doug's

Siamese cat, Buckwheat, taking up the entire side of the gay bar across the street.

One of us—yeah, me—said there probably wasn't much interest in a picture of a pussycat over there.

"Yeah, but isn't it great?" said Doug, proud that he'd managed to project a color slide such a distance.

"No," said Tom. "But it's great."

Buckwheat who, like me, was an ordained minister through a mail-order certificate from the Universal Life Church of Modesto, California, provided additional entertainment another night when Doug decided to see how she'd look spinning at thirty-three and a third revolutions per minute on our stereo system's turntable.

As 1967 rolled toward the holidays, I got transferred from KFOG radio to a new television station. The management needed a writer, and the idea of getting away from the all-night shift suited me fine. However, most of the programming was old movies; we had few advertisers, and I had little to write besides station IDs, movie promos, and introductions to the late-night sign-off sermon.

But in the midst of nine-to-five misery came a breath of fresh air.

It was November 1967, when my roommates came across a new publication—a hybrid of a newspaper and magazine. It was called *Rolling Stone*, and all it cared about was rock and roll.

It was a bracing find. It was the kind of paper with the kind of freedom all of us at S.F. State were fighting for; only it focused almost exclusively on the hip rock scene. Tom and Doug thought I should write for it, but I didn't think of *Rolling Stone* as much of a future. I'd never considered myself a music critic or particularly knowledgeable about rock, and *Rolling Stone* was nothing if not critical and knowing—as well as hip, humorous, well written, and classically designed. It didn't go the way of the underground papers, crazed on psychedelic lettering and littered with mistakes;

it didn't take either rock and roll or itself too seriously. (Its first subscription premium was a wood-handled roach clip, and readers were advised to "act now before this offer is made illegal.")

Even in its raw first issues, sixteen or twenty-four pages of black-and-white newsprint, *Rolling Stone* vibrated from one set of hands to another around our flat on Sacramento Street. When it got to mine, I lapped it up. This was what we were trying to do at the *Gater*. Solid, classic journalism, but unafraid—urgent, in fact—to be contemporary and to mess with the established rules and boundaries.

My roommates worked behind the scenes in music and television. By now, Blair had been replaced by Abe, a Catholic schoolmate of Tom's in Oakland who was road manager for several pop acts, including Peter, Paul and Mary, and Jimi Hendrix. In February 1968, Abe told me about a free concert in a nearby park. The Siegal-Schwall Blues Band was playing, he said, and the show was to promote a movie Dick Clark was making about the Haight-Ashbury.

Dick Clark? It didn't take a genius to flick on the black light in my mind. *"Rolling Stone!"* I thought. I phoned the office, offered the news tip, and got the assignment.

I saw *Rolling Stone*'s offices for the first time when I delivered my report. They were in a part of town unknown to most San Franciscans. It was sometimes referred to as South of Market, a region of warehouses, wholesale outlets, and heavy industry. *Rolling Stone*'s founder, publisher, and editor, Jann Wenner, had scored free rent in a loft above a printing plant. But, once you entered through the lobby and walked along the back wall and up wooden steps to the loft, hot lead, ink, and gigantic rolls of paper weren't the prevailing smells in the air.

The magazine office was just across an alley from a slaughterhouse. That would explain the increasing popularity of incense around the offices.

Rolling Stone had a bare-bones staff: Jann, one other editor, an art director, and a secretary. I handed in my report, looked around a moment, and left.

My story appeared in March, in the issue dated April 6, 1968. Actually, it wasn't even a story. It was just a few paragraphs and ran in a column called Flashes. I got five dollars and no byline. I had no complaints. I was back in print.

A week later, KMPX, an FM radio station that had been taken over by a band of creative hipsters in spring of 1967, went on strike. It was the first "hippie strike," as the papers put it. Of course, *Rolling Stone* had to cover it. I called to volunteer to help on the story, being certain to say that I'd worked on FM radio in town. They teamed me up with a staff writer, but after our first story, he left *Rolling Stone*, and, as the strike dragged over several months, it became my beat.

Covering an intense labor strike called by hippie radio revolutionaries was exhilarating, but the ten- and twenty-dollar checks I received were not.

So I got a job as a writer and editor for Pacific Telephone's employee magazine and took on some part-time work editing the English-language page of the daily *Chinese World*, one of the oldest newspapers in Chinatown. I thought of *Rolling Stone* more as an entertaining side job than as any kind of a career.

·· 1 7 ··

1968

It was through the *Chinese World* that I met Lucy. She had been a contestant in a local beauty contest I was covering. Lucy was a petite redhead with shining eyes and an equally brilliant smile. She and I hit it off right away. I liked the way she tossed off bits of fantasy—she wanted to learn karate, she said, in case she became a spy—and she liked the way I encouraged her.

At the time, I was seeing no one, aside from an occasional date. Mary Keith was still living out of town; Michelle had her musician boyfriend and rock band.

So when Lucy came along, I was free and clear. In my mind, I had not yet had a fully satisfying relationship and had no reason to believe I'd ever achieve one.

Lucy was enticing. My roommates were stunned by her. She was almost the perfect "hippie chick" to have around. Depending

on her mood, she could be cosmopolitan . . . or an air head. She
was friendly and flirty, open to adventures.

It was with Lucy, in fact, that I had my first and only LSD
trip. We'd known each other only a month, but in the rush of
those times, that was a lifetime. We'd already gone out a half
dozen times, to movies, parties, and dinners.

Now, she'd scored some acid and wanted to try it with me. I
felt honored. The wisdom about LSD was that it was best to
have a "guide" with you when you tripped—preferably one who
wasn't on acid. I was too self-conscious to have a sober person
watching me freak out, so Lucy's idea sounded perfect. We'd be
each other's guide. Never mind that neither of us had dropped
acid before, meaning that we could be each other's *worst* choice
for an accomplice.

But I didn't expect to get nuts with acid. With marijuana, it'd
been months before I got my first buzz. With drink, it took more
than a few to wreck me. How devastating could LSD be?

We chose an evening when my roommates would be out.
Shaking and giggling with anticipation, Lucy removed the blotter
of acid from her handbag, and we looked at it for a good long
time before committing ourselves. I set up a stack of appropriate
albums on the turntable—the Beatles, Donovan, Jimi Hendrix,
Jefferson Airplane—and we ingested our LSD.

Well, we flew, Lucy a little higher than me, if recollection
somehow, miraculously, serves. Mostly, we listened to music and
waited for divine revelation, which never arrived. We talked
about how we felt. We very slowly made our way around the
flat. She heard strange sounds around the apartment; I heard
strange sounds in the music I thought I knew so well. I was
aware that I was on LSD and that something earthshaking should
be happening . . . and wasn't. Not so subconsciously, I hoped
that the night would end with Lucy and me in bed, having the
ball of our lives.

It ended, instead, anticlimactically. At about the same time, a
few hours after dropping the acid, we looked at each other sheepishly, as if to say, "Is that all there is?" We napped, then went

out for breakfast and a visit to the Japanese Tea Garden in Golden Gate Park.

Another month and another dozen dates later, I told Lucy that we should stop seeing each other. I was frustrated. As was the case with Mary, Michelle, and several others, I had a swell friendship that looked for all the world like a romance. But I wasn't getting anywhere with her. It wasn't that she was particularly resistant. But I found that if the girl didn't offer a hint of interest—or more—I wouldn't push.

I was insecure; I feared rejection, the loss of a friendship, one I valued enough that I'd be satisfied with just that. But that was tough to sell to nosy roomies who sometimes defined the quality of a relationship by the number of notches on a bedpost.

Or, as we got to asking one another when we saw a roommate returning from a date: "Didja hump her?"

A couple of days after I broke up with Lucy, she called, cheerful as always, and asked what we were doing that weekend. I sighed. "There's a Chinatown Arts Festival I'm going to, and I'll be the emcee." I didn't mention that Michelle would be among the performers. "I'm going with Barry and his girlfriend Kate," I added.

"Great," she said brightly. "When should I be ready?"

·· 1 8 ··

ALMOST CUT

MY HAIR

While I stumbled through my relationships, Barry and Kate had become lovers. He was her first, and, when Barry asked, on their first date, whether she was concerned about being in an interracial relationship, she'd laughed. "I'm on my own," she said. "I can do what I want to do."

Meantime, Shirley had gotten married. Through high school and college, she'd had the same problems I had finding time or permission for a social life; like me, she managed to become active in student affairs. She was a class officer, a member of the yearbook staff. Like me, she almost never went out on dates. And, like me, she socialized with students of all colors; her closest friends in Oakland High were black and white.

But when it came to boys, in high school and in college, she felt compelled to do what our parents wanted. It was a given, she thought, that she'd marry Chinese, so why even bother dating others?

At Cal, she met Rich, an architecture student, on a blind date, and they were soon seeing each other regularly. I was more than pleased. If she married Rich, I thought, that'd relieve some of the parental pressure there was on Barry and me—or, at least, buy us some time. Still, when Rich proposed, about a year after they first went out, Shirley was just uncertain enough to go to Barry.

"I don't think you should," he said. Although Shirley was twenty-two, Barry knew that she was still socially immature, as Sarah, Barry, and I had been at her age. None of us had a serious relationship until we were in our early twenties. Shirley's world, like ours, had consisted only of school and work.

"You haven't had a chance to see much of life," Barry told Shirley. "You should get an apartment, get a car, meet some people . . ." He thought of Kate, who'd been an airline attendant for several years. He was telling her that she ought to go back to school and pick up a degree. Now, he was advising the opposite for his sister.

Go see the world, he said. "You could be . . . a stewardess." Barry was so persuasive that she went and applied for a position with an airline without informing Rich. Only when he pressed her to make a choice between Continental Airlines and him did she decide that she didn't want to fly. In February 1969, they married in a big church ceremony in San Francisco, followed by an even bigger banquet in Chinatown, a "fifty-table" banquet, meaning five hundred guests.

But, for all the red and gold splendor, for all the festive tables weighted down by food and drink, for all the merriment as Shirley and Rich hopped the tables, accepting toasts and *hoong bow*—those little red envelopes of paper money—the banquet was not the event my parents longed to host.

Having gone to many such banquets through the years, our parents felt obligated to return the favor one day, to invite all their friends and their families to a lavish *yum choy* of their own. The most obvious occasion for such an affair was a wedding. But

Sarah had spoiled their plans by marrying a white man. Barry and I had yet to show up at home with a nice Chinese girl. (To the wedding, I brought Margarita, a willowy, artistic Chinese girl who lived upstairs from Tom and me.) And Shirley was so uncertain about how our parents felt about her wedding that she didn't dare ask them to help pay for it. She and Rich, along with his parents, paid for most of it, and they invited all the guests. For all their moments in the spotlight, in the reception line and during the speeches, our parents were still in the wings, waiting their turn.

By getting married, Shirley finally escaped the restaurant. Soon, she would move to El Paso, where Rich had a job in the Army.

Days after their wedding, I got a notice from my draft board. After studying the latest medical information I'd provided, they'd found me "fully acceptable for induction."

I wasn't done yet. Mustering up whatever reportorial skills I had, I located a copy of the U.S. Army's *Medical Fitness Standards for Induction*. In Section XIV, 2-28, rhinitis and sinusitis were listed as causes for rejection for induction. Through friends, I found a sympathetic physician who examined me and determined that I had "chronic allergic rhinitis." and "mild to severe sinusitis." I wrote both the local board and the Surgeon's Office of the Department of the Army, and two weeks later, the Surgeon replied with a promise to evaluate my records.

He found reason enough to send me to the Presidio, the Army's headquarters in San Francisco, for a last-ditch exam.

The evening before, my roommate Tom decided on a spirit-boosting excursion. Margarita, our upstairs neighbor, had told us about a mystical woman who could tell fortunes and talk to the dead. The woman operated out of the Golden Gate Spiritualist Church.

"Let's see if you're going to go fight the Viet Cong or if we'll be writing TV shows," said Tom.

"Sure," I said. Any excuse to go out, and stay out, was fine with me. The more ragged I could be tomorrow morning, the better. Tom took his girlfriend, Fiona, and I brought along Pam, a young British woman I was seeing on occasion.

It was a show. The spiritualist, a large woman in her sixties, stepped onto the stage, silently greeted the congregation, and sat down. A young man then brought a long white scarf to her and, in an overly dramatic style, blindfolded her. She then plucked written questions the audience members had placed into a wooden basket.

We had been asked to put some sort of identifying marker on our envelopes—a name, an initial, a number—so that we'd know when she picked ours. Seemingly sightless, she'd say something like: "I see a red A," and someone in the audience would murmur, "Yes."

If she was so moved, she might guess the audience member's occupation, how many children she had, or how she was feeling that evening. Then she'd get down to business. "I have a message for you. It's ... oh, it's a young voice." In a crowd, someone would gasp or cry out. "It's a little girl," she would go on. More gasps, along with sounds of amazement from the rest of us.

"She says she's doing all right. It took a little time, but her ... grandfather, is it? ... is here."

We heard cries and screams throughout the crowd. We looked at each other, not sure what to think. For one thing, we were all stoned. For another, I entered with a cynical attitude, but, with an appointment with the Army dead ahead, a part of me wanted to believe her. If she could offer some hope, I'd take it.

At the beginning of the evening, I wrote out my question with the idea of testing her. I wouldn't mention the Army, the draft, or even my concern. I wrote: "I have an appointment tomorrow. What will happen?"

About forty-five minutes into the session—plenty of impressive talks with the dead, lots of emotional responses—she picked my question.

I focused all of my energy on her, to give her every opportunity to do well. She told me she had a greeting from an uncle. I had no knowledge of my parents' siblings in China. I muttered an uncertain "No . . ." She tried again. "Could his name be Ed?" I shook my head.

"I think she's at the wrong restaurant, up on the other side," I whispered to Pam.

The spiritualist said: "You are at a crossroads." I sprang to mental attention. "You have one foot in the past . . . and one in the future." She paused. "Things will go in accordance with your wishes."

I breathed a sigh of relief. If there was life after death, and spirits on the other side, hanging out, just waiting for folks like this woman to ring them up, I'd stay out of the Army.

At seven the next morning, I showed up at Letterman Army Medical Center at the Presidio. At the office where I'd been directed, a group of young men stood and sat in the outer hallway, uniformly quiet and nervous. I stepped past them and showed my letter to a nurse.

"Oh," she said. "You're priority." My heart sank a little.

She led me into an examination room, where two doctors were huddled over a clipboard the younger physician was holding. Above and behind them were framed portraits of Lyndon Johnson and the Army Chiefs of Staff.

The nurse gave a manila folder to the older doctor, who flipped through the papers to the latest notes. He turned to his partner. "Could you handle this one?" he said. "I've got a professional actor I've still got to take care of." He and the nurse left.

The young doctor waved at me to sit down while he studied my case. Without glancing from the papers, he asked me to raise my chin. I did, and, holding my head lightly in place, he inspected my nostrils. He used no instruments or special lights.

"Still have this sinusitis?"

I nodded.

He went back to my file, read a line, and looked off to a wall, puzzled.

"Now, are you here for an entrance exam, or are you requesting disqualification?"

My mouth fell open.

"What?"

"Well, I mean do you want in or out?"

I noticed that he was holding a pen, ready to check off whatever I told him.

"Uh . . . if I've got a choice, I'll say out."

The doctor nodded, made a note into my file, and handed the entire folder to me.

"All right, give this to the nurse. You'll hear directly from Selective Service."

I still couldn't believe it.

"I'll hear what?"

"That you're disqualified. Have a nice day."

A week later, I got a letter from the Army Surgeon. He had reviewed my records and found me "medically disqualified . . . for induction into the Armed Forces." Three and a half years had passed since I'd been determined "fully acceptable." I had been ordered to induction three times in twenty months. And now, in the spring of 1969, I was finally free.

I continued to split my time between the phone company magazine and writing free-lance articles for *Rolling Stone*. I wrote about the singer Gordon Lightfoot; the Lovin' Spoonful producer Eric Jacobsen; the writer of the hippie anthem "Get Together," Dino Valente; and the East Bay rock band, Creedence Clearwater Revival. On a visit to Los Angeles, I interviewed a fresh singer-songwriter, Joni Mitchell.

She was my first glimpse into one of the creative nests of the Los Angeles music scene, in Laurel and Topanga canyons, where artists, producers, and record executives had snapped up country homes in recent years. Joni, who'd just bought one in Laurel Canyon, and who was living there with the singer Graham Nash, was part of a woodsy enclave that included David Crosby, Neil Young, Carole King, Frank Zappa, and members of the Mamas and the Papas, the Monkees, and Love.

Joni was a striking young renaissance woman whose first

album had been a success, and who was now working on poetry and painting as well as a follow-up album. She was softspoken, but brimming with self-knowledge, and she spoke with a candor that was still refreshingly new at the time. She had a journalist's keen eye for detail and a songwriter's lyrical feel.

She had come to Laurel Canyon the summer before from the East Coast. "In New York," she said, "the street adventures are incredible. There are a thousand stories in a single block. You see the stories in the people's faces. You hear the songs immediately. Here in Los Angeles, there are less characters because they're all inside automobiles. You don't see them on park benches or peeing in the gutter or any of that."

For new songs, she said, she was relying on her own experiences and on lessons she was learning from friends like Crosby, who produced her first album and who was one of the most political of the Los Angeles musicians.

"I can't help but know what's happening," she said, "but I also know that I can't do a thing about it. It's good to be exposed to politics and what's going down here, but it does damage to me. Too much of it can cripple me. And if I really let myself think about it—the violence, the sickness, all of it—I think I'd flip out."

Rolling Stone packaged the Mitchell interview with a story on Judy Collins and an essay, "The Swan Song of Folk Music," and, to my surprise, put Mitchell on the cover. It was my first cover story—only it wasn't. My byline had been inadvertently left off of the story.

The magazine was still paying between ten and forty dollars for stories, and I was content to straddle the corporate and the rock worlds until early April, when, on the stub of a thirty-dollar check for a Jethro Tull profile, Jann Wenner scribbled an unsigned "Call me soon."

I didn't notice the message for a week or so, and when I called, it was a slightly miffed Jann who suggested we have lunch. We met at a seafood cafe near *Rolling Stone*. I hated seafood, but kept my mouth shut.

We'd spoken a couple of times before, and I had come to think of *Rolling Stone* as a valuable continuing education in journalism. Three months before, I'd been assigned a profile of Valente, the songwriter, and Jann had called me into his office.

Jann Wenner was a short, hyperactive fireball of energy. He was twenty-two years old, exactly one year younger than I was. He had graduated from Cal, where he had covered the Free Speech Movement and written a rock and roll column for the campus daily. He had befriended Ralph J. Gleason, the jazz and pop critic at the *San Francisco Chronicle* who was an early champion of the changing folk and rock scenes.

Jann was not the first rock and roll fan to notice that there was a void in journalistic coverage of the scene; that the mainstream press either ignored or insulted the music, and the fanzines trivialized it. In Boston, there was *Crawdaddy!*, which gave the new rock and roll its first serious criticism—too serious for Jann's taste. And in the Bay Area, there was the *Mojo-Navigator R&R News*, which had more energy than organization, and was doomed to a short lifespan.

When, in the fall of 1967, Jann decided to start a rock paper of his own, he was lucky to have Gleason behind him. Jann was an impetuous young man who was every bit as mercurial as the times and who, just before conceiving *Rolling Stone*, had thought of writing a novel, compiling a rock and roll encyclopedia, and getting a job with the post office. In contrast, Gleason was rock solid, and he provided Jann with invaluable support on several levels. He was one of the investors who gave Jann the $7,500 nut for his paper; he suggested the name for the paper, which Jann had considered calling the *Electric Newspaper*; he led Jann to the printer, who gave *Rolling Stone* its first loft offices rent-free. He wrote a column, giving the upstart publication a respected byline.

But as crucial as Gleason was, *Rolling Stone* was, from the start, Wenner's baby, and he knew what he wanted. Even in this loft, with its view of The San Francisco Screw Company across the street, Jann managed to impart a sense of style, of Victorian chic—hip, but clean and orderly. On my earlier visits, I had noticed how *Rolling Stone*'s offices, like the magazine itself, looked nothing like a scruffy and disheveled underground paper. On the walls, there were no psychedelic posters from the Fillmore or the Avalon; instead, there was only a photograph of Merry Prankster and novelist Ken Kesey and a poster of the Marx Brothers, with Groucho honking on a hookah as if the smoking pipe were a saxophone.

Charles Perry, one of *Rolling Stone*'s first editors, would tell me later that Jann had a rule against nails, Scotch tape, or thumbtacks on the walls. Only plastic pushpins were allowed.

Jann had borrowed from the stately design of a local paper, the Sunday *Ramparts*, with its Times Roman typeface and its Oxford rule borders around each page, for *Rolling Stone*. (*Ramparts*, in turn, had been inspired by the *London Sunday Times*.) Similarly, although he had trouble finding and keeping writers in the early going, given his finances, he knew how he wanted *Rolling Stone* stories to be done.

He coached me before I went off to see Dino Valente. "Don't just ask him questions," he said. Jann spoke with a certainty in his voice far beyond his twenty-two years. He turned to his antique oak desk and grabbed a couple of magazines. They were issues of *The New Yorker*. "Lookit these," he said, handing them over. "This is the kind of detail, description, and reporting I want in our profiles."

I went home, just managed to get through one of the magazine's lengthier articles, and ventured out one evening to Valente's houseboat in Sausalito. I took in his scene—freshly showered before our talk, he sat, shirtless, over a cup of tea and a slice of pie served by three—*three!*—beautiful chicks—and wrote it up.

Before I got my first byline for a feature story, however, my name had to weather a challenge from Jann. When he first saw it on a KMPX story, he'd gone to John Burks, his savvy new managing editor.

"So what is it with his name?" he asked. "Is it like a pen name?

If it's not real, let's have him pick one or the other. No one will believe this is a real name."

"No, it's the real deal," said John, himself a former *Gater* editor who knew me from S.F. State. "Besides, it's the greatest byline in the world. People are gonna be saying, 'Where's this guy coming from?' and be lured into it!"

Rolling Stone ran the Valente story over two glorious pages. Now, two months later, we were having lunch at Blanche's, an outdoor seafood cafe on the waterfront at China Basin, overlooking the San Francisco Bay. Over his favorite dish there, a crab salad with Russian dressing, Jann offered me a job. "Just come in and, you know, do what you think needs to be done." It was a dream job. Rock and roll—and no more suits. I leaned back, squinted at the sun, and asked about money. I was making $700 a month at Pacific Telephone, I said. Jann didn't blink. He knew what he had going and how attractive it was for any journalist who enjoyed covering the pop scene. He had pulled John Burks in for half the salary he was earning at *Newsweek*. Jann offered $135 a week, and within a month, another used desk was being fitted into the loft. It was May 1969.

Rolling Stone came out only once every two weeks, but it was a daily rush. Like the Dylan song said, we knew something was happening, but, unlike "Mr. Jones," we knew what it was.

By now, *Rolling Stone* was getting notice as the first intelligent rock and roll publication in the country. It was professionally written and designed; it reported and reflected, but also criticized, the burgeoning rock scene. This baby, they were saying, had a chance.

But it operated with only a couple of editors and an art director. They were by no means hippies. The art director, Bob Kingsbury, was a bearded, older man—he was over forty—who was Jann's brother-in-law and a sculptor before Jann convinced him to switch to magazine design. John Burks was a tall, bespectacled young man with a Beatle haircut, a thing for jazz, and a solid journalism background. Charles Perry, a proofreader who would later write fables about drugs, columns about wine, and a history of the Haight-Ashbury scene, came in with no newspaper experience. But his portfolio, such as it was, was intriguing. He majored in Near Eastern languages at U.C. Berkeley, shared a house with Augustus Stanley Owsley III, the legendary manufacturer of LSD, and had roughly equal affection for psychedelia, animals, exotic foods, good wine, and colorful neckties.

Along with Jann and an elfin photographer, Baron Wolman, who shot everything from classic studio portraits of rock stars to an on-the-spot dope bust of the Grateful Dead, we made for a motley crew. I took on the title of news editor, and I soon learned two things: First, the news was whatever interested us, whether it came over the phone, by mail, or through an experience the night before at a club, a concert, or a friend's house. Early in my time there, and until our staff grew to more than a half-dozen editors, we had no formal editorial meetings. We'd just talk about what was going on around town, and a story might develop. Outside of our network, we relied on the British pop press, from which we pilfered with abandon for the "Flashes" column and for stories we'd flesh out with our own reporting.

Second, I discovered that titles were meaningless. Whatever we called ourselves, we did a multitude of jobs. We all wrote; we all edited; we all made assignments; we all pitched in with captions, headlines, and story ideas. Once, when Bob Kingsbury went on a vacation, Jann tried to paste up a year-end roundup of rock and roll news, made a mess of it, and had to call Bob back from a ski resort. The summary of the year 1967 ran in the issue dated February 28, 1968.

I did the stories that had to be done—a roundup of rock festivals, a Jefferson Airplane bust, a lawsuit against the Grateful Dead—and a few bigger ones, including our first obit of a major star: Brian Jones, founding member of the Rolling Stones.

It didn't take me long to feel like I belonged. One of my first stories as a staff member was a short piece about concert promoter Bill Graham's record company offering free seminars to budding recording engineers. Most newspapers would have run the press release verbatim. I tossed the story in the air and got some cynical feedback. I didn't know that Jann already had a history with Graham; that, when he was writing his column at U.C. Berkeley, he'd attacked the Fillmore Auditorium promoter as a hippie-hating capitalist.

In *Rolling Stone*'s first year, Graham had already banned the magazine's staff from the Fillmore, then rescinded the order. While Graham became known for throwing people—musicians as well as customers and the press—out of his ballroom when he felt wronged by them, he maintained a civil relationship with *Rolling Stone*, with occasional fireworks.

My story on the free seminar included a thought that one of our editors had tossed out—that the seminars, while offering valuable training to people wanting to learn about engineering, could give the Fillmore's two record labels a stable of cheap young talent.

Graham blew up, and when he next saw me, I was at his auditorium, conducting an interview with a rock band. "*Mis-tuh* Fong-Torres," he said, spitting out the title in contempt. "I do not want to see you, *ever* again, on my property!" I smiled at, the leader of the band, and he gave a small smile back. He'd seen these scenes before.

As my byline became a regular occurrence in *Rolling Stone*, readers took note of my name.

One wrote: "I wonder if you're aware of the sort of impact your name itself has. It's so . . . *distinctive* a name that when I first ran into it three years or so ago, I assumed that it was assumed. In print it appears violent and sinister and full of paradox, like the name of a Shanghai hired assassin with, perhaps, considerable personal style, who savors a blend of celebrity and notoriety. There are all kinds of associations: Bent Fang, warrior of the Torrid Tong; and at the other end, the suggestion of an international mixture of aristocratic bloods—Fong seems Chinese, Torres, Spanish (hyphenation for nobility), the Ben seems, rather than Benjamin, like the Moslem genitive preposition."

All this as the beginning of a six-page query for a story idea.

Unshackled from the corporate world, I dressed more casually than I even had in college. There, taking my role as an editor too seriously, I often showed up at the newspaper office in a white shirt and narrow tie. With my horn-rimmed glasses and short hair, I looked like some engineering student who'd stumbled into the wrong place.

Now, I took to blue work shirts and jeans. I switched to rimless glasses. I grew a moustache and I let my hair grow, leaving it unwashed for days at a time.

Still, like my siblings, I would manage to make my way over to Hayward and to the Bamboo Hut to work a few hours or an entire day on the occasional weekend. With Shirley married and in Texas, Burton took over most of the chores, while Barry and I made guest appearances.

When I showed up one Sunday that summer, my parents were not happy to see me. They did not mince words, and as soon as my mother saw me, she cried out: "*Ai-ya! Nay* kaw *yeong!*" This has no direct English translation, but roughly meant, "You look like *that?*"

"Why so long?" she asked, indicating my hair and looking ashamed for me. "It looks not good." She didn't press the issue, but when she went into the kitchen, she told my father, and he came out to the dining room for a look.

It was the middle of the afternoon, and there were no customers.

"You look like a *girl*," he snapped.

That's all it took. I turned, gave poor Burton a pat on the shoulder—he'd be working alone again—and drove back to San Francisco.

A few days later, Barry heard about the blowup and called. He, too, had grown a moustache, but he kept his hair at early-Beatles length, with sideburns. He was a probation officer and subject to office policies.

"You should tell them it's a job requirement," he said, laughing.

"How do you say 'job requirement' in Chinese?" I asked. It was a rhetorical question. In Chinese, there are no requirements. You just showed up and worked.

"I know," said Barry. "I'll bring them some pictures of some *real* freaks. That should calm them down."

When I next visited home for my mother's birthday in August, the subject of hair-length was left undiscussed. But, then, so was almost every subject. We were incapable of talking about politics, the war, civil rights, or what young people were thinking. My parents, as far as I knew, didn't care. Their only concern was that their children would not become hippies.

When I joined *Rolling Stone*, I told them only that I was working at a newspaper in San Francisco that covered music. There was no easy way—and no point, really—to telling them more. My parents tended to judge people on surface appearances. That's how they had treated Shirley's dates; how they responded to various friends of ours; and why Barry and I rarely talked about our dates. When Barry mentioned that he liked Kate, and that she was not Chinese, Mom had told him, "Please, don't. Sarah already upset us so much."

They meant well. Sure, they had their own concerns about *seet-meen*, the dreaded loss of face; they wanted us to be more Chinese, even if it meant being less American. But they were also concerned for us. They, too, knew about racism and knew that life would be easier for their sons and daughters if they weren't involved in interracial marriages.

I wished I could have engaged them in a real conversation about my feelings. I understand your concerns, I would have said. But I can't let your worries about how people in Chinatown look at you dictate how I live my life.

Here I am, in a profession few, if any, Asians have cracked, and race had absolutely nothing to do with my getting the job. That was true of my jobs at the phone company magazine, at the radio station, and in college.

Here I am, an editor at a magazine chronicling not only music but the massive social and cultural revolutions that are irrevocably changing our world. At the heart of the movement is an ideal, of a more just and equal society in which one recognizes differences in cultures, but doesn't discriminate because of those differences.

And here I am, writing about some of the most creative forces of our time, many of them rhythm and blues artists I have loved since first turning on Top 40 radio ten years ago.

This is who I am, and you're asking that I go out with only Chinese? I'm sorry, but I can't do that. And it's not because I need to rebel against you, to do the opposite of what you want. In an ideal world, I would love a woman who happened to be Chinese, and we'd all be happy. In reality, the women I'm seeing are people you wouldn't want to meet. They're good women, too. It's just too bad they've got that one thing wrong with them.

Once, I used the pages of *East West* to tear into my fellow Chinese—specifically, Chinese a generation older than me—for their racist ways. Somewhere in America, there were Chinese kids who did kowtow to their parents in the matters of professions and relationships. That kind of submission, I said, fostered perpetual racism and other biases. That was the kind of thinking, I wrote, that had to be wiped out—"among people of all colors."

Seeing my raw anger in print, I was relieved that my parents couldn't read English. Barry could, and sent me a note from Hawaii, where he was spending a weekend with Kate. "Continue socking it to them," he said.

While I was getting settled in at *Rolling Stone*, Barry was taking ballet lessons.

"Hey, it's good exercise," he told me, just a mite defensively.

Actually, he added, he wanted to take kung fu lessons at a school operated in the East Bay by Bruce Lee, a young martial arts master who'd just begun to make action movies in Hong Kong. But after a tryout, an instructor suggested dance as a less strenuous step toward kung fu.

Once Barry got a taste of ballet, he was hooked.

One day that summer of 1969, he and Norma, his *Mui-Mui*, went to see Rudolf Nureyev and Margot Fonteyn dance *Swan Lake* at the Opera House. They made a day of it, browsing through downtown stores. At the fine arts and gift shop, Gumps, he found a poster by one of his favorite artists, Ben Shahn. In the poster, a man, blank-eyed, his chin resting on clenched fists, was in contemplation. Shahn's statement: "You have not converted a man because you have silenced him."

"Barry," said *Mui-Mui*, "you must have said this to Ben Shahn."

Barry chuckled and nodded. "This," he said, looking at the poster, "sums me up." He bought it.

After a bite in Chinatown, they proceeded to the Opera House, where Nureyev dazzled them with his soaring jetés. Barry's voice was among the loudest at performance's end, as he and Norma joined in the standing ovation. Moments later, they were outside on Van Ness Avenue when the fresh memory of *Swan Lake* overtook Barry. He'd been learning to jump in his ballet class, and now, near midnight on a balmy summer evening in San Francisco, he jetéd all the way to his car.

Five years after graduating from Cal, Barry was still taking graduate courses. He was working for a doctorate in criminology. But he was equally interested in avoiding military service. He made no secret of his opposition to the Vietnam War.

On October 15, war protestors organized a nationwide Vietnam Moratorium, during which students and workers were encouraged to take a day off to spread information about or to rally against the war. Barry led a group of Contra Costa County probation officers in a picketing of the Federal Building in San Francisco.

"Probation officers have been too quiet too long," he said. "We are presenting ourselves to the public as responsible citizens aghast at the continuation of the conflict. We plan to take the day off and stand as a group of probation officers who beseech the President to end the slaughter with all haste."

* * *

I met Amie Hill at a book party in North Beach. She wrote and produced counterculture-flavored commercials for KSAN, the dominant free-form, progressive-rock station in town, but once I learned of her writing talents, I convinced her to contribute to *Rolling Stone*.

One night, we were on our way home from a nightclub concert. My Toyota had just crested a hill overlooking the lights of downtown, and we stopped to look at the view. We may have been stoned as we sat in silence. Amie spoke: "You know, this is an incredible time to be alive and doing what we're doing. It must be almost like living in Florence during the Renaissance.

"And here we are," she went on, "working at *Rolling Stone*. We see shows for free; we get records in the mail; we get to interview famous people." I had taken her with me on visits with Crosby, Stills, Nash and Young and with Cheech & Chong, and she was doing some interviews of her own. "Life," she said, "is certainly interesting."

For me, life got much more interesting when I met Amie. A native of Pennsylvania, with cascading blond hair framing a classically pretty face, she was a comic hippie in the guise of a fairy princess. A quick draw with quips and wordplay, with a sense of the absurd that I could appreciate, she shot down pretension and silliness—common qualities in would-be hipsters of the day. And when I got too serious, she'd remind me to make room for play.

One evening, we were in her room in her boarding house in the Haight-Ashbury, and the subject turned to dances.

"Now, what the hell is a fox trot?" I said. "I've never known."

Amie smiled. She didn't know, either, but she jumped up and said: "It's like this. Here." She reached out, pulling me to my feet and getting us positioned in front of a mirror. She then invented a trotting dance step and looked so ... foxy and so hilarious that for years afterward, we'd break into it at the sight of a mirror.

From the moment we met, we were soulmates. There was one major difference between us. It wasn't race, although, after our first embrace in my car, she shrank back in mock horror and informed me: "Gee, I never hugged a Chinese before."

It was that Amie truly was a free spirit. I wrote about the hip scene; she lived it. She didn't write for a living; she wrote as part of life. And in the area of relationships, she was the essence of laissez faire. When I told her of women friends I'd known for years who I'd take out on occasion, she was disarmingly generous. "Sure," she said. "We don't own each other. Whatever happens is all right."

"Really?"

"Really. You can even fox-trot with them."

When I encouraged Amie to write for *Rolling Stone*, she was uncertain. I assured her that she'd make it—or fail—on her own merit. She proved her worth, but it wasn't easy. After she'd written two pieces, I suggested to Jann that we assign her to cover Country Joe McDonald's visit to an alternative high school.

"No, I don't want her to do it," said Jann. "Women can't write. Get a guy." Although women had important positions in the advertising and art departments, there were few female bylines in *Rolling Stone*, whether by choice or coincidence.

I told Amie to go ahead and write the story. When she submitted it, I took off her byline and passed it along to Jann. At the next editorial meeting, when he praised the article, I leaned over and whispered the bad news to him.

Amie went on to write for both *Rolling Stone* and a sister publication, an ecology magazine called *Earth Times*. Her work at the magazine, however, outlasted our own relationship. For all the freedom that we gave each other, she needed more. Even though I had dates with other women, I thought of ours as the most stable of our respective relationships. She came to find the stability restricting.

Through the years, we remained close. If one of us had something fun to do and no one to do it with, we called on each other. We wound up going to three Halloween parties together. Once, we went as each other. I wore a blond wig, a fairy-princess paper mask, a bright orange shirt that was a favorite of hers, and her leather vest. She wore my vest, work shirt, jeans, a black, mop-top wig, and a Fu Manchu mask—just in case anyone didn't get it.

DAZED AND

CONFUSED

In the first days of 1970, Gordon Lew called. *East West*'s English language editor needed to take some time off to work on a novel. Could I help out? I was up to my leather vest at *Rolling Stone*, but I couldn't ignore Gordon. I began to show up on production nights at *East West*, which now had its offices in a spartan basement in a Chinatown alley. I edited stories, wrote headlines, stole photos and even stories from *Rolling Stone* and other publications and put them into *East West*. To Gordon's delight, I applied *Rolling Stone*'s inventive design to *East West*. I cropped photographs and cut around flags, rifle barrels, and feet to make them extend into a page's borders, giving the photos what appeared to be an additional dimension. Gordon approved of my relatively radical editorial slant, reasoning that it added a vitality to Chinatown's staid journalism.

In turn, I learned about Chinese problems—in China, Hong Kong, New York, and, most of all, in San Francisco.

By 1970, anyone who spent much time in Chinatown couldn't help knowing that this neighborhood of thirty city blocks was going through its most cataclysmic upheaval since the '06 quake and fire.

It had never been the exotic, Oriental Disneyland so many outsiders—including Chinese-Americans—thought it was, though it had always been a neighborhood with a gold-gilt and neon facade that attracted millions of tourists. Strolling under pagoda-topped streetlamps and lanterns strung across Grant Avenue, eating in restaurants like the Far East and the Cathay House, browsing through curio shops, and looking curiously through the windows of Chinese groceries and herb shops, they got the outsider's look at the Orient of the West. Few knew that they were, in fact, visiting a ghetto.

I first wrote about Chinatown in *East West*. There was no way for me not to be disturbed by what I saw. Families of six to eight shared single hotel rooms, with a plank of plywood over a bathtub serving as a dining table. Clothes were stored in old trunks or stuffed into shopping bags hung on nails. Older single men slept in tiered bunkbeds in dank, closet-sized rooms. Behind more than a hundred unmarked doors, I could peer into garment sewing factories, where women labored for fourteen hours a day, stitching designer clothing at a fraction of the minimum wage. In notoriously inexpensive Chinatown restaurants, the employees could explain the low prices by revealing their salaries, which were on par with the garment workers'.

Beyond what I could see, I reported what I was hearing from social workers and college students who were concerned about conditions in Chinatown. And I recited what had become, among insiders and critics, a litany, a laundry list of disturbing facts and statistics about Chinatown.

The area's population density was ten times the city's average, and, because of the 1965 relaxation of immigration laws, Chinatown—packed with 50,000 residents—was fitting in another 8,000 a year.

The unemployment rate was nearly double that of San Francisco and more than triple the national rate. Many of the immigrants came to the Golden Mountains with schooling and skills, but, without English, they found themselves trapped in Chinatown, working in restaurants and sweatshop garment factories. It wasn't surprising, then, that the suicide rate was three times the national average, the substandard housing rate three times that of the city.

And there was the most volatile problem: displaced and distressed young people. The children of the immigrants faced the same frustrations their parents did—but had to face them in the context of contemporary American life in the sixties. Where they needed friendship, they often found hostility from American-born Chinese, who called them "FOB's"—"fresh off the boat." In turn, the newcomers sneered at the American Chinese as *jook sing*, meaning "empty bamboo."

English left the new arrivals lost. Home wasn't much of one, with parents off at work twelve hours and more every day. Many of them turned to forming social and self-protective groups, modern-day versions of the tongs the early Chinese settlers had organized.

The new generation of Chinese immigrants came into an America pulsing with social change. On college campuses, protests against the Vietnam War and racism gave rise to the Third World Liberation Front and, later, the Red Guard, the Chinese equivalent of the militant Black Panther Party. Chinese youth began to speak up, to demand rights, and—shocking the outwardly decorous first generation—to do so with earthy language. Piety was thrown to the winds.

Soon, Chinatown became an unwitting and often unwilling social science laboratory. College students set up tutorial programs, but many of the intended beneficiaries had no reason to trust any outsiders. They had enough problems with Chinatown's elders, who wrote them off as delinquents and refused to lend a financial hand to them. When community groups called for more playgrounds, business leaders argued that parking lots were more important, to accommodate tourists. When youth groups asked for money to start up a coffee house, an alternative to pool halls and smoke shops, they were told to abide by the old virtues, of study, hard work, and achievement over handouts.

The establishment—the family associations and the tongs,—seemed to think of anyone who called for social change as Communists, the party they'd been fighting since Mao's revolution had banished their beloved Kuomintang, the Nationalist party, to Formosa (Taiwan). The factions, the politics, the mutual distrust, made Chinatown an impossible world to traverse, let alone penetrate; they made its myriad problems all the more difficult to solve.

While I wrote about Chinatown for various publications, Barry continued to study social ills both at Cal and on the streets. While working toward a Ph.D. in criminology at Cal, he was a probation officer in Richmond, where he became director of the Dynamic Youth Program, which worked closely with troubled youth. He was becoming recognized as an authority on delinquency.

At a dinner for the Juvenile Hall Auxiliary in the East Bay suburban town of Concord, he told a mostly white, middle-class audience that his Dynamic Youth Group kids had a "kind of fatalistic attitude.

"With these kids, it's not 'If I get on probation, I want you for my probation officer.' It's *when*. It's not 'If I get pregnant' but *when*. Tragic, really."

The kids, he said, needed alternatives to their everyday lives.

"I tell my volunteers we have to share our lives with these kids. Take them home to dinner or on a shopping trip. They have to see there is more to life than what they find in their community."

Barry took his kids to the beach, to ball games, and to museums. With help from Kate, he took them downtown to department stores. He took a contingent to the ballet, and he arranged two overnight trips to the snow country in Squaw Valley and Lake Tahoe.

Even when he attended a wedding, he thought of his kids.

Norma—*Mui Mui*—was planning to attend the reception banquet for their friends' wedding with Barry, but because she was a bridesmaid, Barry was on his own. He showed up with eight of his Dynamic Youth Group kids and seated them in the back of the church.

Some of them had never witnessed a wedding before. When the bride started down the aisle with her father, one kid stared at the couple and asked, loudly: "Is she marrying *that* old man?" Barry had to work hard to keep from breaking up.

My parents, still disappointed that Barry had chosen to be something akin to a social worker, wished he'd get married—to a Chinese girl, of course. But he was in no hurry to settle down. For a short time, in 1968, he was engaged to Kate. He presented her with a ring, and she accepted—but with an indefinite date. She wasn't certain that she was ready to marry.

That was fine by Barry. As much as he was taken with Kate, he, too, was nagged by doubts and worries about what our parents would think. Not that he didn't know.

One day, Barry wondered out loud to a friend about what it'd be like if he married Kate, and if he died. He was thinking about the New Orleans–style funeral processions that are staged for some Chinatown elders.

"I can just see it," Barry said. "The procession marching down Stockton Street, with this big old picture of me being carried by this beautiful blonde . . ."

When Barry wasn't exasperating our parents with talk about Kate, or dating other non-Chinese women, he tried to be a good first son, taking time out to handle our parents' taxes and other businesses. A few years before, our parents had purchased a four-unit apartment building in East Oakland, and Barry was their liaison with tenants.

As for me, my parents didn't know what to think. They knew I was making a living as a writer, and, in China, literary pursuits are considered honorable. But they kept a discreet distance from information about just what kind of people and activities *Rolling*

Stone covered. They did like the fact that I was spending some time at *East West*. At least I was meeting some Chinese for a change.

Sometimes, while I was in the basement office of *East West*, *Rolling Stone* matters would intrude. Late one night in May, an editor answered the phone and waved at me.

"It's for you," he said.

I grabbed the phone near me.

"Hi," the caller said with a crackly voice. "It's Janis."

It took me a few seconds to get it. I'd been trying to reach Janis Joplin for several days, for a story about her latest band, her second since leaving Big Brother and the Holding Company. She and *Rolling Stone* had a tumultuous relationship, but this night, she was feeling good, and she'd tracked me down in Chinatown.

"Man, I feel so fucking great," she began, "that I thought I'd put a flower around my wrist." She told me about taking off from rehearsals at her house in Marin County to hit a tattoo parlor in downtown San Francisco and get a permanent bracelet of hearts and flowers. "A lot of my Capricorn girlfriends have tattoos," she said. "It's fuckin' beautiful."

She gave me a rundown on her new band, then told me about a recent visit to South America, where she was shaken up by the Rio de Janeiro police.

"It's vicious, man. If you've got long hair they can drag you off and never let you out. There's no judicial system at all there. The cops rape people, put dogs to guys' balls. And people think *we've* got it bad . . ."

Up the Brazilian coast, she found a different scene in Salvador. "No cops," she said. "In fact, there was nothing there. So it ended up for three nights with me and my friends going to this big whorehouse that had this four-piece band, and I sang with them."

I scribbled down everything Joplin said, congratulated her on the new band, and returned to *East West* matters.

Early another evening, a group of young Asians dropped into the *East West* office to have a look around. One of them was a girl named Lenni. She had an undeniable presence: Her hair flowed down to her hips, she wore big, round-rimmed glasses, and she had a sassy sense of humor. She said she liked to draw and wondered if we might be interested in taking a look. We were.

Her whimsical line drawings soon found their way into *East West*, and I found myself staying at her Asian hippie pad and getting to know, for the first time in years, a group of Chinese people my age.

Lenni was spunky, moody, alternately needy and motherly. We got high and reveled in our rebelliousness. We were Chinese—she was grounded in San Francisco's Chinatown and still had friends there; I was exploring and reporting it for the only bilingual paper there. But here we were, playfully flaunting Chinese customs and ethics.

Like Amie, Lenni was far more a hippie than I could even pretend to be. Like Amie, she would find that one steady relationship was too restricting. But in our time together, we were aware enough of how difficult it was to click with a Chinese person of the opposite sex that we even entertained thoughts of a long-term relationship with each other.

As we spent time together, I remembered a remark that one friend had made. "All your women were beautiful," she said. "And none of them were Oriental." It was true that, until Lenni, I hadn't really dated any Asian women.

The fact that, within a few weeks, we were talking about living together told me that, as independent as I was, a part of me was still trying to placate my parents. In their eyes, I was failing them by not having brought home a Chinese girl—a perfect match— for their approval.

The way I saw it, by the very act of trying, of looking past non-Chinese friends for the most important relationships of all, I was being racist. By denying my affection for people of all colors, I was being dishonest with myself. When I found myself attracted to someone and, miracle of miracles, she didn't flee, screaming—well, I wouldn't walk away.

But I also didn't argue when people said that life is simply less complicated when they're paired up with partners of similar backgrounds. And so, when Lenni came along, I allowed myself to be happy that, for the first time since Michelle, I had a relationship that wouldn't get my father chasing after me with a cleaver.

Just as Lenni and I were becoming a couple, Michelle returned to town from New York City. She was visiting her family. She had a jazz musician boyfriend in New York, and I had Lenni, but while Michelle was in town, we renewed our friendship, eating together in Chinatown and North Beach, and catching jazz and rock concerts. Michelle was expanding from music and poetry into journalism, and she noted the changes going on in Chinatown and *East West*'s efforts to chronicle them.

I thought I was doing some good at *East West*, helping with Gordon Lew's goal to foster communications among the many factions in and around Chinatown. Sometimes, it was hard to tell.

One morning in May 1970, Gordon called to say that the newspaper office had been bombed. Someone had attached an explosive to the front door and ignited it. Whoever it was botched the job. Only the door was damaged.

But they weren't done. One afternoon in early June, I'd just emerged from a meeting of the Chinatown–North Beach Youth Council when three young Asian men surrounded me and forced me into an alley.

"Can you speak Chinese?" one of them demanded. As I began to answer—in my broken Cantonese—they pushed me around to one another. I knew what was coming. Instinct told me to pocket my eyeglasses, and just as soon as I did, I was tackled, shoved to the ground, and beaten and kicked for an agonizingly long few minutes. I covered my head and shouted at them: "Why?" But the assailants remained silent through the pummeling, then ran off. I never got a good look at them.

Too shaken, confused, and hurt to even cry, I made my way to the *East West* office, a few blocks away, where an employee tended to me. I had suffered no serious injury.

I learned later that my crime was running a story attributing a recent slaying of a young man to the rise of gangs in Chinatown. I had violated some code of silence that had insinuated itself in the Chinatown underground.

In the days following the attack, Lenni found herself a target as well. Her mother had been getting threatening calls asking about her.

I retreated to the far safer, much more comforting worlds of rock and roll and *Rolling Stone*.

A few days after I'd been beaten, I was at my office, on the phone with Paul Boucher, the program director at KSAN. He had an item for our "Random Notes" column. Tom Donahue, the station's general manager, was orchestrating a movie for Warner Bros. He was taking a busload of rock musicians and friends across the country and filming free concerts at various locations. A number of disc jockeys would go along for the ride. It then occurred to Paul that Donahue's raid of talent would leave him scrambling for a month in the summer of 1970.

"Haven't you done some radio?" he asked.

I knew better than to mention spinning "Dolly Holiday" tapes on the all-night shift on KFOG. I said only that I'd worked on radio.

"Well, you wanna do some fill-in shifts while the weekend guys are gone?"

With that, I was scheduled for a month of shows in August.

But this was free-form radio. I shouldn't have been surprised, but I was when Boucher called me back and asked if I could drop by the studios and go on the air between four and seven o'clock— that afternoon. The entire staff, he said, was going out for a photo session.

It would be baptism by air—and it would be dead air, the disc jockey's nightmare, if I didn't fill it properly. The only assistance I'd have would be a temp answering the phones. Boucher suggested I arrive a bit early, to acclimate myself to FCC regulations concerning program logs, with the transmitter and its assortment of meters, with the record library, and with the control board, which I'd have to run in order to say or play anything.

After an hour of frantic orientation, I was on my own. I began with the most obvious of songs: Bob Dylan's "Like a Rolling Stone." The VU meters indicated that it was actually being broadcast, and I rolled on from there. The three hours passed swiftly enough, as did the following month.

As things turned out, several of the adventurers in the film wound up wandering through Tibet and Morocco after the filming was completed, and had no plans for returning within any measurable time frame. My temporary gig at KSAN lasted eight years.

On the air, I played and did whatever I wanted. I could see someone like Steve Martin, an opening act at a local club, and bring him in for an interview. He was an unknown when I first saw him, and not everyone in the club quite got his act. In 1972, hippies ruled the pop scene, and Martin was this prematurely graying, clean-cut guy in a flannel shirt and pressed slacks. In a time when comedy was stoned and/or socially relevant—Cheech and Chong, Richard Pryor, and George Carlin were headliners— Martin didn't so much break the rules as much as act as if he were unaware of any contemporary standards.

He made balloon animals and put on a fake arrow-through-the-head; he was a smug jerk trying out pick-up lines; he was a show-biz guy who was disgusted with his mom because she'd asked to borrow ten dollars "for some FOOD!" Strapping on a banjo and playing expertly, he called for a sing-along, dividing the room into men and women and then "this half of the room . . . now, *this* half," but also "Now, this two-thirds, and this one-third . . . and this three-fifths, and this two-fifths . . ."

But what killed me was a moment when he picked up a sheet of paper off the stage, announced that it was a list of his jokes and routines, and started checking them off aloud, trying to figure which ones might work for this crowd and which might go over our heads.

He came on my show and—of course—proceeded to do a series of sight gags. "It's nice to be here," he began, seated at his microphone. Then he stood up and stepped away. "No, it's nice to be *here*," he said. He walked over to and behind a bank of transmitter equipment and shouted, "Actually, it's nice to be *here*."

Although *Rolling Stone* demanded most of my time and required travel, I rarely missed a Sunday at the station and made myself available to substitute for others. On occasion, the all-night announcer, Edward Bear, would ring me up late at night to ask if I could fill in for him. When I could, I'd experiment with musical mixtures of pop and jazz; I'd play wild routines by Richard Pryor, with Miles Davis pulsing underneath. On the all-night shift, anything could happen. Women called to invite me over, or to invite themselves over. One morning, a woman who identified herself as a topless dancer offered to do an in-studio appearance. Why not? She was a pale, slim young woman who seemed to do her best communicating with her body. She took off her clothes and began a blend of belly dancing and the sort of free-form writhing commonly seen at rock concerts, something one *Rolling Stone* staffer, Cindy Ehrlich, nailed as "the Woodstock sun grope."

Toto, I thought, we're not at KFOG any more.

I was riding high, working at two of the standard-bearers of the youth culture, traveling around the country with stars of pop, rock, and R&B music, and writing about them. Then, on weekends, I could go on the most popular station in town and play radio.

I had, for now, left Chinatown and its myriad problems to others.

The more effective my brother Barry was with the kids in Richmond, the more he began to hear from friends and co-workers who knew of other places where his services might be put to good use.

"Why," he was asked, "are you working with black kids in Richmond when there's so much to be done in Chinatown?" He had no ready response. He was committed to his work with the Dynamic Youth Group, but he'd also thought of San Francisco as an adopted city. It was his favorite place to visit.

He couldn't help knowing all about the problems in Chinatown. It had been eight or nine years since his term paper on the low incidence of delinquency among Chinese youth and his prediction that a new and more Americanized generation would be more prone to criminal activity.

By 1971, delinquency was too clinical a word for what was going on in Chinatown. People were being killed in the streets; merchants were being extorted; gangs were at war not only with each other but with community leaders and cops.

In spring of 1971, an opening for a director was announced at the Youth Service and Coordinating Center. The YSC, as it was known, had opened only a few months before, in the fall of 1970. It would provide services to delinquent and predelinquent youth in the Chinese community, attempting to divert kids from crime by offering various services. Its staff included a social worker, employment specialist, recreation activities coordinator, police-community relations officer, parole officer, probation officer, school counselor, lawyers, and youth workers.

But by the following May, the original director, a scholar and civil rights activist named Ling-Chi Wang, announced his resignation. He wanted to move on to another community group, and the YSC board began a search for a new director. Barry applied immediately, and he impressed Ling-Chi as an idealistic young man deeply affected by what he'd been hearing about Chinatown and eager to do something about it. "I really want to come back to the community," Barry told Ling-Chi over coffee.

For Barry, the job sounded like the perfect avenue into Chinatown. He had worked with young people in the East Bay; now he'd be working with young Chinese. He had done his work as a probation officer; now, he'd be heading an agency that included law enforcement officers as part of its staff.

He met with the board of directors and impressed them as the perfect new director. Barry had established a reputation as a streetwise youth worker who was, at the same time, a law enforcement professional. On top of that, he came across as a dedicated young man with a sense of obligation to do something for Chinatown.

When the board signaled its interest in him, Barry asked for and got a one-year leave of absence from the Contra Costa Probation Department. He'd be due back in Richmond in June of 1972.

During the interview process, he was told that his would be a sensitive position, that he'd be perceived as an outsider and a cop. Barry knew that Chinatown was no Richmond. Still, as he told one friend, "I have to do it. I'm supposed to work with my own people."

He told Kate that he thought he was entering dangerous territory. One day, he was talking with Norma—his *Mui-Mui*. They had always spoken freely about both their personal and professional lives. But now he put up an uncharacteristic guard.

"It's better for your own safety that you know as little as possible," he said.

On a visit to the restaurant in Hayward, he spoke to our mother about his new job. He knew she'd be alarmed, and she was.

"Don't go," she said in Cantonese. "Full of bad boys."

"They're only bad because they don't have good families," said Barry, in halting Chinese. "You taught us how to be good; I can teach them. I want to try."

Mother shook her head. She knew about the time I had been beaten, and she had read articles about gangs in both Hong Kong and the Bay Area.

"Those people carry knives," she said.

"I know," said Barry. "They have guns, too."

"And for such a dangerous job, you make more money?"

"No, *Ma-Ma*. Less."

Mother guessed that Barry had already accepted the job. If not, he had certainly made up his mind. She gave up.

"Be careful," she said, trying not to sound as wary as she felt.

·· 2 0 ··

INTO A

MINE FIELD

IN OLD AGE, LIFE'S AFFAIRS
ARE SUPPOSED TO LEAVE ONE AT PEACE;
HOW COULD I FORESEE THAT EVERY MORNING
AS SOON AS I AWAKE, THERE'S GRIEF?

—*Yuan Mei, Eighteenth Century*

Barry strode brashly into the mine field that was Chinatown in 1971. He learned quickly that Chinatown was a land of fractious factions, of turf battles, and modern-day versions of the old tong wars. Only now, for all he'd studied about his own people, there was nothing like having them in his face, demanding attention, services, and funds, while at the same time giving him the constant once-over, distrustful of him because he was an outsider, a probation officer, a liberal, a native-born—any identity could be the wrong one.

To those who worked with him at the Youth Service Center, he was somewhat of a mystery. He was a big brother to his staffers, but to older members of the Board of Directors, he was a renegade, a man who didn't appear at all to be a law enforcement officer. He dressed casually, wore his hair long, and developed a full moustache. He spoke the language of youth, of the streets.

And yet, to the kids in the streets, he was an outsider as well. His name didn't even sound Chinese. He came from somewhere over the Bay Bridge. And, as they saw more of him, they heard or noticed that he liked sports cars, that he enjoyed a nice meal out now and then, that he attended ballet performances and music concerts, that he liked to travel, and that he collected antique Chinese and Japanese swords and Asian arts and crafts.

In other words, he was bourgeois.

He wasn't, really. He lived in a sparse apartment on upper Grant Avenue in North Beach, the Bohemian/Italian neighborhood that increasingly interwove with Chinatown. Like most city and county employees, he was underpaid. It's just that he knew what he liked and saved up for the occasional objet d'art or *plaisir*.

While in Chinatown, Barry maintained contact with his friends in Richmond. He'd call to ask about his "kids." He kept photographs of two of them in his wallet. One girl signed her photo, "To a real saver."

Barry enjoyed life in Chinatown. He gobbled up Chinese culture, as if making up for all the years lost ignoring it. When I visited him at his apartment in the fall of 1971, he proudly showed off some of his antique swords. During the holidays, he went shopping for a gift for Father with Patricia, a Japanese friend who was in town from Hawaii.

Barry had encouraged our parents to sell the Bamboo Hut, to retire. Father was near seventy and was beginning to agree that it might be time to slow down. Barry decided on a present that would help keep him busy, and began going through stationery stores, looking for calligraphy brushes and special papers. A few days after Christmas, he invited our parents over for tea in Chinatown and introduced them to Patricia. Although she was Japanese, Mom and Dad put on their most gracious face. Back home in Oakland, however, they fretted.

"Nget-boin," my mother said. *Japanese.* "Worse than that white girl."

"He's working in Chinatown," my father said. "Maybe he will find a Chinese. Must."

In spring of 1972, while attending an Asian Mental Health conference in a San Francisco hotel, Barry met Gail Katagiri, an office worker at Japanese Community Services.

They were an immediate couple, although, in the fishbowl atmosphere of Chinatown politics, Barry's relationship with Gail had its risks. She represented the Japanese community—or "J-Town," as the Japantown area was commonly known. Chinatown and J-Town social agencies often went after money from the same public funds and were not particularly friendly. For Barry to openly escort Gail to community events—as he began to do in June—was tantamount to a political statement. When Gail invited Barry to a Japanese Community Youth Council function, she felt uneasy about bringing him onto her turf. The event was a dance and party to bring together Japanese and black social and youth groups, but, on Barry's arm, Gail felt like she was at a debutante ball, with all eyes on her for showing up with not only an outsider but the director of an ethnic fiefdom from across town.

Around the Youth Service Center, on Columbus Avenue in North Beach, just a few blocks from the heart of Chinatown, Barry kept his office door open, and he established a close relationship with most of his staff. But, as he had in Richmond, he also struck out on his own. He roamed the streets, absorbing all he could about Chinatown and its problems.

His independence put him at variance with the emphasis in Chinatown on group identity. Individuals tended not to be trusted.

Barry knew not to be too inquisitive. At his first meeting with Ling-chi Wang, the original director had advised him against doing what law enforcement people tend to do. "Don't be asking too many questions," Wang said. "You don't want to be perceived as an intelligence-gathering organization."

"Don't worry," said Barry. He didn't want to come across as too cocky; he knew he struck some people that way. But he could handle himself. In Richmond, he had an open-door policy, and he planned to work the same way in Chinatown. With kids hanging around the offices, it'd make no sense for him to be keeping dossiers on them.

He was right. Chinatown youth—some of them affiliated with various gangs—hung out at the Youth Service Center. Some of them got to know Barry, who looked and sounded like a sympathetic figure. But many of them also knew that he was here on leave from his actual job, as a probation officer.

A year into his time in Chinatown, according to a fellow officer, Barry sensed that he was getting in too deep. In mid-June, they had dinner, and Barry seemed confused and depressed. "It just doesn't work," Barry said. "You can't be friends to all sides." Not long ago, he was talking with the leaders of two groups he was working with. "We like you, but get out," said one of them. "You can't belong to both of us."

Gail, who saw Barry constantly, didn't think of him as feeling defeated. Barry felt he could reach the youths with whom he was working; that he knew what they were going through being ethnic minorities trying to gain an education and climbing the ladder while dealing with white society. And he felt that because he spoke a language that separated him from the older generation, he could express his commitment to the community.

Barry didn't appear frustrated to me. On Mother's Day, the family had gathered for dinner at a restaurant in San Francisco's Chinatown, and afterwards, Barry and I stayed in the bar for a drink.

The family had noticed that he was walking stiffly.

"Maw-yeh," he'd said. "It's nothing."

Now, in the bar, he fessed up.

"It's Gail," he said, smiling. "This girl I've been seeing. She's a back-breaker."

We laughed. With both of us mired in work, we rarely saw each other, and I hadn't known about Gail.

"What about Kate?" I'd always enjoyed seeing her.

Barry looked thoughtful. "Well, she's sort of around. I'm not sure. And there's Ellen I've told you about. But this Gail. I don't know. She's one of the most intelligent women I've ever met."

"And she's a back-breaker."

"Yeah. That doesn't hurt. Well, actually, it does."

We laughed again. I thought back to when we were boys, delivering papers and stealing magazines. We brought home our share of *Playboy* magazines. Under covers at night or, if we couldn't wait, in daylight with our door locked, we'd study the photographs, awed by the women.

We'd gone through awkward adolescences—mine more clumsy than his, I imagined. Barry was taller, more handsome, sportier, and all-around smoother than I. He probably actually read the articles in *Playboy*.

Now, in our young adulthood, neither of us lacked female company. While his latest relationship sounded promising, I had hopscotched through a dozen affairs in recent years. It wasn't a case of making up for a late start, and I didn't feel as if I were taking advantage of the libertine times. I figured I was just one of the millions of young men who thought of sex every—what was it I read once—fifteen minutes? Or was it seconds? And when it became readily available in my life, I did more than think. Sometimes, I did anything *but* think.

We toasted our many women, and then he talked a little about work.

"I'm thinking of changing jobs again," he said. His year's leave from the probation department in Richmond was up next month, and he had to make a decision—whether to return to the East Bay or extend his leave.

"Maybe I can stick around just a little longer, and then get back to my kids." He took a drink and let out a sigh. "I don't know."

Since my beating, I had steered clear of Chinatown matters, and had no advice to offer.

A couple of weeks ago, I told him, I covered the visit by the Ping-Pong team from China to Stanford.

"Looks like things are opening up between us," I said.

Barry nodded. "You know what that means," he said. "More people in Chinatown. Just what we need."

A month later, on the evening of June 21, Barry dropped by my apartment. He'd just visited our parents in Oakland, and they'd given him some *joong*—Chinese tamales that our dad made consisting of rice studded with boiled peanuts—and a sweet Chinese sausage called *lop cheung* to give me.

I filled Barry in on work. I was writing an obituary of the rhythm and blues great Clyde McPhatter, and editing a paperback anthology of articles, *The Rolling Stone Rock 'n' Roll Reader*. The weekend before, I'd interviewed Smokey Robinson and the Miracles, who'd broken up and were doing a farewell tour.

Barry, the guy who'd handmade our first record player, liked music but leaned toward folk, jazz, and classical music. Once, I got him tickets to a promotional party for Three Dog Night in Los Angeles.

"The dinner was good," he reported in a letter, but "the music was neither imaginative, creative, unique or memorable. The group was a typical plastic group of the L.A. genre, which tried too hard to be cute. So much for 3 dog nights."

Barry said he was wrapping up his work in Chinatown. "It's been pretty tough," he told me. "It'll be nice being just a probation officer again."

He mentioned that his apartment had been burgled the previous night. Only six weeks before, he had moved out of Chinatown and into the Sunset District, into a tiny, two-room apartment in back of one of the Sunset's typical stucco houses. Someone had made his way down the alley entrance and broken in through the kitchen door. But the burglar had taken only three rifles from Barry's collection of old weapons. His antique swords, a box of jade and rosewood pieces, his skis and bike, his TV and stereo, even some money he had given Gail for a new dress, which was on his bureau—all had been left alone.

Barry shrugged. He seemed mystified but unconcerned. He'd taken Dad to Lake Tahoe as a Father's Day gift, he said, and they'd won a couple hundred dollars. In his mind, the winnings helped balance the burglary.

I felt bad about his losses, and excused myself. From a closet, I fished out a street sign I had found in a junk shop and handed it to him.

"What's this?" he asked. The sign read ADELINE. That was the street where Moon's Chinese Kitchen was located in Emeryville.

"It's yours," I said. He shook his head.

"Thanks," he said, more for the gesture than for the old sign. "I don't really want a reminder of Moon's."

I told him I'd had a minor run-in with Mom. I'd mistakenly assumed that, at age twenty-seven, I knew how to live my life.

"Just go along with them," Barry said, instinctively including our father with our mother. "Be patient. They're the way they are, and the best thing to do is to give in a little."

"I can't do that," I began to argue.

"You have to, because they're not going to change. No matter how old you are, they're older. And they're *Ma-Ma* and *Ba-Ba*."

And Barry was a Number One son who was suddenly sounding like one. He was a youth counselor doing his work.

Five nights later, Barry and Gail were at his apartment, playing Scrabble and having champagne and popcorn. On the stereo was a favorite album, *A New Sound from the Japanese Bach Scene*— classical pieces played on the koto and other Japanese instruments. Barry drank lightly. In a little while, he would be driving to a local radio station to appear on a talk show. The subject: Chinatown ills.

It was about 11:20 when his doorbell rang. The sound jolted Barry and Gail. In his work, Barry received calls at all hours— but a visitor? Barry paused, puzzled, for just a second, then put on a pair of slippers and rose.

He went to one of the antique swords, touched it, and, with a solemn gleam in his eyes, told Gail: "I'd better take this with me. You never know." Then, leaving the sword behind, he entered the darkness of the alleyway toward the solid wooden door at the front of the main house, beside the garage.

It was there, in the dimness of the alley, that five shots rang out in quick succession, and Barry fell backwards.

Several people in the neighboring house heard the shots, and one of them called the police.

In Barry's apartment, Gail also heard a series of pops, but thought, for a split second, that they were firecrackers, that someone was joking with Barry. But that was only a momentary flash. She knew something was wrong. She went to the bathroom and listened out the window, which faced the alley, hoping to hear someone laughing. Hearing nothing, she was overtaken by dread. She stepped out into the alley and found Barry slumped on his side. She knelt beside him.

"Barry," she said. "Don't worry. I'm here." She got no answer. She ran back to the apartment, grabbed a blanket, and covered Barry. Afraid that he might already be dead, she could barely utter a word. She managed a few more words of reassurance, then ran back to the apartment to call the police. An ambulance came within minutes, and the crew quickly placed Barry into their vehicle and sped off to Park Emergency, a small hospital on the border of the Haight-Ashbury.

Police officers soon arrived and cordoned off the area. They noted where Barry's body had fallen. They saw that a large envelope and a white mortician's glove had been left near Barry. They began questioning Gail and several neighbors. The man who called the police had looked out a window that overlooked the alley, but saw no one running or driving off. Neither did his wife or son, whose bedroom adjoined the alley. But another neighbor, hearing the shots and looking out over his backyard toward Barry's apartment, said he saw a short, black-haired man in a gray outfit. He had seen this man walking nervously back and forth in the alleyway moments before the shooting, he said.

The witness said he also saw a taller male crouching on the rear staircase of a neighboring house, acting, the witness said, like a "lookout man." But the family living in that house said they saw no such men.

At *Rolling Stone* that day, I had done my usual deadline-day work. Now, at my apartment, I was editing stories for the anthology. It was getting on toward 12:30 when the phone rang.

The caller identified himself as Dr. Rolland Lowe. He was chairman of the Board of Directors of the Youth Service Center, he said, and he had some news about Barry. He had been shot, about an hour ago. Dr. Lowe's voice was low, his speech deliberate. "He was taken to Park Emergency, and he expired there."

"Weird word," I thought instinctively. What Dr. Lowe was saying took a second to sink in.

"Oh, no . . . *Barry*," I said. Dr. Lowe allowed me a few seconds of silence. He knew I was in shock.

He told me that I should notify the rest of the family; that I would have to go and identify Barry's body at the hospital. He told me a woman named Gail had been with Barry. I jotted down her address and phone number. He mentioned a Mr. Jang, Barry's landlord. I told Dr. Lowe I would go to the hospital, then to Barry's apartment to meet Gail and the police.

Yes, I would do all of this, I thought after I'd hung up. I stood. I could feel myself turning pale. I thought of our parents. They were asleep in Oakland. Oh, God, I thought. To have to awaken them with this news . . .

But these things had to be done. Something had happened, and it required a series of responses, no matter what time of day or night it was. I called Sarah in Mill Valley and told her what I'd heard. I was as straightforward as I could be; I didn't want to allow either of us to fall apart. Sarah, who'd grown to look at life with a cynical eye, and who had a sardonic sense of humor, was not one for sentiment. Without saying so to each other, we decided that grieving could wait, and we plunged into figuring out what had to be done. She would phone our parents and

Shirley, who would go to Oakland if necessary. Burton lived with our parents and would provide immediate support.

I went to my bedroom to prepare to leave. At the foot of the bed, I thought about what I'd just heard. None of it was real, yet. I thought about Barry's recent visit. *That* was real. He'd had a birthday less than two months ago, when he turned twenty-nine. How could he suddenly no longer exist?

"I'm not religious," I thought to myself. "I don't know how to pray." But I wanted to say something. I dropped onto my knees. "Barry," I said silently, "I don't know where you are or how you are, but I'll do everything I can to take care of you. And the family. I hope you're okay, that you're at peace. I'll see you soon."

At the hospital, a police officer ushered me into a rear room, where Barry's body lay on a table. I took a quick look, told the officer, "It's Barry," and began to leave. But I couldn't. I had to touch him once more before letting him go. I put my hand on his shoulder, and a thought flashed through my mind: Maybe this was just a joke, and he'd be springing up with that wicked, mustachioed grin of his.

After learning where his body would be taken, I drove out to the Sunset, to Barry's apartment.

Gail greeted me. We had not met before, but we were suddenly, intimately connected. She was obviously numbed by what had happened. She introduced me to a policeman and went off to talk with a roommate and several friends who had come to comfort her.

When I was finished with the police, Gail told me she wanted to talk. I drove us around until we found a twenty-four-hour coffee shop.

They had met only two months before, but Gail seemed to know and understand Barry's work. She mentioned the burglary of Barry's apartment. "He didn't make a big deal out of it," she said, but there must have been a connection. Barry didn't talk much about work. Barry thought of Gail as part of the precious little private life that he had. Still, she knew about a few recent incidents.

Barry, she told me, had helped a gang acquire a police permit for a dance. Just before that dance, she said, a member of that gang had been shot on a Chinatown street. Barry may have gotten to know the leaders of that gang enough that he somehow angered leaders of a rival gang, she said.

This was all beyond me. I couldn't imagine Barry, with his street smarts, and having had a year of Chinatown under his belt, making such a mistake. All I knew was that in the two years since I'd been beaten, the stakes for running afoul of the gangs had been raised to a murderous height.

Gail and I talked about Barry and a bit about ourselves; sometimes, we just stared off into space. Neither of us could fathom doing something as normal as going to sleep—lying down, resting, succumbing to dreams—when Barry had just died.

While we talked, Ling-Chi Wang was at home, listening to the radio. His wife, a health worker, was scheduled to be on the same talk show for which Barry had been booked. When he failed to show up, the program about Chinatown problems went on without him. Now, it was being interrupted for a news bulletin: A Chinatown youth worker, Barry Fong-Torres, had been murdered.

Ling-Chi turned pale.

An

Uncommon

Death

At the start of Tuesday, I began to telephone people, to let them know what had happened and to ask for help. Before heading for Oakland, Sarah and I met at Barry's apartment. Sarah nearly broke, but managed to hold together. We began to make funeral plans, leaving final decisions dependent on our parents' wishes.

Sarah's husband Dave drove us to Oakland, and by the time we arrived, Shirley and her husband Rich were there, and numerous family friends had rallied around our parents. Grace Fung, their oldest friend and neighbor, was there, along with Helen Moon of Moon's Chinese Kitchen. They were busy wrapping coins and candy into red envelopes, to be handed out at the wake and funeral.

Mother looked ten years older. She'd been up all night, crying.

Dad looked calm, but he, too, had broken down, then spent much of the night awake, sitting in silence. Burton, red-faced with the pain of loss, grieved silently, succumbing to occasional outbursts of anger. For several years, Barry had made it a point to visit whenever possible, once or twice a month, and to take Burton out for some socializing—a quick dinner, a movie, an evening playing pool or pinball at an arcade. He had become one of Burton's few friends as well as a good older brother.

Sarah and I told our parents about possible places for the funeral and burial, and they made their choices. Dad had already written an obituary for the Chinatown papers. I would contact Gordon Lew and ask him to preside over the services.

Long after having moved out of the flat I'd shared with Tom Gericke and various others, I'd continued to drop in for visits. This night, I would stay with Tom and his girlfriend.

All we could do was keep busy. The next day, Sarah and I returned to Barry's place, with Tom and Sarah's longtime friend Annie, to clear out furniture and clothing. While we were there, I got a call from a woman friend in Los Angeles who I'd been seeing; she promised to come up for the services. I found that friends were the hardest people to talk with. Like rolling surf, the emotions built, and overwhelmed.

While Tom and Annie helped clean up, Sarah and I were off to Barry's Berkeley apartment. We had to find an outfit for Barry. It'd either be sportswear or his favorite suit. We proceeded to Mountain View Cemetery, where Father was waiting for us, along with Shirley. She had given birth to a girl, Tina, less than three months before Barry's death.

Some of their friends were buried here, Dad said. We drove to the highest reaches of the cemetery. Around Plot 75, my father marched from the concrete road and onto the gently sloping grassy area. He moved with authority, from spot to spot, like a human chess piece. And then he stopped.

"Here," he said firmly in our native Cantonese. "Barry will have a lot of sunshine here." He looked to the corner of the plot. "There are trees nearby. And he can see Oakland and San Francisco all together."

He studied the marble stones embedded at the head of each grave. He would compose some thoughts, he said, and write them out in Chinese.

Back in San Francisco, looking for Barry's car keys and address book, I came across a sheaf of loose pages from one of those large Chinese calendars Chinatown banks and other merchants hand out, and that many families use—in every room—as inexpensive wall decorations. On the back of several pages, Dad had done some calligraphy with the pen and brushes Barry had bought for him—and Barry had saved them. I couldn't help smiling.

But all around us, tension was in the air. The papers were reporting that inside the envelope left beside Barry's body was a note reading: PIG INFOMERS DIE YONG. The police denied even knowing Barry, and investigators later dismissed the note as a ruse. Still, the idea of Barry being thought of as an informer was discomfiting.

After we found the keys to Barry's car, Sarah and her friend Annie went out to Barry's apartment. She would take the car to Oakland, to store at our parents' place. As Sarah approached the '66 Mustang, she was suddenly gripped with paranoia.

"God," she said, "Do you think it might be wired to a bomb?"

"No," said Annie. "Can't be."

Sarah wasn't so sure. She went to the landlord, Mr. Jang, and used his telephone to call the police and have them dispatch a bomb expert.

Back outside, as time passed and no police appeared, Sarah became impatient. She got out of her own car and headed toward the Mustang. "Stand back," she said. "I'm gonna start this mother!"

Annie jumped out of Sarah's car to join her. "If you're goin', *I'm* goin', too!" she said.

With teeth clenched, Sarah inserted the key and turned the

engine. It started. Without waiting for the police, Sarah and Annie drove off to Oakland.

That evening, I went to my apartment for the first time, but found myself incapable of staying there, alone. I drove around aimlessly, still stunned.

The next day, Thursday, Kate materialized. We had been calling her, to no avail. Now, she'd tracked us down—and just in time to help with final details of the funeral services. To give friends enough time to travel to the Bay Area, and because of the Fourth of July holiday weekend, we set the wake for Sunday evening and the funeral for the next day.

In looking through some of Barry's photographs, we had spotted a shot of the Ben Shahn poster with the saying: "You have not converted a man because you have silenced him." That, I thought, would be an appropriate thing to hand out at the services. But we couldn't find the poster. Kate recognized the work. Barry had hung the poster in his office in Richmond. We went to her apartment, in the Marina district of San Francisco, where she had a book containing the poster.

Through the recent years, and through the various women she knew Barry had seen, Kate had the feeling that she came first, and that, someday, they'd get together.

"I'm just so sad that we lost touch," Kate said. "He changed my life tremendously. He got me to go back to school, to think I could do much more than fly." She looked away for a moment. "I keep thinking that he gave so much, and that he got short-changed himself."

She went on: "He was always so in tune to other people, so concerned with them, where they were psychologically and emotionally. And he was always so giving that often his own needs were not met."

What Kate said eerily echoed something I'd heard from Gail, who remembered Barry being the picture of confidence and self-assurance—almost, sometimes, to the point of arrogance. Except for one moment.

"He felt that time and time again he'd give so much of himself, either to Chinatown or to a woman, and what does he get? He said, 'You hear people saying you should serve the people and help the community. But when does Barry Fong-Torres get something? What's the payoff?' It was the only time I saw him with tears in his eyes."

On Monday afternoon, four hundred people crowded into the Albert Brown Mortuary. As people entered the chapel, *A New Sound from the Japanese Bach Scene* played on Barry's own turntable.

I watched the guests filing by Barry's open casket on their way to their seats. They looked sober, disturbed, pained, sullen, sad. Friends who spotted me would nod, and with those nods, I read anxiety, empathy, respect. There were many familiar faces: My friends from *Rolling Stone* were there; two of the delivery men from Moon's Chinese Kitchen attended, along with Moon Moo and Bong, our old bosses. There were family friends—there was our old barber, Git Moo, and our family physician, Dr. Yee; friends of Barry's from childhood on—"Fungus" and *Mui-Mui*; board members, co-workers, and peers from his and other youth agencies; leaders of youth groups in Chinatown. There were the kids he'd worked with in the Dynamic Youth Group in Richmond.

Gordon Lew stepped to the pulpit and recited Barry's biography:

Barry's life exemplifies a life of service and dedication. To the betterment of society, to improve the distorted relationships between men, and specifically in service to problem youths, Barry gave of his time, his talents, his energy, and, finally, his life.

We are sad and troubled.

We are sad to lose a dear friend.

We are sad to see a fine and beautiful life cut short.

We are sad to see parents in their middle years bury their children.

But we are also frustrated and enraged. For this was not a common death. This was not the tenth Chinatown gang murder; this was the first. The first murder committed against someone who was not a gang member. The first against the head of a social service organization. The first against an innocent victim.

Barry's death was not a common death.

He was not born and raised in Chinatown. He didn't have to come to Chinatown to work in this critical area or at such a difficult time. But he came. When his year's leave was up, he could have packed up and gone. But he stayed. He came because he cared. And he stayed because he was concerned. Barry's death was not a common death. This is the death of a person of care and compassion. And whenever such a person dies, heaven and earth mourn deeply.

Looking at the recent events from our community's standpoint, Barry's death is like the ringing of bells and the sounding of gongs . . . In the villages of China, the sounding of gongs is a signal of emergency. Certainly, no one would deny that this is an emergency. But do not forget, the sounding of gongs is also a rallying call.

It calls those of us who have been avoiding participation in community affairs to become involved.

It calls those of us who have been silent to speak out.

It calls those of us who have been condemning the lack of communication within our community to lend a hand to bridge the gaps.

It calls those of us who have been walking side by side with him to pick up the responsibilities and march on.

Barry's death is not a common death.

His death could be a turning point.

When the mourners arrived for the service, family friends handed out small copies of the Ben Shahn poster. Now, as they left the chapel, they each received one of the red envelopes of coins and candy that Grace Fung and Helen Moon had prepared.

The coin symbolized a wish for good fortune; the sweets, erasure of the bitter taste of loss.

At the Mountain View Cemetery, a man with a vaguely familiar face came up to me. It was William Fung—"Fungus" of the model airplane destruction derbies and the water balloon wars. Bill had served as one of Barry's pallbearers.

With our backs to the grave, we had before us a sweeping panorama of Oakland, our hometown, and San Francisco beyond.

Bill looked down. What could he say?

"I feel ashamed," he managed. "Here's Barry, doing so much good, and I'm just having a family. I'm just ... existing." He gripped my arm, then turned away.

I found myself feeling ashamed for wholly other reasons. Looking around the chapel at all those sad and sober faces, and, now, near the top of Mountain View, I suddenly felt something that can only be described as *seet-meen*. For no logical reason, I felt consumed by a sense of personal failure because my brother had died the way he did. He had been taken from his family, his friends, and his community in such a public way, one that invited clusters of reporters, with their notepads, cameras, and questions, one that tainted him guilty, until proven innocent, of compliance with the gangs or of being an informer.

Despite the comforting blankets of sympathy, the words from those who knew better, I felt as though we were the accused, the indicted, the wrongdoers.

After the services, we, the children, went to our parents' apartment. By Chinese custom, parents do not attend funerals for their children. Younger members of the family take on the responsibilities of seeing off the departed. Instead, our parents saw friends at the wake at the mortuary the evening before.

There, they also saw Barry for the last time. Sarah and I decided against a suit; Barry always looked sharp in sports clothes. We chose a black turtleneck shirt and a muted green sport coat. He wore two necklaces—one made by a friend from Hawaii; the other, from Kate. The day of the wake, we found his favorite jade carving and placed it in his hand. At the mortuary, our father left a piece of poetry he'd written for Barry with him. Throughout the hour of visitations, my mother wailed as we'd never heard her before. No one could console her; not any of the dozens of friends and cousins, people from the same villages from which our parents came. They found themselves shaking their heads and groping for words.

But no one had more difficulty than her own children. In the worst of times, we didn't know what to say—at least not in words that each other could fully understand.

I wanted to tell them about the things I most wished I could believe; that there was a spirit world beyond ours, and that Barry was there. I wanted to be able to tell them the specifics of the case, as much as had been pieced together so far. Bits of information and misinformation as they were, I felt they had the right to know what was being said. And I wanted them to know that I had contacts through whom I could stay abreast of the case. The police couldn't know everything, but there had to be people who did.

But I was helpless; I could neither articulate those thoughts nor act on them. They had, right away, forbidden me from getting involved in any investigation.

There was no discussion. Just, *Mm-haw.* "Don't."

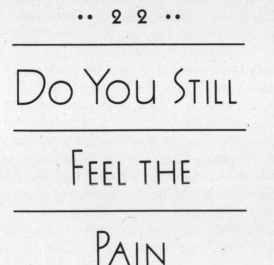

·· 22 ··

Do You Still

Feel the

Pain

On July 3, the San Francisco Board of Supervisors adjourned its regular meeting out of respect to the memory of Barry and informed our family of its "deep sympathy and heartfelt condolence."

Backstage at Winterland Arena, the Jefferson Starship had just played. Tonight, the producers had placed several tables along the walls and laden them with catered food and drink for the guests of the Starship.

I was not in that room. At her invitation, I had followed Grace Slick, lead vocalist with the Starship and someone I'd known since her days with the Airplane, to the band's quarters. I had long thought of Grace as one of the few rock musicians truly worth talking with. As fucked up as she could get on drink and drugs, she mesmerized me with her candor, her humor, her fury.

There was something she wanted to say. She sat and locked me into her frosty blue eyes.

"I'm sorry about your brother," she said. "I just wish I could get whoever did it. I'd lock 'em up in a room. Just them and me. Give me fifteen minutes with them. And you know what I'd do? I'd do what they did to your brother." She lifted a glass and drank.

I nodded and thought that this was a woman I would always love, as if she were my own sister.

A few weeks after Barry's death, my mother called in alarm.

"You should come home," she said. "*Ba-Ba* has his gun out. He wants to find whoever killed Barry."

I rushed to their apartment. My father had bought the gun—a .32 Winchester revolver—in the forties to keep at his restaurants. We'd get a glimpse of it now and then, and, once, a very young Burton climbed a stepladder to take it out of a hallway shelf so that he could play cowboy. The pistol wasn't loaded, and Burton was discovered before he could locate any bullets. The gun, we were warned, was off limits.

Now, I was taking it away from my father. He put up no resistance. Mom gave me the gun, which was in a wrinkled old paper bag, and Dad just sat in his high-back lounge chair, staring off into nowhere.

Our family had little reason to invest our faith in the police department or city officials. A few days after Barry's assassination, Mayor Joe Alioto called a meeting of police officials and intelligence agents. He promised to give Chinatown his "immediate attention," but said he wasn't particularly interested in reestablishing the Chinatown police detail, which went after gambling dens and prostitution rings. That unit was phased out two years before, reportedly after Chinatown leaders exerted political pressure on the police department.

The mayor said he wasn't sure what steps the police would take, but he took pains to assure outsiders that, despite the fact that Barry was the tenth murder victim connected to Chinatown problems in two years, the area was "the safest place in town for tourists and Caucasians."

Meantime, the investigators at the Hall of Justice were stumped. Despite what appeared to be an abundance of clues at the scene of the shooting, they seemed clueless.

Kate was called in for an interview. The homicide investigator who questioned her seemed to have no understanding of who Barry was. He appeared to be more interested in what a nice white girl was doing running around with a Chinaman like Barry. He asked her whether or not Barry might have been a heroin dealer. He gave Kate the once-over more than once, and he asked her about her work as a flight attendant, about whether she might like to continue their conversation over lunch.

Gail was equally outraged by her interview. First, the officer floated a theory involving a rivalry between Chinatown and Japantown, then asked questions not only about her and Barry but about her former boyfriend as well. In fact, he said, they'd like to talk with him.

"You think this is a love triangle thing?" said Gail, appalled at the officer's seeming ignorance of recent Chinatown history. He dropped that line of questioning.

Aside from the obvious connection between Barry's killing and his work with Chinatown youth, the police actually had reason to link Barry with gangs. Two weeks before the shooting, an officer told Gail, Barry filed a report saying he'd been jumped on Stockton Street in Chinatown by three young men. Barry said he couldn't identify any of the assailants, and the police officer made it clear that he didn't believe Barry.

Gail was shocked; she'd seen Barry regularly and he'd never mentioned or showed signs of a beating. When I saw him on June 21, he said nothing—and, with me having been the subject of a similar attack two years before, he likely would have mentioned it to me. But if, as the police suspected, Barry was holding back information about his attackers, why would he have bothered to file a report at all?

Our family never heard from the police. But we knew that Barry had never been a police informer. And it was unlikely that he'd upset one gang by aligning himself with another. He was too smart, too tuned in to politics to get himself into such a crossfire.

The police developed several theories and came to favor one: A Chinatown gang had tried to muscle into positions of power within the Youth Service Center, so that it could gain a greater control of funds. Barry resisted its efforts. The gang leader put out a contract on him. But the police department's homicide division never proved that or any other theory. The case remains officially open.

Despite Mayor Alioto's cheerleading for Chinatown as a "safe place for tourists and Caucasians," the violence continued. Three months after Alioto's declaration, a gang invaded the Palace Theater looking for members of a rival group. Shots were exchanged, and four youths were arrested. Two ringleaders were at large.

While the gangs continued to wage war on each other, youth workers became an endangered species around Chinatown.

Barry's death, Gordon Lew had said, was like the sounding of gongs, calling for involvement in community affairs, for picking up Barry's responsibilities and marching on. But Barry's assassination scared off a lot of good people. Kate stayed in touch with a prominent attorney connected to Chinatown. "Ever since Barry," the lawyer told her, "a lot of people got out of youth work."

Gail continued with her social work in J-Town and maintained contact with Chinatown workers, who told her they were either lying low or getting out. "Look," said one of them, "you bust your ass and give everything for the community, and look what happens."

The Youth Service Center redefined itself shortly after Barry's death. No longer would it deal with youth in trouble with the law. Instead, it would focus on prevention, and on helping kids before they got into trouble. In other words, it would have nothing to do with gangs.

Nine days after Barry's murder, I returned to *Rolling Stone*, but I was only half there. Sarah and I were now working out a memorial scholarship fund in Barry's name; we had an attorney working on workmen's compensation payments to our parents. The minutiae of a sudden death are unending.

Phone calls were a jumble of business, sympathy, and advice. Dexter Waugh, a reporter for the *San Francisco Examiner* who'd known Barry and covered his funeral, wanted to write about him for a magazine. We talked about a series of articles about Chinatown that had appeared in San Francisco's morning paper, the *Chronicle*.

Dexter said one of the reporters on that series, a Chinese-American woman, had to leave town because she was getting threats.

Two days later, the reporter, who said she was in hiding, called and warned me to stay out of Chinatown for six months— minimum.

I immersed myself in *Rolling Stone*. The magazine, now nearly five years old, had moved to larger offices in the South of Market, and there were forty of us on the staff. As corny as it sounds, we were family. To some outsiders, we were the Manson family, and we were by no means simply an oversized nuclear unit. There were love affairs among us, many broken hearts, and more than a few disownings and runaways. In a deadline-driven business requiring creativity, chutzpah, salesmanship, and plain hard sweat, we worked well together. In off-hours, we played well.

And now, we had our first death in the family. In our twenties, most of us had more experience with rock and roll deaths—Otis Redding, Jimi Hendrix, Janis Joplin, Jim Morrison, Brian Jones— than with direct, personal loss.

For my co-workers, Barry's death forced open a part of my life that had been unknown to them. They knew me as a hard-working editor and writer of everything from "Random Notes" to ten-thousand-word cover stories; as a Wenner loyalist who survived various staff upheavals by eschewing office politics; and, as editor of the music section, a tough sell to publicists and artists' managers. I was also known as a mimic of Top 40 deejays, concert promoter Bill Graham, Hunter S. Thompson (who'd catapulted into stardom with his drug-soaked "gonzo" journalism), and Jann himself. And I didn't mind a laugh at my own expense. One day, Sarah Lazin, an editorial assistant, looked out a rear window to the employees' parking lot and discovered her space empty.

"Hey," she called out. "Has anybody seen my little yellow Rover?"

"I'm right here," I yelled.

But the voices and wisecracks shielded most of my personal life. Sure, the staff knew about relationships—on that level, secrecy was impossible—but I rarely exposed my emotions.

For a couple of years, the editorial side was in the hands of Jann, Paul Scanlon, and me. Paul wore his heart on his sleeve, and Jann hid none of his feelings, idiosyncrasies, or habits from his staff.

I kept my stuff inside, and when I had a bad day—whether because a writer or a story had fallen through, or there was a rift in the family—Jann and Paul would sit in Jann's corner office wondering what was going on with me.

"Who knows?" Jann said one night. "He's just inscrutable."

If I'd let my fellow workers in on what I was going through that summer, they'd have thought I'd gone nuts. By most appearances, I was back to my breakneck pace, doing cover stories on Three Dog Night and Santana, and plotting a major interview with Ray Charles.

But beneath my inscrutable surface, I was a different man, and had been since the earliest hours of June 26.

·· 2 3 ··

LOVE THE

ONE

YOU'RE WITH

Barry remained an undercurrent in everything I did. Doing the Santana story, I interviewed Bill Graham, who was their manager, and when he said something about how close Carlos was to his brother Jorge, I thought of Barry and broke into tears. Lazing away a weekend morning in front of the television, I was watching the Olympics when the Arab terrorists attacked Israeli athletes—and thought of Barry being shot.

In those first days after Barry's death, I received a sympathy card from Dianne Sweet, a former schoolmate at college. I remembered her being a Homecoming Queen attendant one year and being Homecoming chairman the next. She'd bring press releases and photographs to the newspaper office.

Dianne remembered me as a short, bespectacled editor at the

campus daily who looked more like a high schooler than a college student.

At S.F. State, Dianne majored in sociology—more because it was a "loose" major, one that allowed more choices of elective classes, than because of any career goal. She didn't know what she wanted to do, but became a counselor at the Youth Guidance Center.

Now, she was a probation officer in San Francisco. She'd married and divorced. She lived just a few blocks from me. And she'd begun listening to KSAN. On Sundays, her routine included gardening in the afternoon, with the radio on in the background. She reacquainted herself with me over the radio, where she liked my choice of music and my penchant for being absolutely personal. Whatever I was doing or feeling got on the air. Fresh off a visit with Ike and Tina Turner, I'd tell about the friend who looked at their garishly decorated house—with its guitar-shaped furniture, astrological clocks, and fake waterfall— and said to Ike: "You mean you can actually spend $70,000 at Woolworth's?" If there was a big 49ers game going on, I might flick on a portable TV set and air some of the play-by-play over the mike.

In spring of 1972, Dianne called me at the station to get a lost-dog notice on the air. She was listening in a few weeks later when I did a woe-is-me show after a breakup with a woman I'd been seeing, and invited me over for a glass of wine.

I found her lovelier than ever; she had a glamorous glow that conjured lustrous movie stars of the past, like Jennifer Jones and Elizabeth Taylor. Her voice was melodious; her home, warm and settled, evoking a New England cabin.

She claims she found me—in my rimless glasses, Beatle hair, moustache, flowery shirt, and bell-bottom pants—far less dorky than she remembered.

She had sent a sympathy card. I contacted her and visited again, bringing over a few albums for her. Dianne thought of herself as conservative; during and after the fabled Summer of

Love, she was engaged, then married to a jazz fan. She'd missed out, and her only link to the scene was KSAN. She didn't even know much about *Rolling Stone* or my work there, but she was interested. She invited me to a party with her fellow probation officers a week or two later. Before the night was over, we knew we'd be seeing more of each other.

What Dianne didn't know was that there was, on the immediate horizon that summer, another woman.

It was Michelle, the girl I'd known and loved in college. She heard about Barry's death a week after and wrote. We had not seen each other for two years, back when, she remembered, I was still limping from my Chinatown beating, and we were talking about mutual dilemmas in an inherited ghetto.

"I have always been more than fond of you," she wrote. "There are so many parallels between your family and mine, and this latest blow hits home." She promised to get in touch the next time she visited from New York.

She came for a week in September. We talked one night until 4 A.M., and, a few days later, I took her to Oakland for dinner at my parents'. It was the first time I'd ever done such a thing, and they seemed stunned. I could feel them judging Michelle, the way they scrutinized all our friends. But I could also sense them reining in their critical devices. This, after all, was *Ben*—with a *Chinese girl*! Michelle said all the right things, as many of them in Chinese as she could.

I had already visited at her family's apartment. It was like old times, seeing her sisters and brother. I remember immediately liking the idea of adding a new brother to my family circle.

After dinner, back in San Francisco, Michelle and I summarized our thoughts. We had a tremendous affection for each other, and we were in harmony on the essential things in life; those things included our families. If we were to be together, it had to be because we wanted each other. But we also knew that the bonus—the happiness of our respective parents—was a big factor in our decision.

We had reached a turning point in our lives. We had discussed marriage. There was only one obstacle: real life.

Michelle had a home in New York, where she lived with a musician. He was not husband material, but, still, they were together. New York was also important to Michelle's work. Having given up music for the moment, she had turned to journalism. Now, she was exploring broadcast work and had hooked up with a radio network as a reporter. She couldn't easily give up such a job.

In San Francisco, I told Dianne about Michelle. Dianne was nonplussed. She wasn't all that interested in a full-time relationship with me, and she even saw the challenge of being an "other woman." She enjoyed going out to concerts, for which I always seemed to have great seats and backstage access, although one of her favorite shows had been a Boz Scaggs concert in Berkeley for which, she happily reminded me on occasion, she secured better tickets through the box office than I had with all my connections. Dianne and I also caught Elvis Presley at the Oakland Coliseum. It was my first time seeing my rock and roll idol; Dianne had seen him at the Oakland Auditorium in 1956, when he was at his first frenzied height.

While I was in Chinatown reading my Elvis fan magazines, Dianne had caught the real thing. I was impressed.

In November, I took her to Palm Springs, where most of our top editors, along with a few people from advertising and the magazine's book division, were gathering at the summer home of millionaire Max Palevsky, who'd become an investor in *Rolling Stone* two years before, and his wife Linda. The staff had a few meetings, but we spent most of the long weekend either lounging by the pool or getting wrecked.

Hunter S. Thompson arrived on the second day, a Saturday. He showed up with his usual duffel bag of high-tech writing and rock and roll equipment. While the cooks and servants prepared dinner, he made the rounds, handing out pills of unknown make and effect. Thinking he'd already taken a couple, the dozen or so in our party played good sports and downed ours.

By the time we made it to the dinner table, we were uniformly wasted. At one point, I held my fork and knife over my prime rib and asked for directions.

Hunter, meantime, was sober for perhaps the first time in his adult life. He hadn't taken any of the pills. We abandoned dinner and staggered into the living room to watch some films Max had acquired; one was the work of Robert Downey, director of the irreverent *Putney Swope*. Whatever the film was, it was sensory overload for some of us, and we escaped to the pool. There, the last sight I remembered was Hunter, in Hawaiian shirt and Bermuda shorts, carrying a case of Roman candles in his left arm. With his right hand, he was trying to light a match, so that, in the darkness, he could read the directions on the box.

Inside, Dianne walked by the kitchen, where she noticed a tray loaded with individual desserts, ready to serve. The staff had apparently been frightened off by our behavior and fled the house. Dianne took a photograph of the abandoned tray, a souvenir of the time she got to know the people of *Rolling Stone*, up close and personal.

She was beginning to think of the two of us as a couple— until, on the eve of Thanksgiving, I took off for New York to meet with a few writers and editors and, of course, to see Michelle.

"You look tired," Michelle said, first thing. We were at the hotel room I had for two nights, while I was conducting magazine business. We rested, then took a subway to Chinatown for dinner—quick, just to see each other; to catch up. Friday would be our one full day together.

She spent Thanksgiving with her musician boyfriend and their social circle; I had dinner with a fellow *Rolling Stone* editor, then repaired to a funky little Greenwich Village apartment that Josh, one of our ad salesmen, had turned over to me for my last two nights in town. There, I edited my Ray Charles interview transcripts.

The Ray Charles story was a perfect example of the way things happened at *Rolling Stone*, a way I couldn't imagine happening at any other major magazine. In editorial meetings, all of the editors were expected to have story ideas based on news events and on which artists were on the charts, on the road, or on the way.

But we could also fantasize about stories we'd like to do—Elvis, Sinatra, Streisand, Brando—and chase our dreams right onto the pages of the magazine. All we had to do was make a case and secure the story. At the end of one meeting, I simply raised my hand when Jann asked for "any other ideas."

"Ray Charles," I said.

Done.

Charles was going through a dry spell at the time, but that didn't matter to us. He was musical history. And he was pleased to hear that we were interested in him. I met him in San Francisco, watched him making a new album in Los Angeles, running most of the control board himself, and caught up with him in Washington, D.C., where he did a concert.

In his hotel room, we did the formal interview, which turned out to be another Ray Charles show. Dressed in a turquoise flannel jumpsuit, he padded around in Chinese slippers. On a sofa, he never sat. He writhed; he almost fell onto his knee in search of a restful position. And whenever he was challenged or in any other way aroused, and wanted to punctuate a point, he'd stand and shout, "HEL-lo!"

I asked about Joe Cocker, the British blues singer who had a voice and delivery that were direct descendants of Charles, and who was getting the young record buyers Charles used to have.

He stood up.

"Listen, I'll tell you somethin'. Back maybe thirteen to fourteen years ago, they had ads in the paper where they were tryin' to find anybody to sing like me ... I guarantee Joe Cocker ain't *never* appealed more to the young people who raised me up. He appeals to the young *white* because he's white. Shit, man. That ain't a mad statement, that's just the truth."

He went on: "I say two things. First of all, in order for that guy to copy me, he gotta wait 'til I do it first. Now the second thing I feel, well, if you take this guy over me and he's just an imitation of me, then that says to me that I must be pretty damn good. Because I don't know nobody that you wanna copy that ain't worth a damn. All right, HEL-lo!"

The final manuscript was due whenever I got back to San Francisco. I couldn't find any scissors in Josh's apartment and wound up folding and tearing the transcripts, then taping them down, eleven thousand words' worth. On Thanksgiving night.

It was at Josh's, the next night, that Michelle and I finally made love. It had been seven years since we first went out; two years since we reconnected in Chinatown; two months since our heart-to-heart; two days since I got to town.

We had spent the afternoon shopping in the West Village. Over Irish coffee, we assured each other that we didn't need to rush. My anxious mother had given me a ring to present to Michelle as a gift from her, but when Michelle suggested getting me a ring, I suggested we wait until the next visit. She might still be a year or two away from getting to San Francisco. But our intentions were clear, and when we returned to Josh's place, we climbed onto the loft bedroom as if it were our wedding night.

After an initial bout of shyness, we made slow, easy love, each of us making a trip down to change records on the turntable until, finally, we resorted to the radio.

The next day, I was back to San Francisco, where, at the airport, I was greeted by Dianne. With her was her dog, Puppy, a sweet-tempered blend of Pekingese and poodle who was the reason she called me that spring day at KSAN.

I loved that about Dianne—that she would name a dog "Puppy," simply because she hadn't come up with an actual name. (She also had a cat named "Kitty.") I also liked how settled she was in her home life and in her profession.

I liked Dianne enough that I hurt her deeply one evening, just after returning from New York. I couldn't keep secrets from her, and I told her about my long-term plans with Michelle. Our common backgrounds and our families were factors, I said. But, not wanting to sound like I was entering into some modern-day arranged marriage, I hastened to say that I loved Michelle. By doing so, I was implying that I loved Dianne less.

But I did more than imply; I said it. Maybe I was hoping for a clean break. Michelle had no set timetable for a return to San Francisco, and I'd be keeping Dianne in a limbo of the worst kind. Maybe I was being an immature jerk, the way I'd been years before when girls were a new phenomenon, and I had no idea of how to handle or conduct myself with them.

What was my weakness, that I'd be so unsubtle, so unkind? Was I so insecure that I'd have to inflict pain on people I cared about, at a time when they needed gentleness?

There had been times when I was at the other end of a tough break. But just because I'd hurt didn't excuse my hurting others. Those moments, I wanted to think, weren't the real me. They were the unformed me, still awed to attract attention from the opposite sex, still anxious to please, still so artless when it came to severance that I'd choose naked candor, hurtful truths, over diplomatic words that would soften any blows. I was making my living with words, but, at times, no one would have guessed it.

Fortunately, Dianne wasn't in her line of work for nothing. She had resilience and patience, and, for reasons still unclear to me, she loved me. She resolved to stay with me and weather whatever lay ahead of us, and by the beginning of 1973, we had settled into a routine, seeing each other regularly.

In the summer, Michelle came to town. She was working on a television documentary about Chinatown gangs for the PBS station in Washington, D.C. As part of her research, she spoke with a brother of one of the best-known gang leaders in Chinatown and, at one time, a suspect in Barry's murder. One day, she visited, and I was shocked to see her wearing a button with a photo of the young man.

"I can't *believe* you'd be wearing that," I said, my voice breaking.

She said she'd heard some persuasive things about the gang leader, that he was being persecuted by the police and the Chinatown establishment.

"No matter," I said. "This is a guy who might've been involved in my brother's killing. And besides, you're here as a journalist. What kind of objectivity is *that*?" I pointed at her button.

But Michelle stood her ground. Just as I was immersed in what was being called the New Journalism at *Rolling Stone*, in which strict objectivity was regarded as an impossibility and, in any case, often took a backseat to personal observations and involvement, she was a reporter with an activist edge. With her background in Chinatown, and as a musician, poet, and essayist, she found it second nature to be a champion of the underdog.

Disputes aside, Michelle blended easily into my family, and, during her visit, she visited my parents in Oakland and Sarah and Dave in Mill Valley. Michelle and I were inevitable.

But she was still based in New York; she was slowly extricating herself from her domestic situation, and she asked that I be patient.

I was in no position to be tapping my foot, demanding that she move. Michelle knew about Dianne, of course, but I didn't tell her exactly how much impact Dianne was having on my life. We now had friends who thought of us as a couple and knew nothing about Michelle. And, with Dianne's help, I was beginning to have my first real home.

She had done what she could with the contemporary sparseness, the white walls and gray carpeting of my apartment. In fall, she convinced me that I should move into a place with more character, and found me a Victorian flat near the heart of Japantown. While she let me decide on most of the furnishings— it still made no sense for her to invest too much of herself into my life—she was becoming a true and loving partner.

She shared in the fun of my work at *Rolling Stone*: a visit to the set of our favorite dance show, *Soul Train*; a trip to Vegas and a night on the town with Dick Clark, who she used to watch after school every day. We toasted my ASCAP–Deems Taylor Award for the Ray Charles interview and my being named to *Esquire* magazine's "Heavy 100 of Rock" list. She joined me sometimes at KSAN, and, one weekend in spring of 1973, survived a twelve-hour live broadcast from a Marin County studio, where bands ranging from Sammy Hagar to Sha Na Na performed.

I loved Dianne, but there was still one thing she did not share with me, besides my house and my name: my family. My parents knew nothing about Dianne; they were still waiting, as I was, for Michelle.

To Dianne, the specter of Michelle was unreal. She found it ludicrous that I could have this marriage pact with a woman who was living with another man in New York; that this wedding would take place whenever she managed to get out to San Francisco.

I agreed that the whole scenario sounded bizarre. But Dianne couldn't understand the cultural underpinnings to our plan, and I couldn't bring myself to again define the kind of love I had for Michelle. As unbelievable as it all seemed to Dianne, things were coming to a head. In April, I went to New York to appear, along with Grace Slick, David Crosby, and Jerry Moss of A&M Records, on Geraldo Rivera's first national television show, *Goodnight, America*. The subject was drugs and rock and roll. I saw Michelle, and she promised that she'd move to San Francisco by summer.

She arrived in mid-August, and we got right into gear. All the old familiar feelings—the the warmth, the comfort, the expectations—returned.

Two weeks after her arrival, however, I got a call from her. She was shaking. She said she'd seen me the previous afternoon with Dianne. We were in my car, stopped at a corner in Chinatown, she said. She couldn't believe it.

The day in question, I was helping plan a bachelor party for a fellow editor at *Rolling Stone*. Along with several other friends, I was at a restaurant on the Embarcadero the entire afternoon.

Also, I had not seen Dianne in more than a month. With Michelle's impending arrival, Dianne had put her foot down. She didn't want to see me or hear from me while my "fiancée"—she said the word so that the quotation marks were obvious—was in town. And Dianne didn't want to hear from me unless it was *she* who'd be the fiancée. Now, Michelle—who hadn't ever even seen Dianne—was accusing me of something I hadn't done. Despite my protests over several conversations, she refused to entertain even the possibility that she might be wrong.

One evening, she called Dianne, saying the two of them should get together, since they had something in common. Before Dianne could respond, Michelle casually referred to having seen Dianne and me together recently.

"You must be mistaken," Dianne told Michelle. "I haven't seen or talked to Ben in weeks."

In her attempt to prove that I'd been dishonest with her, Michelle had resorted to trying to deceive Dianne. Our relationship was unraveling, but Michelle still wouldn't back down. I was in an untenable situation. My only way out would be to say that she was right and ask her forgiveness. That, of course, was no way out.

There was something going on that she wasn't telling me. It had to do with doubt. Michelle and I had a sense that if we were committing ourselves (and our families) to marriage, it had better be perfect. Somehow, she feared it might not be, and conjured up a reason and rode it to the end of our relationship.

She didn't admit to that. In our last talk one evening at my flat, she insisted that she saw what she saw. "It was your car, and it was you with this woman."

I remembered how Michelle had responded when she first saw my dark green Audi in the *Rolling Stone* parking lot. As she looked it over, it was clear that she thought it too conservative, too square. She definitely knew my car.

I didn't want to go through another defensive recitation.

"You know what you're giving up," I said. "It's not just us."

"I know," she said. "My family likes you."

"And mine likes you. It's gonna be tough on them."

"Well," she said, "it's not easy for me."

Maybe I could have pushed further; forced her to talk with the editors who were with me that day; called for a cease-fire. But I was beginning to have my own doubts. If this was how she was responding to something she was wrong about, what did it portend for the future?

It was over.

But even as we broke up, the heat and anger had left us, and we felt love for each other, an affection and intimacy that had kept us in sync through the years we'd been apart and that overrode even this most critical of disputes.

She gave me a mischievous smile that I read instantly, and we made love one last time.

A few weeks later, I called Dianne to tell her the news. Now, we could talk about just us. If we were getting back together, she hoped it'd be for the long-term. After thinking over everything—and everyone who'd been in my life—I agreed. With all that had gone on around us, we'd been great together.

By October 1974, she had moved into my flat, and, soon, we set a wedding date: May 1, 1976. I couldn't face my parents alone with the news. Once more, I dragged Gordon Lew into my life, and we visited them in Oakland. They were, to put it mildly, devastated, and responded with bitter silence, which, in turn, angered me. They would never say so, but they would file the event away as yet another tragedy in their lives.

In the end, as they did with Sarah, they came around in their own way, saying that we should have a Chinese banquet. To my way of thinking, banquets were false fronts of festivity, staged by parents for other adults, many of them strangers but who, through the vast network of Chinese relations and associations, were somehow owed a debt. The children—often the putative honorees of such banquets—had the least to do with them. Their own friends were often left off the invitation list. "So many villagers and cousins to invite!" they'd be told.

Dianne and I opted for a small family ceremony—conducted by Gordon Lew—and a raucous reception, with all parents invited, in a disco on Nob Hill.

* * *

The following year, Shirley and Rich separated. Over the years, they had simply grown apart. They dissolved their marriage in 1980, but both chose to continue to live in the same town, the better for Rich to visit their daughter, Tina, on a regular basis.

That same year, Burton married. With help from our parents, he met a Hong Kong woman, Cynthia; they corresponded, and after Burton went to Hong Kong to meet her, they agreed to marry.

Now, finally, my parents had a wedding they could truly celebrate. This one would be their show; their chance to stage the kind of banquet any respectable Chinese family is supposed to put on at least once in their lifetime.

They did it up big. The banquet took place at the Silver Dragon in Oakland. The restaurant had first opened a quarter century before at 710 Webster, as the replacement for our father's New Eastern Cafe. It had moved up a couple of blocks to a new, two-story building with a banquet room occupying the second floor. After a City Hall ceremony on January 20, 1980, they and three hundred guests—or thirty tables, as the Chinese count large numbers of diners—convened at the Silver Dragon. Gordon Lew and I offered toasts in Cantonese and English, and Cynthia and Burton went on the traditional table-to-table visitation, to raise tea cups, to receive good wishes and gifts of good-luck money.

Forty years after my mother's arrival in this city, forty years after her own wedding banquet, she and our father finally had another. They had paid their dues; one of life's largest circles had been closed.

Our parents could also think back with some satisfaction at the trip they made to China—to her mother—in fall of 1972, just a few months after Barry's death.

Mother had thought about canceling the trip, but Sarah encouraged them to go ahead with their plans, made soon after Richard Nixon's visit to China that February wedged open the door to tourism to China. Mother had wanted one more visit with Grandmother, now in her nineties.

"You have a chance to see *Po-Po*, and you should," Sarah reasoned. In Canton, Mother shopped for food that she knew her mother would like. She made the trip without telling *Po-Po* in advance, so that she wouldn't be anticipating her every day. She and Father, carrying three large baskets of food with them, took a five-hour train ride into the village. When she arrived at the family house, Grandmother was taking a nap.

"My cousin was there," my mother remembered. "She started jumping. She told my mother, 'Stop sleeping! Your daughter's come home!'

"My mother said, 'Don't bother me. I must be dreaming. How could my daughter be home?'

"I said, 'It's true! I'm home!'

" '*Ai-ya!*' *Po-Po* screamed. 'My daughter! My puppy!' "

Mother and daughter embraced. "She was so happy," my mother said.

My parents returned with photographs of themselves in Japan and Taiwan as well as China, including a couple of pictures of themselves printed on souvenir plates. They had goldfish key chains for all of us, and they had purchased a scroll for Barry, which I hung at the shrine they had set up in a corner of their living room. It was a shelf filled with framed photographs of Barry, a copy of the Ben Shahn poster, a scroll that had belonged to Barry, and, always, a few sweet oranges on a Chinese plate.

In early December, I visited my parents again, and Mom took me aside.

"Do you dream about Barry?" she asked.

A chill went through me. I led her into a back bedroom, down the hall from Father, who was in the kitchen reading a newspaper.

"Yes," I said. "He has come back." I didn't know whether details would comfort or alarm her, but I decided to go on.

"Sometimes he's very young. We're on Eighth Street." Tears began welling in my mother's eyes. In mine, too. "The other night, I dreamt of him again—like it was today. He was fine. He said he had come back, but could not stay long."

Crying, my mother said, repeatedly: "So *yeem-goong*." So sad.

"I try to hold back when *Ba-Ba*'s around," she said. "He is still so bad about it." With a tissue, she wiped away her tears.

It had been nearly six months—the amount of time the *Chronicle* reporter had told me to stay out of Chinatown. I knew what her answer would be, but I asked my mom once more: Do you want me to check with some people I know who might know something?

Her face filled with dread. *"Mm-haw,"* she said. "Don't."

I promised her that I wouldn't do anything to endanger myself or the family. Still, at home and in my office, I saved and devoured articles about Chinatown and gangs, and stopped at every name, wondering . . .

I would not write an article about Barry for twelve years. Even then, it was an essay about the unending nature of loss, about the impact Barry continued to have on me. But I couldn't help mentioning him once in *Rolling Stone*, in early 1974.

I was on tour with Bob Dylan, who was on the road for the first time since 1966. Backed by the Band, an edgy Dylan had executed an emotionally charged two and a half hour opening show before 18,500 fans in Chicago Stadium. The next night, I was in the audience again, and I was nervous. My assignment was to cover the beginning of this twenty-one-city tour and to write two articles. The first, to be filed from Chicago, would cover the opening shows. The second, to be written on return to San Francisco from Montreal—the fourth city—would be a cover story, and it would feature an interview with Dylan. But I had no assurances of getting one. Just before the tour, *Rolling Stone* ran a piece about ticket sales and a lucrative deal Dylan had signed with a new record company. The article was headlined "Bob Dylan Sells Out," and no one connected with Dylan was about to extend himself to the magazine. I had about a week— on the road, bouncing from hotel to hotel—to nail him down.

But this second night in Chicago, I lost myself in his music, and near the end of "It's Alright Ma (I'm Only Bleedin')," I took a direct hit to the heart.

As I wrote at the time, it wasn't so much the song—as great as it was in its simplicity—as it was the delivery. Dylan made a statement through a tone he was painting with his bitter-truth voice, a feeling of knowing resignation, the uplift deriving from the knowledge that here was a guy who'd seen it all, saw through it all, and, as Robbie Robertson of the Band put it, "had a way of phrasing it and condensing it down."

I watched this small figure, behind his guitar, looking up and bawling, "I got *nothing*, Ma, to live up to," and I shivered. Then he pulsed through another verse:

While them that defend what they cannot see
With a killer's pride, security
It blows the mind most bitterly
For them that think death's honesty
Won't fall upon them naturally
Life sometimes must get lonely

I found myself wiping away tears and thinking about Barry, who was a fan of Dylan's, and wondering if he could hear him, on the road, rising and roaring again. Against all objective logic, I liked to think that he could.

GOING HOME

ONE JOY DRIVES OFF A HUNDRED GRIEFS.

—Chinese Proverb

In 1977, *Rolling Stone* announced plans to move to New York, and I decided to stay in San Francisco. I was now my parents' Number One Son, and I could not move three thousand miles away. I became the magazine's West Coast editor, and I maintained a small office in town and oversaw a few writers in Los Angeles.

Through the years, Jann Wenner itched to prove himself as more than just *Rolling Stone*'s founder. He'd tried different magazines, started a book publishing arm, got into radio, fielded numerous offers for television shows based on the magazine, and hungered to go Hollywood. With my background, I was a natural accomplice in many of these adventures, editing anthologies of interviews and articles, writing and narrating radio specials, helping write a television show—*Rolling Stone: The Tenth Anniversary*

Special—that aired on CBS in 1977, and, two years later, going Hollywood.

On the heels of *Animal House*, a film inspired by the humor magazine the *National Lampoon*, studios began looking for other magazine tie-ins. Paramount came to *Rolling Stone* and made a three-picture deal with Jann. Hunter S. Thompson, the doctor of gonzo journalism, would write a drug-running story; Cameron Crowe, whom I'd brought into the magazine a few years before, when he was sixteen, would write a high school movie; and my assignment was a comic love story centered on the San Francisco music scene of the sixties.

I had never written a screenplay or, for that matter, fiction before. My efforts would be supervised by Jann and another *Rolling Stone* editor, neither with any film experience. My script, which I named *Somebody to Love*, wound up in the dumpster Hollywood calls "turnaround." Meantime, Hunter's script never got started, and Cameron's wound up at another studio, where it enjoyed great success as *Fast Times at Ridgemont High*.

I returned to *Rolling Stone* for another year, but by 1981, I was itchy. The West Coast was an outpost; no longer could I stick up my hand at a meeting and get the go-ahead on a story idea. Now, they had to go through some kind of process in New York. I began to wonder about my time at *Rolling Stone*. Whatever I wrote got in. But did I have any credibility outside this oasis I'd been on for almost a dozen years? The only way to find out was to leave, to strike out as a free-lance writer.

My fear was that *Rolling Stone*'s reputation would create a backlash; that there were just enough envious editors at other magazines, editors who might have been rejected by us at some point and who'd look forward to slamming a door in my face.

I found no such editors. I was fortunate that in my last years at *Rolling Stone*, I'd expanded beyond music. My last couple of features at the magazine were on Steve Martin and Rodney Dangerfield; previously, I'd profiled Diane Keaton and the star of *The Buddy Holly Story*, Gary Busey. Having shown some range beyond rock and roll, I had no trouble getting work from several major magazines, among them *Parade* and *Esquire*. And within a year, I got the assignment of a lifetime.

In the spring of 1982, Charles Jennings, a film producer in Portland, invited me to go to China for three weeks, to either write about or help write the script for a TV documentary called *Cycling Through China*. The idea was a troupe of American entertainers—Ben Vereen, Kate Jackson, Lorne Greene, and a variety show of others, a magician, a mime, a former Harlem Globetrotter, and several musicians—bicycling through villages and cities, big and small, from Macao to Guangzhou, performing and spreading goodwill wherever they went.

I agreed to go. With Gordon Lew in tow, I visited my parents, who knew that if I were headed for Guangzhou, I might be close enough to our ancestral village to visit. They armed me with letters, photographs, and instructions. They would write our remaining kin there to alert them of my arrival.

But, on the eve of my first trip to China since I was three years old, I wanted more. That's why I had Gordon with me. I wanted to talk with my parents in detail about their lives in China. In preparation for the trip, I'd read several books about the country, and the stories about the Communist revolution and about the Great Proletariat Cultural Revolution between 1966 and 1976 astounded me. I'd been so lost in my own life that I'd had no idea of the horrors visited on millions of people—most of them innocent—by their own people, their own leaders. Of course, during those years, few outsiders knew what was going on. Even *East West* had to rely primarily on Western news agencies for the occasional account.

I wanted to ask my parents, not about their immigration to America but about what I now thought of as their escape from China. I wanted to know things that our language barrier had kept me from asking all these years—about how, as we reporters are prone to ask, they *felt*. I would write out what they said for an oral history for our family, I told them. But, mostly, I wanted to know these things for myself.

They were happy to talk. Sometimes, they were taken aback

by how much I wanted to know, how many details I wanted about their pasts. Neither of them was a natural storyteller; neither had the kinds of embroidered fables I'd read in books by second-generation Chinese writers. But my parents talked as if they'd been waiting to do so for years. They told of their childhood dreams and fears; their willingness to give up their families and villages to find a better life in a land less troubled than their own. They talked about their arranged marriage and their separate journeys to America, thirteen years apart, about coping with life in this very strange country, and about the hard work that went into raising us.

"Nowadays, parents have time to talk to their children," my mother said, directing her remarks to Gordon. "I often scolded them when they were bad. But I wanted to teach them to be good people. I scolded Hoong-Doy [Barry] a lot because he was very naughty. When he grew up, he excused me. Once, I said that it was hard to teach children nowadays. He said it was not the kids' fault. It was the parents who didn't teach their children the way I had taught mine."

That was Barry the social worker talking. What did they really think of the path I chose, into media?

"I had no objections to that," my mother said. "Media is somewhat considered literature. And most Chinese like literature."

And what about their missing Sarah's marriage to Dave?

My mother hesitated. Gordon by now was a trusted friend of the family, but, suddenly, she was aware of being interviewed about very personal matters by her own son.

She sighed. "I wasn't feeling well," she said. "We were busy working at the restaurant, so we didn't go to her wedding."

If she hadn't been my mother, I would have torn her answer apart. Instead, I asked how Sarah responded to her lack of enthusiasm for the wedding.

"I told her I couldn't change my mind. Some people would disown her. But I couldn't do that. I loved her so much. She was a very good child.

"Deep in my heart, I want my children to marry Chinese only."

My parents answered all my prying questions, but they also made sure I would be ready for my trip to their villages, and that, once there, I would know our relatives and do right by them.

"I have an elder sister," my mother said. "Fourteen years older than I. She carried you on her back when you were three. And I have an aunt and a sister-in-law there."

"Have some five- and ten-dollar notes," my father interrupted. "Give everybody a dollar bill."

"*Ba-Ba,*" my mother continued, "has a brother. He sent some money to him for the New Year, but there has been no response. He is more than eighty years old. He will be very glad to see you. When we saw him, he was very happy. He said it was like a dream to see us."

"I will write him," my father said. "You should go to see him if you have an opportunity."

"You should visit *Ba-Ba*'s birthplace," my mother said.

Such simple requests. I shook my head in amazement. Never in my life had I thought I'd ever get this close to them or to their pasts.

Our troupe's visit took place as the Chinese were conducting their first, cautious test flights toward a more modern and open society. Six years before, Mao Zedong had died. Deng Xiaoping and Hu Yaobang, at the head of the new leadership, steered the country toward industrialization; the shambles of the Cultural Revolution were being repaired—in part by the trial of the "Gang of Four," who were accused of conspiring to overthrow the government.

China went through a period of reevaluation of Mao, and, just before our arrival, a session of the Chinese Communist Party issued a resolution that, while praising its late chairman, also found him guilty of serious ideological and political errors in the sixties and seventies.

Citizens were being encouraged to be candid about mistakes

of the recent past—although criticisms of the party itself were still actively discouraged. Still, they couldn't help noticing radical changes around them. Workers were being pushed to increase factory production; the country itself was reaching out to foreign investors; China and the United States restored diplomatic relations in 1981. China opened its doors to tourism and to the dollars, goods, and knowledge that visitors might bring. And, finally, China allowed the return of various forms of art and literature that had been prohibited since the Communist Revolution.

A tour of American entertainers, then, was a perfect fit with the emerging China of the early eighties.

Our group landed in Hong Kong and ferried to Macao, the Portuguese territory that serves as a gateway into southeast China. On the ferry, which we shared with stacked cages of ducks and chicks and penned greyhounds headed for Macao's racetracks, our crew began to dance to the Doobie Brothers' "What a Fool Believes" as the mountains of China came into view.

While they danced and photographed each other, I strained at the rails to see China, and I thought about Barry. It was so easy to do, wherever I was. Every day, for ten years, something would trigger his memory. It could be anything: an unrelated conversation with a member of the family; a chore that took me into the Sunset District; a glimpse of an antique sword in a store window; a flier from handgun-control advocates; a mention of the year 1972 or the month of June. I'd even flinch when I saw a comedian doing Jimmy Cagney, inevitably employing the seething stock line, "You dirty rat . . . you killed my brother!" Certain songs evoked Barry. Elton John's elegiac ballad "Daniel" was a big hit in spring of 1973, and every time we played it on KSAN, I thought of Barry.

> Daniel my brother, you are older than me
> Do you still feel the pain of the scars that won't heal?
> Your eyes have died, but you see more than I
> Daniel, you're a star in the face of the sky . . .

It was five in the morning when I awoke in my hotel room in Macao. I peered out a window into the predawn darkness. The hotel plumbing emitted strange, intermittent, *boop-boop* sounds that reminded me of a video game, and they blended in with the distant crowing of roosters. "And so it begins," I thought. It was melodramatic, I knew, but that's how I felt, up before dawn and knowing I couldn't sleep, as close as I was, finally, to my parents' homeland.

Each of us found our own China. Several of the performers thought the people enjoyed freedom—even within the rigidity of Communism. Others were awed at how quickly the doors had opened to the West, as signified by a hotel disco playing Beatles music and by packs of teenagers wearing satinlike jackets emblazoned "Rider Fellas." My roommate, Mark, a wellness physician in Portland, went out to a beautiful park one early morning and joined dozens of people doing their t'ai chi exercises. There, away from the streets, Mark found that he didn't have to be a spectacle, an object of curiosity. He felt invisible. On returning to our room, he announced to me: "I found China."

For me, China was crystallized into one day: our fourth day in the country.

It was a Monday in mid-March. Our troupe was in a little town called Shigi, and, out on my own, I found myself admiring a tray of *don tot* when I was interrupted. *Don tot*—custard tarts— are a staple of *dim sum* trays these days, but for me, these particular tarts were nostalgic. I had first seen such tarts in China in 1948, when I was three.

Now, in 1982, I was back, and people were gawking. My skin may be yellow, but to the townspeople of Shigi, I was clearly not Chinese. They didn't need to note my latter-day Beatles bowl haircut or my Nike sportswear to make that judgment. They could tell by my *posture* that I was a Westerner.

I stood there, gazing longingly at these pieces of pastry, when two women approached and offered to buy me one. I was stunned. In the three days I'd been in China, I'd become accustomed to being treated by strangers like some relative who'd gone astray. But now I had been challenged, obligated to respond in kind. That is, in Cantonese. "No, thank you very much," I said, in *tze-yup*. By refusing, I had done the proper thing. But instead of insisting—which is the next proper thing—the two women let out roaring laughs that stopped just short of harshness. They knew exactly where my parents were from, one of them said. They could tell by the way I spoke.

I was in luck. I had hoped to take a side trip from Shigi to find my parents' ancestral villages—in the Hoi Ping region, not far from where we were, according to my maps. The women weren't sure, but they read the name of the village on the back of a photo my father had given me of his brother. They consulted a couple of bystanders who were watching us. One of them said the village was close enough to get to by car, and pointed to a shack across the street. A small sign, in English, read: CARS FOR HIRE.

I tried to express my thanks again, and they laughed again. "Go home," one of the women said, in the dialect that I heard as an echo of my own. "Go home."

I asked Sero, a Hong Kong woman who was a production assistant on the show, to accompany me and help interpret. At our hotel, the head clerk on our floor told me what to bring.

"Buy a chicken and some pork," she said. At stores, she instructed, I should ask for candy—*lop jook*—and incense—*tong shuen*. I'd need red paper for the money I'd give out. How much? "A few dollars—doesn't matter, as long as the bills are clean." She reminded me how rarely Chinese people got to travel.

"Three hours away," she said. "That's *far!*"

At 8:20 the next morning, Sero and I met our driver and loaded my gifts into the trunk. Soon after she gave him instructions, our blue Toyota was hurtling out of town and over what passed for highways. We rolled past straw-hatted peasants and teams of water buffalo working the rice paddies and farmlands all along the way. Technology had been slow coming to China, and the land was worked the way it always had been.

We hit a stretch of road lined with tall trees, and for a brief moment, I felt as if I was in Beverly Hills, until, beyond the trees,

I could see streams and farmland, and I was back amidst the communes of China. Our taxi clambered onto a ferry to cross several tributaries and rivers on the way to Chek Hom. Wherever we were, we saw people at work; women hauling wooden wagons loaded with baskets of coal; men and women carrying entire garlic trees.

"Look at her," Sero said, pointing out her window to a young woman walking calmly down the road with a load of straw the size of a baby grand piano on her shoulders.

I shook my head in amazement. "In America, two young men probably couldn't lift that," I said.

Sero smiled. "The people here are very healthy," she said.

We overtook bicycles weighed down with crates containing anything from geese to fresh produce. We sped past buses and rumbling minitractors, past construction workers on bamboo scaffolding. Everywhere, it seemed, China was being built.

We stopped briefly in Sun Wi, which happened to be Sero's ancestral village. While she chatted with some of the people, I watched a crew of construction workers in white hard hats taking a break, chewing on *jeh*, sections of sugar canes I remembered Dad giving us at the New Eastern Cafe.

China is a country of basic truths. With Sero by my side, I asked a young woman what she did for a living.

"Work," she replied.

As we entered Chek Hom—my mother's village—the portraits my parents had drawn vanished into the dusty air, replaced by actual people, deeply lined and tanned, going about their business in town. Some stood idly around in front of decayed buildings; others hawked goods—*jeh*, peanuts, garlic, greens, and roasted meats—along the streets. At the sight of our car, they all stopped and stared.

Sero turned to me. "Your cousin's going to be a star for a whole month," she said, "between you coming from America and this car."

At our designated meeting spot in town, a young man who

introduced himself as my cousin's son greeted us and got in to direct the driver to my aunt's house. Even as we made the final few turns, the cynic in me remembered warnings I'd received, both in San Francisco and here: Overseas Chinese are often mobbed by villagers, counterfeit cousins hopeful of a gift of cash. But with this man, there was no question. When he spoke, I could hear an accent within the dialect, a rhythm of the words that I'd heard all my life. He sounded just like my parents.

I had no idea what to expect. In our few days in China, we had yet to visit a commune, and, on the road to Shigi, I had seen housing only from a distance. The sight was distressing. I remember stately, fortresslike buildings that looked as if they'd survived fires, but even more arresting were the mud huts covered with a mosaic of tar paper and remnants of old clothes.

We stopped on a wide dirt street, and I knew I was in a residential neighborhood. Clothing hung off bamboo racks in front of almost every door and from second-floor balconies. My cousin's son led us to a white, two-story rowhouse. We entered through a blue metal door and into the dark front room, where a half-dozen people were waiting for me.

The Chinese are not a demonstrative people, and it was my cousin—the mother of the young man who had delivered us— who stepped forward to greet me with a handshake, and to introduce me to my other relatives. Her mother was my mother's only sister, a woman who was seventy-four. Her hair gray and thin, she sat in a straight back chair and smiled from behind her eyeglasses, and looked more like *Po-Po*, my grandmother, than *Ma-Ma*.

My cousin also introduced an uncle—Mother's only surviving brother of three—and two in-laws. All in their seventies, they wore single-colored shirts with Chinese collars, slacks, and sandals, while my cousin, in her early forties, wore a bright, patterned, Western-style blouse.

Before long, I had met a dozen relatives, including two babies. It was a blizzard of relations; I lost track immediately, and I was actually grateful when several of them left after exchanging pleasantries. I wanted to absorb as much as I could, to report back to my family, but it seemed improper to whip out a tape recorder or notepad. And so I was what they expected: the good, obedient son of Tui Wing and Kwok Shang, here to visit from *Mai Gok*.

I took in the front room with pleasure. I hadn't yet seen the whole house, but there was a vibrancy about this room that indicated that my mother's family—*my* family—was doing all right. The room burst with colors, mainly lucky red and gold, on paper scrolls. I looked, with new appreciation, at prints of Chinese watercolor scenes, the kind I saw on calendars Chinatown banks and merchants handed out, and that my parents hung in every room. A portable stereo system sat atop a cabinet.

As in every Chinese family home, a place of honor was reserved for portraits of deceased elders. On the back wall was a large, framed photograph of my grandmother. It was the same picture I'd seen so often as a child in Oakland. And along a side wall, several long frames held montages of photos, one of them devoted to my immediate family. There we were—in grade school, graduating from high school, getting married—our life histories hanging on a wall in a house in southern China. I looked around at the anxious, smiling faces before me and realized that I had many more cousins than the ones I'd met at all those Chinatown banquets.

Over tea, we talked about family, about life in San Francisco, about our common desires for reunions. "Their letters and those pictures," my cousin said, indicating the wall, "that's how we stay in touch. We look at them every day and think about you."

I told my cousin that it would be wonderful to have them come to America, to see my parents and our family. She and her mother laughed gently at my naiveté. They couldn't even leave the county without going through miles of red tape.

I soon realized that Sero, sitting and sipping tea, didn't have much to do. Every bit of Cantonese I'd ever learned, pitiful scraps that they were, seemed to be coming back.

"Come see the house," my cousin said. I soon realized that the front room was the showcase. Wherever I went, I got the feeling I was in a cave. The kitchen, like most in China, was open-air. Between the kitchen and front room was a small area set aside for worshipping departed relatives. We came to a stop. "Time to pay respects," she said. She mentioned a few names I didn't know, and, following her lead, I bowed three times. And once more, for Barry.

Upstairs, several simple bunks crowded a bedroom. It looked like a cozy jail cell, but my relatives said they were happy to have this house. And, they added, they had it because we had sent money over the years.

I asked my aunt about life under communism. When the Communists took over, the family lost ownership of its house and its fruit farm. "During the Great Cultural Revolution," she said, "we were not allowed to wear earrings and bracelets. If people saw you wearing them, they would take them from you." A few years ago, she said, the government sent her son and daughter-in-law to another county. "I got ill and there was no one to take care of me. I didn't look like this before. I was fat and strong. I had to stay in bed for two years. This was the only bad thing." She thought a moment, then continued: "And things were scarce. Money had no value. No matter how much money you had, you could not buy anything. That was not good."

Although the fruit farm was still state property, the government had returned the family's house to her. Life, she said, had improved in recent years, again thanks largely to money sent from our family in the United States.

I asked my aunt if she'd wanted to go to the Golden Mountains years ago. She sighed. "Yes, I would have loved to go. But no one married me and took me over. I was very miserable. If I were able to go, I would have been very happy. I am too old now. There is no more opportunity."

I wanted to locate my father's older brother. Aunt told me that they hadn't seen him in some time. With my cousin accompanying us, we took a short ride, then walked a narrow farmland road into my father's village. It was much smaller than my mother's, the homes all squat, low, brick buildings fronted by dirt yards littered with tree branches and other debris.

In a dark shack, we found my uncle sitting on a rumpled, straw-matted wooden bed, as if he were in solitary confinement. He looked like he'd just been awakened in late afternoon.

So this was my father's birthplace. Dirt floors, mud-brick walls, no windows, no electricity. Now I understood why he slept in the temple, why he escaped to Manila, why he made the journey to the United States.

It took my uncle several moments to comprehend my visit, to grasp the fact that the son of his brother had suddenly materialized. I told him, in my fractured Cantonese, that I was happy to see him and that my father sent his best wishes. I asked if he had a message for him.

He groaned. "Send some money," he managed. Several of his neighbors had gathered at the doorway to look at his visitors, and my cousin spoke with them. She learned that my uncle and aunt had received money from my parents, but he was no longer capable of writing. Still, he needed money for food and medicine.

Whatever I hadn't given to my mother's relatives, I now left with him. I only wished I had more with me, and I felt suddenly guilty for buying some video games in Hongkong. I promised Uncle that I would send more money.

Back in my mother's village, it was time to say goodbye, and there was no getting around it: Through the long grips of each other's hands, and through the tears of farewell, I didn't feel as if I were leaving *for* home. I was leaving home.

I sat, dazed, in the car, unaware of all the bumps on the way back to Shigi. I had been to where my mother and father came from. This was what they'd been trying to tell us all those years, about how tough they'd had it, and about how lucky we were.

All that talk that we'd come to think of, and even dismiss, as clichés.

A few afternoons later, Wenda Fong, one of the show's producers, looked up and down the dirt roads of a small China town and sighed.

"There but for fortune go I," she said. I knew what she meant.

·· 25 ··

FULL CIRCLES

THE BEGINNING AND THE END
REACH OUT HANDS TO EACH OTHER.

—Chinese Proverb

Sometimes, we get pissed off at Barry. It's not his fault, but now that he's dead, he can do no wrong. And in our parents' view, he never did any wrong. If he were alive, he'd always do right.

If our mother or father need a ride somewhere, or for one of us to come home to read a mysterious letter—and we happen to be too busy—we hear the refrain: "You don't care. If Barry were alive, he'd be here. We wouldn't even have to ask."

And all we can do is roll our eyes and wait for the phone call to end. We knew Barry. Sometimes, he was too busy, too.

To our parents, we are forever their children. That is to say, they always know better than us. They pass judgments on how Sarah is raising her children, on how much we've spent for our homes, or furniture, or a gift for them. Once, Shirley and I were on the deck of her house in Pacifica. She was near tears over the latest row with our parents. "It's Chinese-this and Chinese-that," she said. "Don't they know we're in America?"

"Well," I said, "they've only been here about forty years.

"It's pointless," I continued, "to go crazy over how they are. They are the way they are, and they'll always be that way. There's no point arguing. If you want to not talk with them or see them for a while, go ahead and argue. Otherwise, you might as well just give in. Just tell yourself that you know you're right. But for your own peace of mind, compromise. The bottom line is that they're our parents, and they're the only ones we have."

I went back inside to joke with Mom and Dad, trying to defuse the angry vibrations around the house. A few minutes later, alone for a moment, I replayed my words to Shirley. There was an echo in there somewhere. I'd heard some of those words before.

Now, I remembered. *Be patient . . . they're the way they are . . . the best thing to do is to give in a little.* Those were words of counsel from Barry, spoken the last time I saw him, that June evening in 1972.

One day, not so long ago, I saw my former girlfriend Michelle performing in a play in a local theater. Backstage, we agreed to meet for lunch.

When the subject turned to us—and to what happened to our relationship—she turned momentarily uncomfortable, as if she'd been in the waiting room and had been summoned by the physician.

Our relationship, she began, seemed ideal, perfect in every way. I was the first person she'd considered as a possible mate for life. "And I always wondered," she said softly, "what it would have been like if we had gone through with it, how my life and yours would have been different."

I looked away for a moment. Of course, I'd wondered about those things, too, as I watched, from a distance, her progression through life. I'd get press releases about her plays, her books of poetry, her readings with jazz ensembles. I'd hear that she'd been married and had two daughters. And I'd wonder what would have happened if she hadn't seen what she thought she'd seen that day in Chinatown.

I told Michelle that I had a theory about how that episode exploded into our breakup. Maybe she thought of us—even with all the things we had in common—as being in different orbits. She had an artistic/community/political edge; I was a mainstream/commercial journalist and radio announcer. We were on different levels, and that difference was bound to create conflicts.

She nodded. For years, she said, she'd felt guilty for the pain she'd caused me. "It was almost as if I was looking for something, looking for a justification, because of some underlying doubts I was having. I'd reach a place in relationships where I'd have a certain uncertainty, and instead of trying to resolve it, I'd do it emotionally."

In the mid-seventies, Michelle married a Chinese man. She loved him, sure, but she also loved the idea of quieting her parents' constant implorings for her to find a nice "Chinese boy."

It didn't work. "After I went through all that trouble, they *still* weren't happy," Michelle said. "They didn't like him, and then there were problems with the in-laws.

"I came to the conclusion that no matter what you do, they won't be happy anyway, so you might as well do what you want to do."

I need to see where Barry died. It has been twenty years since June 26, 1972, and I have not been back to that basement apartment in the Sunset District since the days following his death, when Sarah and I went over to pack his belongings.

With a weary heart, I drive out by myself. I have the police report to guide me, and when I reach the address, on a block like any block in the Sunset, with stucco homes of unvarying designs, I see that the house is being painted. The door to the alley where Barry was found that night is open. I walk through and find two young Asian men at work. While I try to peer through the windows of the basement rooms, they eye me with suspicion. A moment later, one of them shouts, "We go. You go too. Or talk to owner."

I walk up the front steps of the main house and ring. An elderly Chinese man answers and stays behind his glass door. I tell him that my brother used to live downstairs.

"What's your name?" he asks, in *sam-yup* Cantonese.

"Fong," I say. "How long have you lived here?"

"Thirty years," he says. I know who he is: Mr. Jang, the landlord.

"My brother was Barry," I tell him.

He opens the door and puts a gentle hand on my shoulder, nodding. "Sorry," he says.

I tell him that I am writing about Barry, and he agrees to show me the apartment. "He was good," he says as we enter through the garage. "Trying to do good work. And then those *kwai-jai* ..." In my native dialect, that translated into *ky-doy*—bad boys.

I take a quick look around, just enough to soak in, once more, the modesty of Barry's surroundings when he was working in Chinatown.

Back at his front door, I thank Mr. Jang.

"It is bad," he says. "All these years and it is still bad. More *kwai-jai*. Today they found that little boy . . ." The headlines told of the police discovery of the body of a nine-year-old Vietnamese boy who'd been snatched from his mother the night before. The abductors were three young Asian men, and investigators were looking at a possible gang connection.

My mother called one afternoon about a financial matter. Suddenly, she blurted out how nice it was that we all turned out to be good kids. I didn't quite know what she was talking about.

"I was at the eye-fixing doctor," she said. "The girl asked me how I got the name Torres. I told her. Then I asked, do you know my boy, Ben Fong-Torres? 'Oh, yes,' she said. 'Big name.' I said, do you remember a Barry Fong-Torres? 'Yes,' she said. 'I remember. Such a shame.' "

Well, my mother continued, "I guess they should know. The eye-fixing doctor is in the same office as what's his name, the doctor who called you that time to tell you what happened to Barry."

Ah . . . Dr. Rolland Lowe. I didn't get the connection between people recognizing our name and what good children we turned out to be. But I was glad to hear that she thought we'd turned out all right. I always thought we did, even though our parents' definitions of success, and of whether their children were good or bad, varied from ours.

Sarah and Dave have been married for more than twenty-five years. That's a successful marriage by almost any measure. After raising two children, Lea and Jason, Sarah, who in the seventies and eighties worked at drug and alcohol treatment centers in San Francisco and Marin County, enrolled in school and became a paralegal.

Shirley has remarried—this time to a Caucasian man. She took care to set her wedding date for August 8, 1988. To the Chinese, eight is the luckiest of numbers.

Although most of the children vowed that the closest we'd ever get to the restaurant business would be as customers, Shirley has gone back—on her own terms. She has made a business in the Chinese food industry—first as a cooking teacher, then as a cookbook author and operator of a Chinatown walking-tour company. She often thinks of Barry as she leads tourists through the back and side alleys of Chinatown, and she'd like to think that what she's doing is an extension of Barry's work: increasing an understanding of Chinatown.

One evening, Shirley and her "Wok Wiz" tour were featured on a local television show, and Mom caught it by accident.

She phoned Shirley the next day. "Why didn't you tell me?" she asked. Shirley, an accomplished self-promoter who is regularly in the local press and on broadcast media, hadn't thought Mom would care about yet another appearance.

No matter, said Mother. "You were very good," she said, in Cantonese. And then she switched to English. "Con-gra-du-la-tion," she managed.

Shirley was shocked. She rarely got a compliment from her mother, much less in English. After they hung up, Shirley cried.

The traditions endure. Long ago, our family stopped getting together for Thanksgiving. After Barry, there didn't seem to be much to give thanks for. But we still gather for Chinese New Year's, the time for renewal and hope. I still don't know the difference between *Hon neen* and *Hoy neen*, those different days of the New Year's celebration, but Dianne and I show up every February, spreading tangerines and oranges in groups of the lucky number eight, along with little red envelopes for the kids.

At dinner, over the Buddha's monk stew, the chicken, and all the other requisite dishes, Mom will offer a toast to our health— and especially to *Ba-Ba*, who is ninety years old, and, after an adulthood of looking far younger than his years, is now, finally, frail.

He still jokes. Already weakened by age and various operations, he has recently been diagnosed with a serious lung ailment. For more than a decade, Mom has tried to get him to stop smoking, and, at family gatherings, he has mooched cigarettes off Sarah. Now, he looks over the table at his daughter. "Gimme a cigarette," he shouts. *"Ai-ya!"* says Mom. *Ba-Ba* will never change.

After too many years of dealing with an apartment building in East Oakland, and of driving, more and more erratically, into Chinatown, our parents moved back there, into a condominium a block or so away from where the New Eastern used to stand.

Now, when I visit, it isn't automatically a holiday or a birthday.

I drive one or the other to a doctor's office on Pill Hill, or to the Mountain View Cemetery in early May and late June, the anniversaries of Barry's birth and death.

For the visits to Barry's grave, I buy flowers at a shop on Piedmont Avenue, just outside the cemetery gates, and my parents will bring food, usually *dim sum*, and a little whiskey, and arrange it near the flowers. We gather to form a human shield against the mountaintop breezes so that my mother can light the incense they've brought, and to set afire the ceremonial paper money they've placed in an old pie pan.

The marble grave marker has Barry's name flanked by two vertical lines of Chinese calligraphy, written by our father. My mother reads the phrase in *tze-yup*, then translates it for me: "He had a generous spirit and wanted to help the community." Then, the second phrase: "Despite his passing, his spirit endures."

While my father and I stand nearby, my mother tells Barry that she has brought food and drink, that she is sending him money to spend. She still wants him to prosper. That is this Chinese mother's message to a Number One Son.

From time to time, and not necessarily on Barry's two bitter-sweet anniversaries, I visit him at Mountain View. I have come to like it up there. It is peaceful atop the mountain, with the troubled, still unsettled city of Oakland down below.

At Plot 75, I do a little tending at Barry's grave, but mostly I commune with him—with his soul, in which I have come to believe.

I tell him the latest news. Way back when, I told him about Michelle and Dianne, and I heard him chuckle. *Hey, Ben, you weren't the first juggler in the family!* . . . I've chronicled the growth of our nephew Jason and our nieces, Lea and Tina. I relay something Dave said to me about Lea, now a young adult, and Jason, who's in college. He was struck by the good fortune he and Sarah had with them, that they grew up escaping the drugs and other traps modern life set in the way of young people. He thought it had something to do with their being raised, in part, in a Chinese environment, with all of its culture and values, chief among them the importance of family unity and of respect for one's elders.

I tell Barry of my own coming to realization of what all those years in restaurants meant. For so long, we were so angry at the contradiction. We had to bring home the best grades, but we had to cram our studies between customers—when we were distracted—and after closing time, when we were dead tired. But there were no excuses for mediocrity. Our parents worked hard and made sacrifices. So could we. It was as simple as that.

The funny thing is: It was.

We were raised on work. Sometimes, it got unhealthy, so that we felt guilty staying away from the restaurant one weekend, forcing more work onto Mom or a sister or brother. Our thinking—at least mine—got so twisted that I not only accepted the obligations of our family but even wanted them at the same time that I was fighting for freedom. What kind of son, I'd ask myself in a demanding tone, would desert his parents?

No, we're not so angry any more. Not even knowing it, we learned about values and priorities. We learned responsibility and discipline. Work became second nature, and it has only benefited our lives.

I think and laugh about little things, too, that remind me of how I will always be connected to *Ma-Ma* and *Ba-Ba*. At Chinese restaurants, when I order a rice plate, and the meat and vegetables are placed alongside the rice, I instinctively spoon them atop the rice—the way Dad always made his rice plates.

And there's the way I kiss. I'm talking about the casual cheek-peck we Californians plant on anybody we've met more than once. Anyway, Dianne told me once that I always did a combination of a kiss and a sniff.

"No way," I said.

"Sorry," said Dianne, "but you do. And it's exactly how your Mom kisses." End of argument.

Crouched on one knee, flicking away random leaves around his headstone, I tell Barry what I'm up to, still hoping for his approval. And I think of him at his best, decorating the back of Shirley and Rich's getaway car at their wedding; taking Burton out to the game arcades; hanging out with Sarah and Dave and serving as a human swing to their newborn Lea; going off to the ski slopes; traveling with Kate; giving *Mui-Mui* advice.

We all managed to escape the rice room. I can see Barry arching an eyebrow. *Really?* Well, okay. Maybe, in actuality, we only took vacations. The *mai fong* is still there. A bank now occupies the New Eastern's old spot, but the rice room remains as vivid in my mind as the first smell of soy sauce, of barbecued pork, or of a preserved plum.

We no more escaped our pasts than our parents escaped China. They stayed tied to their old ways, and now we begin to see those ways, those things that used to strike us as so odd and embarrassing . . . so *Chinese* . . . in a new light. Those chicken-wired walls of the rice room may have contained us in a life we found restricting. But they were also windows to a far wider world than many others saw.

I say so long to Barry and return to my car. I drive down Piedmont, hit Broadway, and turn left on Seventh Street, into and through Chinatown, toward the freeway. I decide to swing over a block, to Eighth Street. On my right, I see Grace Fung's big house, all worn out, like a grand old lady left alone too long. A block later, on the left, is 206.

The old set of flats looks exactly the same as when we moved out in 1959. Pink beige with a wine red trim. Concrete front steps that had replaced the rickety wooden ones. I think about stepping out of my car and taking a peek into the side alley, where, beyond the garbage cans, I might see the old clothesline to which I attached my first radio, and the bedroom window from which Barry launched his water balloon at Fungus.

But just knowing it's all still there is enough. I turn on the radio and turn right at Jackson Street, toward the freeway back to San Francisco.

Plume

VIVID BIOGRAPHIES